SELF-

Scholar, former editor and minister, Arun Shourie is one of the most prominent voices in our country's public life.

Also by Arun Shourie from HarperCollins

Does He Know a Mother's Heart: How Suffering Refutes Religions

The World of Fatwas: Or the Shariah in Action

Worshipping False Gods: Ambedkar, and the Facts Which Have Been Erased

Falling over Backwards: An Essay Against Reservations and Against Judicial Populism

SELF-DECEPTION

India's China Policies
Origins, Premises, Lessons

ARUN SHOURIE

HarperCollins *Publishers* India

First published in India in 2008 as *Are We Deceiving Ourselves Again?* by
ASA Publications

This expanded edition published in 2013 by
HarperCollins *Publishers* India

ISBN: 978-93-5116-093-9

2 4 6 8 10 9 7 5 3

HarperCollins *Publishers*
A-53, Sector 57, Noida, Uttar Pradesh 201301, India
77-85 Fulham Palace Road, London W6 8JB, United Kingdom
Hazelton Lanes, 55 Avenue Road, Suite 2900, Toronto, Ontario M5R 3L2
and 1995 Markham Road, Scarborough, Ontario M1B 5M8, Canada
25 Ryde Road, Pymble, Sydney, NSW 2073, Australia
31 View Road, Glenfield, Auckland 10, New Zealand
10 East 53rd Street, New York NY 10022, USA

Typeset in 11.5/14 Adobe Garamond
by Jojy Philip, New Delhi 110 015

Printed and bound at
Thomson Press (India) Ltd.

For

Adit's angels,
Samiran Nundy, Prema Padmanabhan, Nasli R. Ichaporia,
who have kept us afloat

Contents

1

Bal chhutkyo bandhan padey...

'A nation has security when it does not have to sacrifice its legitimate interests to avoid war,' Walter Lipmann wrote long ago, 'and is able, if challenged, to maintain them by war.'[1]

Consider Aksai Chin: The unanimous resolution that the Parliament passed in the wake of the Chinese attack in 1962 notwithstanding, are we prepared to go to war to recover the area? Or, is it more likely that we will rationalize *not* going to war by giving credence to doubts: 'Do we have an interest in the place? Is such interest as we have in it, vital? Is it legitimate?' How many of us even know that this vast expanse that China grabbed at the time is *two and a half times the size of Kashmir?* 'The only unfinished business in regard to Kashmir is to recover the part of Kashmir that Pakistan has usurped'—words of one of our prime ministers. Does anyone seriously believe that we will do anything substantive to recover any part of Pakistan-Occupied-Kashmir in any foreseeable future? What about Arunachal? Are we confident that, when challenged over it by China, we will be able to hold it by war? Is *China* clear on that? Building up capacities to defend our interests apart, bearing sacrifices for them apart, are we one even on what our vital, legitimate national interests are?

[1] Walter Lipmann, *U.S. Foreign Policy: Shield of the Republic*, Little, Brown, Boston, 1943, p. 51. Throughout this volume, unless otherwise specified, italics have been added.

I remember the incident as if it were happening in front of me, just at this moment. Not long ago, at the India International Centre, during a discussion on India's Tibet and China policy as part of the release of the original edition of this book, a commentator—a prominent fixture at discussions on China, on defence—said, 'I am a south Indian, for heaven's sake. I have not grown up with this feeling of Delhi being the centre of things. How does what happens to Tibetans concern us? If the Tibetans want to strive for their independence, good luck to them; let them do so on their own. Why should we allow ourselves to be dragged into their problem?' Indeed, I have heard the same sort of dismissive righteousness on Kashmir—'The fellows want to go? Let them go, for heaven's sake. Let them go and suffer for their sins. *That* will teach them a lesson.' Five years later, the same 'analyst' was holding forth on television. We should reach out and get the Chinese to invest in India, he declaimed. They will then have a stake in India. They are the only ones who have the money. They can build our infrastructure like no one else can…

Nor is there any shortage of analysts like him in regard to our border with Tibet and China. They are suffused with a unilateral objectivity, espousing which is taken as the hallmark of 'independent thinking' in India. Books have been put out showing how in regard to Aksai Chin, for instance, the Indian borders were successively advanced northwards and eastwards by British surveyors in late nineteenth and early twentieth century. That the Chinese have similarly enlarged the entire concept of 'China' is not mentioned at all: is it not a fact that the original China was only one-third of what China is today? I hear similar 'objectivity' in regard to the eastern border, in particular in regard to Tawang. This cannot but dissipate national resolve; it cannot but further expose Tibetans to Chinese oppression; and it cannot but ultimately endanger India.

And there is unilateral silence too: China conveniently

shifts its statements on Jammu and Kashmir as its calculations change; but we must never whisper a word about the true position of Tibet in history; we must not whisper a word about what the Chinese are doing to beat down Tibetans; we must stick to Article 370, but not say a word about how the Chinese are systematically reducing Tibetans to a minority within Tibet—and the Uyghur within Xinjiang, as the Mongols have already been reduced to a helpless minority within Inner Mongolia. The Dalai Lama must not be seen anywhere near an official function. No official functionary must be seen attending any function that has to do with the Dalai Lama—lest the Chinese...

Recall what happened in 2008.

The brutal—the customarily brutal—way in which the Chinese government suppressed the protests by Tibetans in Lhasa in the months preceding the 2008 Beijing Olympics once again drew attention to the enormous crime that the world has refused to see: the systematic way in which an entire people have been reduced to a minority in their own land; the cruelty with which they are being crushed; the equally systematic way in which their religion and ancient civilization are being erased. Protests by Tibetans in different cities across the world, joined as they were by large numbers of citizens of those countries, had the same effect.

No government anywhere in the world did what the Manmohan Singh government did in Delhi, no government reacted in as craven and as frightened a manner as our government did. The Olympic Torch was to be relayed across just about *two kilometres*—from Vijay Chowk to India Gate. The government stationed over *twenty thousand* troops, paramilitary personnel, policemen and plainclothes men in and around that short stretch. Tibetan refugees were beaten and sequestered. Government offices were closed. Roads were blocked. The Metro was shut down. Even members of Parliament were stopped from going to their homes through the square that adjoins Parliament, the Vijay Chowk.

Do you think that any of this was done out of love for the Olympics?

It was done out of fear of China.

Dread as policy—that is all such steps are. But, of course, there is the rationalization, rather a premise: that if only we conduct ourselves properly, the dragon will turn vegetarian.

On every issue—the WTO, economic liberalization, terrorism, Maoist violence, Arunachal, death for rapists, even for terrorists, name it—the pattern of discourse leaves the people feeling that there are two sides to the question: call 'X' knowing that he is *for* a step, call 'Y' knowing that he is *against* it; have each interrupt the other, interrupt both. The 'debate' done, rush to the next 'breaking news'. As every issue has two sides, where is the reason to act, to bear sacrifice? In a word, by the pattern of discourse itself, to say nothing of the doings of governments and the political class as a whole, national resolve is scattered. The consequences erupt every other week. And every time, the same sequence is played out.

'Acne'

Delhi was surprised when news broke out that Chinese troops had come 19 kilometres into Indian territory and pitched tents in the strategic Daulat Beig Oldie. The rulers in Delhi acted true to form—as the news could not be suppressed, they set out to minimize what the Chinese had done: 'Acne', they said; a 'localized problem', they said.

Soon, the Indian foreign minister was in Beijing. He was happy as can be—he had been able to call on the Chinese prime minister, after all.

Did any clarity emerge as to why Chinese troops had intruded 19 kilometres into our territory? he was asked. 'Frankly, I did not even look for it,' the foreign minister said. 'How we responded is clear to us. It is not clear why it happened. They were not offering that background and we were not asking for it at this stage.' How considerate!

Had China admitted the provocation? Again, the minister was empathy itself: 'You cannot expect any country to say we provoked.'

Not just that—he proceeded to furnish explanations that even the Chinese had not advanced! 'It happened in a remote area,' he said. 'To get the message to government, it is a long haul. It will take a little time to analyse.'

And he was statesman-like: 'It is not helpful at this stage to apportion blame between them and us'—so statesman-like as to be completely neutral between the arsonist and the fire-fighter!

Has China given any assurances that such intrusions will not occur in the future? 'I don't think it is fair to ask for assurances... We already have agreement to address this kind of issues.'

'There was appreciation of the manner in which India responded,' he told correspondents, 'and persuaded and moved in a manner that the solution was found.'[2] Why would China not be full of appreciation? He was doing exactly what China would want: minimizing what China had done—making out that the incursion was an isolated, one-off incident, implying that some local Chinese commander had done something on his own, and that Beijing had not got to know in time what he had done.

Soon, he was giving expression to his ardent desire—that he aspired to live in China, 'though not as India's foreign minister,' he added—we should be thankful for small mercies, I suppose.

'Acne'? 'A localized problem'? 'Not fair'? 'Not helpful'? 'Frankly I did not even ask for it'? 'It happened in a remote area. To get the message to government, it is a long haul'? Of course, neither the prime minister nor the foreign minister mentioned that this was not just an inadvertent strolling into Indian territory. This time tents were pitched. The point of

---

[2] Press Trust of India dispatch, *The Indian Express*, 10 May 2013.

ingress that the Chinese had picked itself showed that it had been chosen carefully. 'The PLA has carefully chosen its spot,' Major General Sheru Thapliyal, a former commander of 3 Division, told the defence analysts Ajai and Sonia Shukla. 'Along the entire 4,057 kilometres of the LAC, India is most isolated at DBO, being entirely reliant on airlift. In contrast, the PLA can bring an entire motorized division to the area within a day, driving along a first-rate highway.'[3]

Nor did they mention that this setting up of tents was but the latest instance of what China has been doing. It would not have been 'fair' to mention, as the foreign minister would say, that China has been steadily eating into the territory on our side of the Line of Actual Control; it would not be 'fair' to mention that they have already taken over the Galwan Valley and the Chip Chap Valley—and that by doing so they have already pushed the Line of Actual Control substantially further into India. Nor to mention that, further south, as Ambassador P. Stobdan pointed out in the wake of the incursion, since 1986 they have systematically scared away Indian herdsmen from the grazing lands within Indian territory, occupied the pastures and built permanent structures. It would not have been 'fair' to point out the cruel facts that the Ambassador listed:

> ... In Eastern Ladakh, the 45-kilometre long Skakjung area is the only winter pasture land for the nomads of Chushul, Tsaga, Nidar, Nyoma, Mud, Dungti, Kuyul, Loma villages.... The Chinese advance here intensified after 1986, causing huge scarcity of surface grass, even starvation for Indian livestock. Since 1993, the *modus operandi* of Chinese incursions has been to scare Indian herdsmen into abandoning grazing land and then to construct permanent structures.
>
> Until the mid-1980s, the boundary lay at Kegu Naro—a day-long march from Dumchele, where India had maintained

[3] Ajai Shukla and Sonia Trikha Shukla, 'Shadow on the Line', *Business Standard*, 4 May 2013.

> a forward post till 1962. In the absence of Indian activities, Chinese traders arrived in Dumchele in the early 1980s and China gradually constructed permanent roads, buildings and military posts here. The prominent grazing spots lost to China include Nagtsang (1984), Nakung (1991) and Lungma-Serding (1992). The last bit of Skakjung was taken in December 2008...[4]

'Acne'? 'A localized problem'? *Taken by itself*, each one of the usurpations was! But taken together, the unremitting advances have a pattern—to go on pushing the Line of Actual Control, and hence 'Chinese territory' right up to the eastern banks of the Shyok and Indus rivers, and to absorb the entire Pangong Lake into China.

The reactions of Indian officials to these successive incursions have also been to a pattern:

- Suppress information
- Deny

Who is misled when information is suppressed? Who is kept in the dark when what has happened is denied? Who is led to believe that nothing serious has occurred, that 'the situation is under control', that 'all necessary steps are being taken'? Not the Chinese—after all, they know what they have done; they know the plan of which each step is a part. Not other countries, be they the US or Vietnam: apart from the fact that those governments have sources of information better than our people do, the general patterns—of what China is doing, and how we are reacting—cannot but be evident to them. The people who are lulled are the people of India. And the object of lulling them is straightforward—not just that they should not come to think that their government has been negligent, but that they should not pressurize the government into doing anything more than what it is doing.

---

[4] P. Stobdan, 'The Ladakh drift', *The Indian Express*, 26 April 2013.

- Wait Micawber-like for something to turn up
- Wishful construction—read into Chinese statements and manoeuvres what we wish to hear and see
- Paste a motive, fling a doubt at the messenger, discredit him: 'O, you see, he is from Ladakh. O, you see, he is from Arunachal—persons from an area on the front always tend to exaggerate the threat, to exaggerate what has happened on the ground.'
- Minimize what the adversary has done. In 1959, it was 'a small matter', 'a remote place' where 'not a blade of grass grows'. This time the expressions of choice have been 'acne,' 'a localized problem.' That is exactly what is being said and done about the dams that the Chinese have already started building across the Brahmaputra.
- Exculpate the government of the country: 26/11? O, it was the handiwork of just the Lashkar-e-Tayyaba. As we just saw, the ingress into Daulat Beig Oldie called forth the exact replay: communication from those remote areas is so difficult; must have taken time for the local commanders to get instructions from Beijing…
- Manufacture explanations—sometimes these are so ingenious that even the adversary has not thought of them! 'You see, the real problem is that the LAC has not been delineated on the ground'—of course, don't mention that it is China which has not let the delineation proceed by just not exchanging maps.
- Take the high road: 'We are not here to satisfy the jingoism of others,' said the foreign minister this time round. Whatever happens in the end, proclaim it to have been 'a triumph of our diplomacy', use the media to put out that whatever has happened is exactly what *you* planned should happen. And leave them to rush to the next story—spot fixing in IPL, Sanjay Dutt surrenders, should Srinivasan go because his son-in-law has been charged for betting in IPL…

And at each turn, 'But what else could we have done?' This is what was asked in 1950 as China invaded and subjugated Tibet. Sixty-three years later, the same question remains: 'What else can we do about Tibet?' It is what was asked in 1959 when news of the Chinese road through Aksai Chin broke out: and 1962 showed that, given what we had *not* been doing, there really wasn't anything that we could have done. It is what was asked after each bout of terrorist strikes in Kashmir. It is what was asked in the wake of 26/11. It is what was asked when two Indian soldiers were beheaded. It is what is asked every time news of China's incursions bursts through. 'What else can we do? Our Army could break up the tents in minutes with just a small contingent. But the Chinese, being Chinese, would set up tents elsewhere. We could send a few more soldiers and just throw the fellows out. But, given the roads and other infrastructure that they have built across Tibet right up to the LAC, they would be able to move a much larger force... The whole border would get inflamed... Is that what you want?'

How come no one—certainly not us—is ever able to put the Chinese in that kind of a dilemma? How come no one dares to chop off the heads of two Chinese soldiers?

One does not have to look far—just three/four instances mentioned in passing by Jacques Martin will provide the answer. The mere rumour online that a company that owned shares in Carrefour, the French retail giant, had given financial assistance to the Dalai Lama and the Tibetan Government-in-Exile was met with such fierce protests across China that Carrefour put forth explanations, offered an apology, the works. A wheelchair-bound Chinese athlete was accosted during protests in Paris at a torch rally to protest the fact that the Olympics were being held in Beijing. President Sarkozy seemed to suggest—even if vaguely—that France may not participate in the Beijing Olympics in view of China's record on human rights. China's reaction was such a fusillade that

Sarkozy wrote personally to that Chinese athlete, sent his senior-most diplomatic advisor to Beijing, and France participated in the Beijing Olympics. Earlier, Peugot-Citroen had carried an advertisement in a Spanish newspaper in which a scowling Mao looked askance from a hoarding at a Citroen car. The Chinese claimed the advertisement hurt their sentiments. It was hurriedly withdrawn and the company expressed regret. The American actress Sharon Stone seemed to have remarked that the earthquake in Sichuan Province was karmic retribution for how China had treated the Tibetans. Christian Dior had been using her visage in its advertisements. It was threatened that its products would be boycotted. It swiftly dropped her from its advertising in China.[5] Beheading two of China's soldiers? Who would even think of doing so?

Nor is it just a matter of reputation, of appearances. The fact is that, at each turn—the attack on Parliament, 26/11, the beheading of two of our soldiers, another chunk of our 'sacred motherland' swallowed up—we *cannot* do anything—*because we have not built up capacities over the preceding twenty-thirty years.*

> *Bal chhutkyo bandhan padey kachhu naa hote upaaye...*
> *Strength wanes, shackles tighten, no stratagem, no entreaty works...*

And don't miss another detail.

The two roads that weren't

Recall what Major General Sheru Thapliyal had said—that the spot that the Chinese chose for the incursion was carefully selected: we can access it only by air or by foot or mule track while they can bring a large number of troops at short notice

[5] Martin Jacques, *When China Rules the World*, Penguin, London, 2012, pp. 406–08.

on the first-rate highway they have built. On going into the events, Ajai Shukla found that we had actually planned to construct not just one but two roads to this very spot. What happened speaks to the current state of affairs.

Construction of roads along the borders is the responsibility of the Border Roads Organization (BRO). This organization has two components. The military component is manned by officers from the Corps of Engineers. The civilian component is manned by the GREF, the General Reserve Engineering Force. The two components are at loggerheads. Officers from GREF have been going after roads and sections being built by taskforces that are headed by Corps of Engineers officers. Relations between the two components have deteriorated to such an extent that when the military side holds dinners, etc. to mark important anniversaries in the evolution of the organization or when it organizes some function to mark, say, the completion of a difficult project, the civilians boycott these. Not just that. Recently, when the new head of the organization—Lieutenant General A.T. Parnaik—came to assume charge, he could not enter his office: the wives of the civilian employees were on dharna, demanding that the control of the organization be handed over to civilians. The general had to be taken to his office through a rear entrance.

Anyhow, back to the area that the Chinese came into in 2013. Around 2007–08, the Border Roads Organization finalized a plan to build one summer and one winter road to Daulat Beig Oldie—the reason for two roads was that some long stretches become inaccessible in the winter, and others in the summer: for instance, a lake on the way freezes in winter and you can drive over it; but it melts in the summer and you cannot motor across it.

The original plan envisaged that the two roads would be completed in 2012.

Construction commenced. Soon, new difficulties, in that they had not been envisaged in the original plans, were being enumerated: high altitude, geological instability, unexpected features at ground level, need for realignment…

In 2010, an officer of GREF, one Ghasi Ram, set out to inspect the portions that were being constructed by taskforces headed by officers from the Army's Corps of Engineers. He duly found fault—the alignment could have been 'Z' to 'Y' instead of 'X' to 'Y', etc. Complaints were lodged, and inquiries instituted.

And that brought all construction to a halt.

And, what with decision-making within the organization paralysed and the flow of funds halted, no one has been able to get the construction started again, even though three years have passed.

And Ghasi Ram? He was shifted as chief engineer to a project in Rajasthan. There he had to be removed for incompetence. He is now in Tripura…

But his work lives on! The date by which the two roads were to have been completed has been shifted from 2012 to 2016–17—that is what senior officers in the Border Roads Organization say in Delhi. On the ground, officers say that the roads will be useable only by, hold your breath, 2022.

Sad to say, even that is not the end of the matter. The Chinese were not holding themselves back. India soon found that the road infrastructure across the Line of Actual Control would give the PLA an enormous advantage in war. Accordingly, around 2005, Shyam Saran, who besides being the former foreign secretary and special envoy of the prime minister, and currently the chairman of the National Security Advisory Board, is a keen trekker, was tasked to visit various areas along the India-China border, check up on road construction work, identify the gaps, and pinpoint what more needed to be done. He identified 73 roads that had yet to be built and completed. What with developments of early 2013, and the public outrage these triggered, high-ups felt the need to review what had been done on Shyam Saran's Report.

The party assigned to assess what had been done couldn't get the Report. 'You know how difficult it is to retrieve paper in our system,' I am told as exculpation.[6]

You think the Chinese don't see this? And see the opportunity in it?

China turns the worm

In a sense, the nineteen-kilometre incursion was ill considered, certainly ill timed. The Manmohan Singh government had been battered out of shape by scandal after scandal; by stricture after stricture from the Supreme Court; by the departure of allies; by ministers having had to resign so that the prime minister would not have to; by an ally-on-the-outside, Mulayam Singh, also declaiming that the response of the government had been weak-kneed, that the Chinese must be made to vacate our territory, that they cannot be trusted. In a sense, *this* was the perfect moment for another lunge—an illegitimate government, one preoccupied with just trying to survive from day to day would hardly be able to react. But *precisely because* the government had become so illegitimate, *precisely because* the prime minister was seen as vacillating and weak, it could not do nothing in the face of public anger at what the Chinese had done.

As a result, in talks with Chinese Prime Minister Li Keqiang, during Li's visit to India between 19 and 21 May 2013, Manmohan Singh took up the incursion. Newsmen were briefed that he had made the border a 'focus' of the exchanges, telling Li that peace and tranquillity on the border is the 'foundation' of the relationship of the two countries. At their joint press conference, Manmohan Singh alluded to the two of them having discussed the Depsang episode, and to have noted that the existing mechanism to deal with such occurrences 'had proved its worth'. Li noted

---

[6] On the preceding, Ajai Shukla and persons concerned, personal communication.

that there were differences, that peace and tranquillity should be maintained jointly at the border, and that steps should be taken to strengthen the existing mechanism. The two agreed to 'encourage' their special representatives to proceed to bring the second stage of the three-stage border negotiations to a conclusion, and to speed up demarcation and delineation of the border.

One omission showed that the Government of India had stood its ground, another reference showed that at least India had taken up a vital issue, though China stood its ground. The joint statement did not contain the ritual reference to 'One China'. The joint statement that was issued in 2010 by Manmohan Singh and Wen Jaibao had also not contained the customary phrase. This was a step forward: Indian media were told that India was not going to go on endorsing the Chinese position regarding, say, Tibet being a part of China, when China was espousing the Pakistani position on Kashmir—exemplified, for instance, by its insistence on giving stapled visas to residents of Kashmir.[7]

The other issue was that of diversion of waters from rivers flowing into India from Tibet. Manmohan Singh took this up. He urged that the existing arrangement for exchange of hydrological data be expanded to include exchange of information on projects that are being taken up to dam the rivers. China agreed to inform Indian hydrologists more frequently about the water levels and flow in the rivers. It did not agree to establish any mechanism to exchange information or do anything else about dams and infrastructure

[7] Of course, within minutes of the joint statement being issued, our officials were bending backwards to assure all concerned that the omission did not mean that the Indian position had changed in any way: it was just that as this position—that Tibet is an integral, inalienable part of China—is so well known, there was no need to reiterate it! they told correspondents. *C.f*, 'India plays down omission of "Tibet" from joint statement', *The Hindu*, 21 May 2013.

that are being built across and around the rivers. The Indian Ambassador to China 'characterized the Chinese response as sympathetic,' *The Hindu* reported—how touching, their sympathy for us. He told the media, 'I think they recognize that we have concerns. They pointed out that they would not do something which would damage our interests. And essentially what we agreed upon was that we would strengthen our cooperation based on our existing mechanism.'[8] What that 'sympathy' will turn out to mean, what they would construe our interests to be, we will only learn in the future. But, at least the issue had taken up by Manmohan Singh.

In a word, *in spite* of our media, *in spite* of our governments and the political class in general, public mood has changed—and this time, the alarm and anger at the incursion registered even on this government-that-is-hardly-there. China has turned the worm.

People have come to realize that China is the principal threat to our country. That the gap between China and India has grown so vast in the last twenty years that we cannot at this time protect our interests on our own. That we must forge agreements and alliances with other countries that feel similarly threatened by China. The US-bashing of just a few years ago is hardly audible today: on the contrary, people are relieved at the announcement that it will focus on the Pacific.

This is, therefore, a good occasion to remind ourselves of the lessons that Chinese conduct should have drilled into us by now; to recall the constructions by which a good and great man, a nationalist—Pandit Nehru—deluded himself and thereby brought such tragedy down on the country. It is a good time to look at the chasm that has developed between China's 'Comprehensive National Strength' and ours, and what this chasm holds in store for us. It is the right time to glance at the reactions to China's meteoric

---

[8] 'The focus was on border', *The Hindu*, 21 May 2013.

rise, and what we have to do to avail ourselves of those changes in perception.

This study

In this brief book, I trace the policies, assumptions, and, I regret to say, delusions by which a great man, quite the idol of our generation at the time, Pandit Nehru, misled himself, and thereby brought severe trauma upon the country, a country that he loved and served with such ardour.

The literature on the 1962 debacle is, by now, vast. In this essay, I reconstruct the evolution of Panditji's policies in regard to China solely from his own writings and speeches. He was a prolific writer. He was a one-man orchestra in a sense, handling a vast array of matters, and so what he wrote covers a very wide front. More than that, Panditji saw as one of his primary functions to educate his colleagues at the Centre and in the states, and, of course, the people. Thus, his *Selected Works,* containing his official notes and correspondence, and the occasional speech, already cover 49 volumes. And, as yet, they cover the years only up to mid-1959. To keep them abreast of what was happening, and to acquaint them with the reasons on account of which particular steps were being taken, Panditji wrote every fortnight to the chief ministers. These letters cover five volumes. In addition, there are five volumes of his selected speeches. This last set, in particular, is just a very small selection. For Panditji toured incessantly, and spoke to the people day after day. He spoke ever so often in Parliament also.

I have confined myself to just these notes, correspondence and speeches. In a sense, therefore, this essay is an annotated walk through what Panditji said and wrote about China, our boundary with Tibet and China, and about events in Tibet itself.

Several authors have gone through this corpus and studied it in the light of what can be gleaned from other, ancillary sources also. The books of that devotee of Tibet and India, Claude Arpi, *The Fate of Tibet*[9] and *Born in Sin: The Panchsheel Agreement*,[10] as well as Ajay B. Agrawal's *India, Tibet and China*[11] are representative. Like other scholars, both Arpi and Agrawal have studied Panditji's writings and speeches extensively. They have also gleaned important information from other sources.

As my purpose here is a limited one, namely, to extract lessons from Panditji's own assumptions and world-view, I have confined myself to Panditji's writings and speeches alone. That is an argument for reading in addition the works of these authors. A single example will illustrate that reason.

Confining myself to Panditji's notes and correspondence, etc., I would have missed looking up, say, the correspondence and notes of Dr Rajendra Prasad, our President through much of that period. Agrawal's book led me to look them up. They traverse nineteen volumes. We find K.M. Panikkar, who was our Ambassador in China and of whose assessments we shall have occasion to read a good deal in what follows, giving the same sort of assessments to the President. Of course, there are certain things that the Chinese government is doing within China which we do not like, Dr Rajendra Prasad has him say, but we are not concerned with them. The point of concern to us is, 'They are friendly with our country and want to strengthen this friendship. It is in their interest also because they know well that in case they have bad relations with India, India and Burma together can create problems for them and they cannot harm India in any way.'

'They talk irrelevantly [irreverently?] about Tibet,' the President records Panikkar as telling him. 'It is not possible

---

[9] Claude Arpi, *The Fate of Tibet*, Har-Anand, New Delhi, 1999.

[10] Claude Arpi, *Born in Sin: The Panchsheel Agreement*, Mittal, New Delhi, 2004.

[11] Ajay B. Agrawal, *India, Tibet and China*, NA Books International, Mumbai, 2003.

for them to attack India from Tibet. Some of their military personnel are stationed in Tibet. '*Some*'? By this time, July 1952, China had swamped Tibet with a conquering army. 'They have a problem of supplying rice to these troops from China; supply through India is easier, which they are now doing'—the tell-tale and incredibly tortuous reasoning behind this supply of materials to Chinese troops through Calcutta, we shall soon encounter. The conversation moves to the consulate in Lhasa and the pilgrimage to Mansarovar: 'So, there is no fear from China but we hope to maintain friendly relations with her.'

In a word, the exact sort of assessments which Panditji internalized at such grave cost to himself and the country. The President and Panikkar talk of the need to do more work among the tribals of the Northeast: 'I agreed with him,' Dr Rajendra Prasad records, 'that considerable attention would have to be paid towards the northeast borders as the matter is of grave importance to us.'[12]

Later in the year, on 20 November 1952, H.V.R. Iyengar, who is to discharge several vital responsibilities in the coming years, calls on the President. The President has called him to be briefed on the administrative conditions in the country. The conversation shifts to China and Tibet. Iyengar tells the President, 'China is making a lot of roads, etc., in Tibet. But it would not be right today to say that it has any ulterior designs towards India. Of course, it would be an error to say anything about what may happen in politics in the future because relations between countries can turn hostile at any time. Even so, there is no reason to entertain any doubts at this time…'[13]

Assessments, indeed the very vocabulary is very different seven years later, and it is to an important document of this

---

[12] *Dr. Rajendra Prasad, Correspondence and Select Documents,* Volume 15, Valmiki Choudhary, (ed.), Allied, New Delhi, 1991, pp. 235–36.

[13] Ibid., p. 363.

later period that Agrawal's book led me. As we shall see, by then the Chinese have constructed a road through Aksai Chin and thereby hacked off a large chunk of our territory. Information has had to be prised out of the government, and Panditji personally. Indeed, they are unable to keep it under wraps any longer as the Chinese release an official announcement that the road is being inaugurated on such and such a date! Even as Panditji is minimizing the road and its consequence, the President learns from other sources that the Chinese have built yet another road. This one is further to the south and west of the original road, and hacks off even more of our territory.

He writes to Pandit Nehru on 5 December 1959. He begins by recalling that he had written 'a pretty long Top Secret letter' on 23 September, in which he had made several suggestions about the long border with China. 'Now that Tibet has practically ceased to exist for our purpose,' the President writes, 'we are face to face with a long Chinese border extending over 2,500 miles.' Apart from administrative work, and work to improve the lives of the people of the area, 'I think a plan should be prepared for making arrangements for security and defence.'

The border in the Northeast at least has the McMahon Line to delineate it, the President says. In the Ladakh region, on the other hand, the border is nebulous. The sentences that follow are worth reading in the original:

> We know that one big road has been built in the Aksai Chin area and it runs through our territory and the road is being used, and presumably the Chinese are in possession of the entire area to the north of this road, perhaps to some distance to the south of it also. *I understand that there is another road or track more or less parallel to it further south and running across our territory.* If this road has been built or is being built, it will undoubtedly be in constant possession and occupation of the Chinese, and not only the entire area between the two roads,

> but also practically the whole of that part of Ladakh would be fully occupied by them as far as occupation is possible in that terrain. I do not know to what extent the Chinese have already penetrated in this area into our territory. We may resist any further entry, but whenever there is any question of our reconnoitering the area and our police or military personnel passing into it, the Chinese would treat them as trespassers and shoot them or capture them as they did with some of our personnel some days ago. It is right that we should do our best to negotiate and settle this dispute with China in a peaceful way. But I do not know what will happen if such negotiation either does not take place or proves fruitless. They are already in possession of thousands of square miles of our territory and if negotiation does not take place or does not succeed, they simply sit quiet and remain where they are on our territory. We have therefore to think also of the steps which some day or other we may be called upon to take to recover our territory. That enterprise cannot be undertaken unless there is preparation for it. As it is, the Chinese have the advantage in the first place of terrain in their favour and nearly ten years' advance in preparation by building roads joining with our territory, apart from the big road or roads going east and west across it.

The President urges that apart from the measures that have to be taken to thwart incursions, 'a plan for defence of a long-term nature should be made'. Roads, communications, etc. have, of course, to be attended to. But, in addition, we have to heed what the Chief of Staff said at the last Governors' Conference, the President writes. The Chief had said then that 'the forces [are] just not enough to meet the other requirements as they existed before the border with China became a live issue, and it [is] not easy to deploy forces to the NEFA [the North East Frontier Agency] Frontier from the reserves…'

Concluding his letter, Dr Rajendra Prasad writes,

> We are now forcibly awakened to the fact of the existence of a long border which has to be protected as best we can,

and, what is more, we have to prepare for the recovery of the thousands of square miles already encroached upon in case all negotiations fail, unless we are prepared to write it off. We shall continue to hope that there will be a peaceful settlement and we shall do our utmost to get that effected, but we cannot rest only on that hope and that effort of ours, and as any effective steps to be taken will require very long preparation, the sooner such preparations are begun, the better.[14]

The President is saying things that seem innocuous, in retrospect even obvious. And yet, as will become evident as we proceed, he is urging positions that Panditji has been loath to embrace. In the form of suggestions about steps that should be taken, he is putting forth a deep criticism of the approach that Panditji has insisted on following for years in regard to China.

Panditji replies two days later. The President is at a loss. He takes some time to think through the matter. He writes to Panditji on 18 December, 1959.

Rajen Babu has also drawn attention of the prime minister to reports of corruption, and Panditji has told him that he, Panditji, is satisfied with the functioning of the government. The President's letter is a brief one, and is worth reading in its entirety—for we see through it what is to become a most corrosive course: Panditji has told the President that when the latter comes across information, he should *not* put it in writing; instead he should send for Panditji and talk it over:

Rashtrapati Bhavan
New Delhi
18th December 1959

My dear Jawaharlalji,

I received your letter No. 2585-PMH/59 dated the 7th December 1959 in time, but have not yet acknowledged it as

---

[14] *Dr. Rajendra Prasad, Correspondence and Select Documents,* Volume 19, Valmiki Chaudhary, (ed.), Allied, New Delhi, 1993, pp. 169–71.

I have not been able to make up my mind as to what to write. I must say that I am somewhat disappointed. The question of corruption has been too prominently and too long before the public to brook any further delay in making a probe into it. I think Deshmukh has given enough details about cases to be traced and once the Government makes up its mind and gives immunity to informants against vindictive action, proofs will be forthcoming. I would therefore suggest that thought be given to finding out cases. It is not enough that you are satisfied that all is well. A popular Government's duty is to give satisfaction to the people also.

Apart from what I have said, I have been worried by *your suggestion that I should send for you and speak to you if I have anything to communicate rather than write.* I am afraid this will stultify me in performing my constitutional duty to bring to the notice of the Government any matter which I desire to communicate to it in the way I consider best. I am afraid it may well begin a convention regarding the method of communication which will embarrass not only me but also my successors. I hope you will not mind my frankly expressing this fear which has been weighing on my mind and is responsible for the delay in replying to your letter.

Yours sincerely,
Rajendra Prasad[15]

Why this anxiety about things being put in writing? That information should not 'get into the wrong hands'? That history should be kind? We shall glean the pattern as we proceed. And, just as important, we shall see how that pattern continues to the present day.

In any event, the point I was mentioning was that the reader will learn a great deal more by reading the books of Arpi, Agrawal and others.

But even that cannot bring home the lessons that we must drill into our collective mind, lessons that ministers and civil

[15] Ibid., pp. 172–73.

servants responsible for our defence and foreign policies most certainly must drill into their minds. Those lessons will only seep in when the reader reads the notes and correspondence of Panditji in the original. I, therefore, hope that this brief book will persuade him to do so.

Meanwhile, like all who are interested in policy and research, I remain in debt to the editors of the Panditji's *Selected Works*, his *Letters to Chief Ministers* and his speeches for the systematic way in which they have organized this voluminous material, and to the Jawaharlal Nehru Memorial Fund for publishing the volumes. Close to fifty years have gone by since Panditji passed away. It is good to know that the series will be completed in the next three years. And also that the volumes are being digitized.

Records of debates, etc., that take place in Parliament are, of course, up to date. But they are so very voluminous, and the indexation is so general—even on a single day, the subject may have come up in exchanges during the Question Hour, or as the result of a Short Duration Discussion, or an Adjournment Motion and not just in a scheduled debate—that even the most stout-hearted researcher is liable to be deterred, and even the most diligent one may miss an important contribution. We really should digitize the records, and have them indexed in much greater detail than is the case at present.

But, for the moment, Panditji, and China, Tibet and our borders. The chasm that we have let develop between China and India, and what this portends for us. Lessons that we haven't learnt, and should.

2

Wish as policy

'On the issue of the reform of the United Nations Security Council, President Hu Jintao reiterated the assurance given by the Chinese Premier to the Prime Minister in April last year that *China understands and supports India's aspirations to play a bigger role in the United Nations, including the Security Council, and that China would be happy to see India succeed in its endeavour to become a Permanent Member of the U.N. Security Council'*—the minister of external affairs, Pranab Mukherjee, said in the course of his statement on 28 November 2006, in the Rajya Sabha about the discussions of the Indian prime minister and the Chinese president.

Along with his statement, Pranab Mukherjee placed on the table of the House, the Joint Declaration that had been issued by Manmohan Singh and Hu Jintao about their discussions. In regard to the Security Council, this Declaration had the following to say:

> The reform of the U.N. should be comprehensive, ensure balanced representation of developing and developed countries in the U.N. Security Council, and add to the efficiency and efficacy of the U.N. and its Security Council. The two sides *shall conduct consultations* on the question of U.N. reform, including the reform of the U.N. Security Council.

How does 'shall hold consultations' become 'would be happy to see India succeed in its endeavour'? The Joint Declaration continued to record,

> *The Indian side reiterates its aspirations* for permanent membership of the U.N. Security Council.

What could be more plaintive? And what did China say in turn?

> China attaches great importance to the status of India in international affairs. It understands and supports India's aspirations to play a greater role in the United Nations.

What could be more condescending? And how does the last sentence translate into the claim of Pranab Mukherjee that '*China would be happy to see India succeed in its endeavour to become a Permanent Member of the U.N. Security Council?*' Could 'a greater role in the United Nations' not as well mean a greater role in UNESCO or in UNICEF? Could it not mean that China would be happy to see us contribute more soldiers for peacekeeping operations in Africa? Similarly, read the sentence again in the Joint Declaration which states that the reform of the UN must be comprehensive, etc. Among other criteria, it says that the reform of the UN system, including the Security Council, must 'add to the efficiency and efficacy of the UN and its Security Council'. Has it not been the Chinese position that extending the veto to a larger number of members in the Security Council will *impair* 'the efficiency and efficacy' of the Security Council?

That such clarifications were necessary was triply manifest: Joint Declarations of this kind are routinely drafted to glide over inconvenient facts; China has a record of reading the most restrictive construction into, not just declarations but even into solemn covenants—witness how it has been conducting itself in regard to the commitments it has made under protocols that prohibit transfer of nuclear and missile technologies and components; and Indian governments, on the other hand, have a record of misleading the Indian public and Parliament into reading more into such declarations than is warranted—even during these very months, as documented in *Where Will All This Take Us?*,[1] the Manmohan Singh government was reading all sorts of meanings, not just unwarranted meanings but total falsehoods, into US legislation on the nuclear deal.

Soon enough, to no one's surprise, the Government itself put out documents that detailed communications between the additional secretary, Ministry of Foreign Affairs, in Islamabad, and Pakistan's envoy in Nigeria, which established that, in June 2007, that is, just months after those homilies about understanding India's aspirations for playing a greater role in the UN, China had gone to great lengths to coordinate efforts with Pakistan to ensure that the African governments stuck to a stand that would make it impossible to make any advance towards according a greater role for India, Japan, Brazil and Germany in the Security Council.[2]

But no secret documents were required. The statements that China had been issuing in public, the 'principles' it had been spelling out from time to time, were carefully crafted to puncture the case of both India and Japan. Using publicly available information up to just 2004, Mohan Malik, for instance, documented how the five 'principles' that were being advanced by Chinese 'analysts' nullified India's case point by point.[3] 'Top priority [should be assigned] to achieving equitable geographic distribution' in the Security Council, Malik quoted the Chinese foreign ministry analyst as advocating: as Asia is already represented by China, this 'principle' excludes India and Japan! China also

---

[1] Rupa, *The Indian Express*, New Delhi, 2008.

[2] *The Indian Express*, 15 June 2008.

[3] For the following account of 'principles', J. Mohan Malik, 'Security Council Reform: China signals its veto', *World Policy Journal*, Volume XXII, No. 1, Spring 2005.

advocated that, to ensure balanced representation from regions, the aspirants should conduct consultations 'until a final consensus is reached through a secret ballot within the regional group'—Pakistan is going to partake of a consensus in India's favour? Next, 'whether the newly elected permanent members shall be granted the power of veto', shall be decided by 'discussion and consensus among the present permanent members'—China will allow a consensus to emerge which puts India and Japan at par with it?[4] All this and more was in the public domain. But here was the minister of external affairs reading into the Joint Declaration what was manifestly not in it.

Mukherjee reported that Hu Jintao 'stressed that China had taken a "long-term and strategic view" of the relationship with India, desiring to build a strong and cooperative relationship based on shared and common interests'. Really? That is why it has ringed India? What do a nuclearized and armed Pakistan; a fully militarized Tibet; a military pact with Bangladesh; Myanmar as a dependency; naval facilities in Myanmar, Bangladesh, Pakistan and now Sri Lanka, signify? A 'long-term and strategic view' of India no doubt! Is it because of this 'long-term and strategic view' of India that China has been supplying technologies, materials, components, technicians and more for Pakistan's missile and nuclear programmes so much so that the scale and persistence of the assistance have led the director of the Wisconsin Project on Nuclear Arms Control to testify, 'If you subtract China's help from the Pakistani nuclear

---

[4] Malik also cited a series of statements by Chinese analysts and diplomats to the effect that China would just not allow India to become a permanent member of the Security Council. He cited the statement of the then prime minister of Pakistan, Shaukat Aziz, to the effect that, during his visit to Beijing in 2004, he had obtained a firm commitment from the same Hu Jintao that China would not let India get a permanent seat in the Security Council.

program, there is no Pakistani nuclear program?'[5] 'Economic cooperation emerged as a major thrust area of the visit...,' Mukherjee told Parliament. As in the way China has trounced India in bid after bid for oil-bearing tracts—from Ecuador to Kazakhstan? As in its strenuous efforts to stall India's access to ASEAN?

'Prime Minister and the Chinese President exchanged views on the boundary question and expressed satisfaction at the progress made by the Special Representatives,' Mukherjee said. 'Both leaders agreed that an early resolution of the boundary question would not only advance the basic interests of the two countries, but also invest our strategic partnership with further strength and dynamism, and should therefore be pursued as a strategic objective. They directed the Special Representatives to intensify their work to expeditiously explore the framework of a boundary settlement on the basis of the Agreement on Political Parameters and Guiding Principles signed in April last year.'[6] Hardly had a few months passed when Mukherjee personally got a taste of China's commitment to these 'principles': one of the 'guiding principles' that had been agreed upon was that the due interests of settled populations on each side of the border would be safeguarded; we were led to believe that this was an acknowledgement by the Chinese that Arunachal, in particular Tawang, would remain as they are—with India; in June 2007, the Chinese foreign minister told Mukherjee that the 'mere presence' of settled population does not affect China's claims across the border! Mukherjee did not say then, and has not said since, that, in fact, China has

[5] Cited along with much else in J. Mohan Malik, 'The Proliferation Axis: Beijing-Islamabad-Pyongyang', *The Korean Journal of Defense Analysis*, Volume XV, No. 1, Spring 2003.

[6] The agreement, 'Political Parameters and Guiding Principles for the Settlement of the India-China Boundary Question', was signed during the visit of the Chinese prime minister, Wen Jiabao, to India in April 2005.

systematically repudiated not just this 'principle' but each one of the 'guiding principles'.[7]

Just days before Hu Jintao was to arrive in India, the ambassador of China in Delhi, Sun Yuxi, declared that

---

[7] Ajai Shukla summarizes the position in regard to each of the principles as follows: *Article I:* 'The differences on the boundary question should not be allowed to affect the overall development of bilateral relations. The two sides will resolve the boundary question through peaceful and friendly consultations. Neither side shall use or threaten to use force against the other by any means. The final solution of the boundary question will significantly promote good neighbourly and friendly relations between India and China.' *Fact:* The differences on the boundary question have indeed been deliberately dramatized, and widened so that they *are* affecting the overall development of bilateral relations. Recall that, in November 2006, the Chinese ambassador to India, Sun Yuxi, stated publicly that, 'In our position, the whole of the state of Arunachal Pradesh is Chinese territory. And Tawang is only one of the places in it. We are claiming all of that.' Some way to promote 'the overall development of bilateral relations'! Similarly, a dispute has suddenly been raised in the 'Finger Area' of north Sikkim in a deliberately confrontational manner. This itself has the potential to explode into violence. This was considered a settled area, but now China has laid claim to 2.1 square kilometres of this tactically important high ground which overlooks the Tibetan plateau. Chinese patrols are now intruding up to the halfway point. The message in the 'Finger Area' is that China is willing to use strong-arm methods to take control of an area it considers important, either tactically or as a way of snatching bargaining chips for itself. ...

... *Article II:* 'The two sides should, in accordance with the Five Principles of Peaceful Coexistence, seek a fair, reasonable and mutually acceptable solution to the boundary question through consultations on an equal footing, proceeding from the political perspective of overall bilateral relations.' *Fact:* Consultations are not proceeding from the political perspective of overall bilateral relations. China is proceeding entirely as if its assertions of the moment alone matter. Having obtained Indian acceptance that Tibet is a part of China in exchange for recognition of Sikkim as a part of India, China's reopening of border disputes in Sikkim cannot be better designed to exacerbate bilateral relations.

Arunachal is a part of China. He repeated the claim in Chandigarh a few days later. The cry was taken up in November itself at meetings of Chinese think tanks—the Institute of Asia-Pacific Studies of the Chinese Academy of

---

Article III: 'Both sides should, in the spirit of mutual respect and mutual understanding, make meaningful and mutually acceptable adjustments to their respective positions on the boundary question, so as to arrive at a package settlement to the boundary question. The boundary settlement must be final, covering all sectors of the India-China boundary.' *Fact:* China has steadily moved away from a package settlement, as it feels the international climate has moved in its favour. Far from any sign that it is prepared to make any 'mutually acceptable adjustments' to its position on the boundary question, it is enlarging its claims. In the western sector it has taken a maximalist position; in the eastern sector it is demanding Tawang, which it knows India cannot part with.

Article IV: 'The two sides will give due consideration to each other's strategic and reasonable interests, and the principle of mutual and equal security.' *Fact:* Surely, that could not have meant continuing to arm Pakistan, to ring India, to actively impede Indo-ASEAN cooperation, to ensure that it is consigned to a subsidiary role in the Shanghai Cooperation Organization, to actively thwart India's bid for a seat in the Security Council.

Article V: 'The two sides will take into account, *inter alia,* historical evidence, national sentiments, practical difficulties and reasonable concerns and sensitivities of both sides, and the actual state of border areas.' *Fact:* China is interpreting 'historical evidence' entirely its own way, as it has insisted on doing in regard to Tibet itself. It is ignoring the actual state of the border areas, for instance while pressing its claims to Arunachal.

Article VI: 'The boundary should be along well-defined and easily identifiable natural geographical features to be mutually agreed upon between the two sides.' *Fact:* The claim on Tawang entirely violates the agreement to go by 'easily identifiable natural geographical features'. If that were the basis, the McMahon Line—broadly along the watershed—the very line which China has accepted in its agreement with Myanmar, would be the border in Arunachal.

Article VII: 'In reaching a boundary settlement, the two sides shall

Sciences and the China International Institute for Strategic Studies. Arunachal is 'Chinese territory under India's forcible occupation,' analysts declared. They talked of 'China's Tawang region', of Arunachal as 'Southern Tibet' which must

---

safeguard due interests of their settled populations in the border areas.' *Fact:* As we have seen above, China has turned away from this agreed principle also in pressing its claim to Tawang.

Article VIII: 'Within the agreed framework of the final boundary settlement, the delineation of the boundary will be carried out utilizing means such as modern cartographic and surveying practices and joint surveys.' *Fact:* This clause comes into effect only after the two sides agree upon the basic principles by which delineation is to be done. As the principles have been thrown into uncertainty, this stage is deferred to the indefinite future.

Article IX: 'Pending an ultimate settlement of the boundary question, the two sides should strictly respect and observe the line of actual control and work together to maintain peace and tranquility in the border areas. The India-China Joint Working Group and the India-China Diplomatic and Military Expert Group shall continue their work under the Agreements of 7 September 1993 and 29 November 1996, including the clarification of the line of actual control and the implementation of confidence building measures.' *Fact:* The repeated and continuing incursions by China exhibit what it understands by 'the two sides should strictly respect and observe the line of actual control and work together to maintain peace and tranquility in the border areas'. As for meetings, they continue without getting anywhere as China insistently refuses to exchange maps on the Line of Actual Control.

Article X: 'The Special Representatives on the boundary question shall continue their consultations in an earnest manner with the objective of arriving at an agreed framework for a boundary settlement, which will provide the basis for the delineation and demarcation of the India-China boundary to be subsequently undertaken by civil and military officials and surveyors of the two sides.' *Fact:* The special representatives are in deadlock. Arriving at the 'Agreed Framework' is now in the indefinite future; China is effectively repudiating even the prior stage of 'Political Parameters'.

be brought under the control of the 'Tibet Autonomous Region'. All this was on record. Several commentators, including persons like me, had repeatedly drawn attention to these claims.

Mukherjee told us in the Rajya Sabha:

> I am aware of the concerns expressed by Hon'ble Members about remarks made by the Chinese envoy on the eve of the visit about the status of Arunachal Pradesh. As you are also aware, I unambiguously rejected the Chinese contention, stating that Arunachal Pradesh is an integral part of India. Let me also state that the matter was taken up immediately with the Chinese Government through our Ambassador in Beijing and our disappointment and concern over the Chinese statement clearly conveyed.

But the question was: what did the Chinese say in return? I kept inquiring from various quarters in government. They wouldn't say!

The Chinese soon gave their answer—in deed! A 107-member delegation of new IAS officers was scheduled to visit China on a study tour in May 2007. One of the officers happened to be from Arunachal. The Chinese refused to give him a visa: since he is from a part of China, why is he to be given a visa? The entire tour had to be cancelled. The following month, as we just noticed, they told Pranab Mukherjee that the fact of settled populations could not come in the way of their claim—the reference was pointedly to their claim over Arunachal, in particular over Tawang. In January 2008, Prime Minister Manmohan Singh was to visit Tawang, among other places in Arunachal. The Chinese protested: he shouldn't be visiting Arunachal as it is a 'disputed area', they maintained.

Events in regard to Sikkim tell the same tale. It has been assumed all along that as a consequence of discussions during Mr Vajpayee's visit in 2003, China had finally recognized Sikkim to be a part of India. In return, India had paid the price of stating that the 'Tibet Autonomous Region of China is a part of the territory of China.' Misgivings in this regard were brushed aside. We are acknowledging no more than has been stated for years, it was said; in return, we have got China to give up the claim implicit in its maps—maps which show Sikkim to be part of China.

Astute observers had pointed out even at the time that, in fact, China had not changed the position in its maps, that it was maintaining that Sikkim is 'a historical issue' between China and India, and that China 'hopes' it will be resolved as bilateral relations improve—in no way did any of this suggest that China had agreed to the Indian inference.[8] In November 2007, Chinese troops demolished two posts of the Indian Army at Doka La, at the Sikkim-Bhutan-Tibet border junction. Two weeks had not passed and Chinese troops brought materials to build a road in the 'Finger Area' in north Sikkim. In January 2008, the Chinese government issued a démarche lodging a formal protest at movements—routine movements—of Indian troops within Sikkim. In March 2008 it made a formal claim to the 'Finger Area'. In June 2008 it formally brought Sikkim back into the discussions during Pranab Mukherjee's visit

[8] P. Stobdan, in the *Indian Express,* 6 October 2004. Observers were later to point out that by agreeing to this formulation, the Government of India, in fact, jeopardized India's position twice over: 'In 2003', Abanti Bhattacharya of the Institute of Defence Studies and Analyses, pointed out, 'the Vajpayee government went further than any other government before by stating that the "Tibetan Autonomous Region of China is a part of the territory of China." This has two critical implications for Indian security. First, it excluded Inner Tibet (present day Sichuan, Yunnan and Qinghai provinces) from the geographical notion of Tibet, thus recognizing Inner Tibet as Chinese land. Second, it provided China a greater opening to advance its claims on Arunachal Pradesh. For, Outer Tibet or the Tibetan Autonomous Region (TAR), according to the Chinese definition, includes Arunachal Pradesh, which it refers to as its "southern state".' Abanti Bhattacharya, 'India should revisit its Tibet policy', *IDSA Strategic Comments,* 4 April 2008.

to Beijing—the same visit during which the Chinese prime minister cancelled the meeting that had been scheduled with Mukherjee. And Mukherjee had but to leave China, and, within days, China again sent its vehicle-borne troops into the 'Finger Area'.

All this comes as a continuation of a series of pins that China has been thrusting into India over the last three years. The director general of the Indo-Tibetan Border Force reported that in 2007 alone there had been over 170 incursions—again, right from Ladakh in the west to Arunachal in the east. Several of these had been deep into our territory.

As the incursions have proceeded, the Chinese have kept inventing occasions to push India—from hacking into Indian networks, including those of the Ministry of External Affairs, of the National Informatics Centre, of the National Security Council Secretariat, to summoning the Indian ambassador in Beijing, well past midnight, to demand that Tibetans in Delhi be reined in.

Surely, none of this could be by inadvertence. Quite apart from the fact that these measures have been executed *by China*, which does nothing without calculation, and the very fact that in the last three years there has not been one incursion but over 300, the very fact that these have not taken place once or twice but have continued for three years, and the very fact that China has accompanied the incursions with a barrage of 'diplomatic' shoves show that all this is by design, that it is in furtherance of a definite objective.

To make India *feel* small.

To make India *look* small—in the eyes of countries in Asia in particular.

To convince people of the Himalayan states, as well as Indians living along our border with Tibet, that, even if it can, India will not stand up to China, and that, therefore, they better look up to and towards China for their future.

To keep India off-balance.

To put pressure on India to settle the boundary question on China's terms.

The aggressive thrusts that China has been executing would further each of these objectives.

And what has been the response of our government?

First, strenuous efforts to keep the people from getting to know the facts, to shut up any official who speaks up.

Second, when the facts do burst out, to downplay what is happening. The incursions are no reason to 'press the panic button', government rationalizers say; such things keep happening, the terrain is such that straying here and there is natural, they say. Why is it that *our* soldiers never stray into Chinese territory? No, no, please don't make so much of our ambassador being called in the middle of the night, a government high-up told me. There was a specific situation, and that was the only reason she was called; others also have been summoned at such times.

Third, to keep sending notes—'What is the Government doing about the incursions by Chinese in Arunachal?' the Indian defence minister was asked recently. 'Whenever there is any issue, it is always taken up through the appropriate channels and that system is continuing,' he replied. And there is a variant of this response: to keep expressing our 'disappointment and concern'—as in Pranab Mukherjee's statement to members of the Rajya Sabha about what the government had done in response to the Chinese ambassador's claim that Arunachal is a part of China: 'Let me also state that the matter was taken up immediately with the Chinese Government through our Ambassador in Beijing and our disappointment and concern over the Chinese statement clearly conveyed.' Remember these 'measures', these modes of 'response'—taking up issues through 'appropriate channels'; remember these words, conveying 'our disappointment and concern' as we proceed.

The fourth mode of response of the government has been

to be at its craven best in the belief, presumably, that, if only we are humble enough to the python, it will not swallow us. Annual reports of the Ministry of Defence used to describe, ever so summarily, but at least describe a bit, the advances that China was making in its military prowess and what implications these had for India's security. The 2007 report omitted the subject all together, trilling on about the way China was being a good and friendly neighbour to one and all! Government officials have been barred from attending functions where the Dalai Lama is present. The government, having seen the Bangladeshi writer, Taslima Nasreen, out of India by its pusillanimity, the minister of external affairs has lectured the Dalai Lama as if he were another Taslima and told him not to do anything that can be dubbed 'political'. The nadir of this approach has been the cravenness with which the government handled the passage of the Olympic Torch. Close to *twenty thousand troops* were brought in to seal off a route that is scarcely longer than a kilometre; government offices were closed; Parliament was sealed off from the road; the Metro was shut down... But why look for specific examples like these? Look at the cover of this book. *That mudra* is the Government's response to everything Chinese.

Do you think the Chinese do not notice? Do you think they do not arrive at operational deductions from the cravenness? Soon after that shameful display by our government of spinelessness and tremulousness in handling the Olympic Torch, I had gone to speak at a seminar organized by the International Institute for Strategic Studies here in Delhi. One of America's prominent security experts, indeed one of the principal architects of the Indo-US nuclear deal, was there too. He had just arrived from Beijing. 'You Americans should learn from the Indians,' he said the Chinese had told him, half mocking him—for, though an American now, he is of Indian origin. 'Learn from the Indians? What should we learn from the Indians?' he said he had asked them. 'See how *properly respectful* they are. You Americans should learn from them!'

And yet all this is of a pattern. Indeed, one hallmark of our policy vis-à-vis China has been continuity! The reactions to Chinese audacity, the evasions, the 'hope as policy', the very words—conveying 'our disappointment and concern' through 'appropriate channels'—are what we encounter when we look back at the steps that led to our being slapped in 1962.

3

'We may have deceived ourselves'

In his communications to the Tibetans, in notes to officials, right up to 1949, Pandit Nehru refers to 'the Tibet Government', to 'our two countries'. When, soon after India becomes independent, he convenes the Asian Relations Conference, the Government of Tibet is invited to send, and it sends, its representatives. In January 1949 a delegation comes from Tibet. He meets the delegation, offers to assist Tibet in its development and promises to send experts on village and cottage industries and on mineral development—experts who, he tells the delegation, will 'work under the direction of the Tibetan Government'.[1]

K.M. Panikkar has been India's ambassador to the nationalist government in Nanking. He has been warning Delhi about the strategic significance of Tibet for India, and how vital it is that its autonomy be maintained.

The communists seize power. Panditji is the first to ensure that India recognizes the new government. He also urges

[1] *Selected Works of Jawaharlal Nehru,* Second Series, Volume VIII, Jawaharlal Nehru Memorial Fund, New Delhi, pp. 470–72, at 471. Henceforth *SWJN.* The volume number shall be indicated in Roman numerals and the page number in Arabic numerals. Thus, for the previous reference, *SWJN,* VIII.471. The literature on the subject is quite extensive by now. It should be compulsory reading in our colleges and in institutions where our policymakers, in particular foreign service and defence officers are trained.

countries like the UK to hasten recognition. Although it is Chiang Kai-shek who has supported India's struggle for independence, and although it is with him and his associates that Indian leaders have been in cordial contact, once the communists seize power, Panditji is confident that they will be well disposed towards him and, therefore, towards India. '...Thirdly, they might be induced not to be hostile to us,' he writes in a note to the foreign secretary on 5 December 1948. 'I have some slight reputation with the leaders of Communist China because of the Medical Mission we had sent. I have corresponded with Mao Tse-tung and other leaders in the past. All this might help...'[2] Panikkar is now accredited to the communist government.

From the day they seize power, the Chinese communists declare that they will 'liberate' Tibet. Panikkar is too busy witnessing history unfold. He attaches no significance to the declarations, and to what they would, when acted upon, imply for India. Panditji immediately begins championing the cause of the new government. He urges the British, the Americans, in fact everyone he can reach, to force the nationalist government to vacate its seat in the United Nations, and that seat—which means necessarily the seat both in the General Assembly and the Security Council—must be given over to the communist government.

Even six months after the Chinese have been proclaiming their determination to 'liberate' Tibet, Panditji is maintaining that, in fact, an invasion of Tibet is not likely. On 9 July 1949 Panditji writes a note to the Secretary General, Ministry of External Affairs:

> Whatever may be the ultimate fate of Tibet in relation to China, I think there is practically no chance of any military danger to India arising from any possible change in Tibet. Geographically, this is very difficult and practically it would be a foolish adventure. If India is to be influenced or an

[2] *SWJN*, VIII.416.

> attempt made to bring pressure on it, Tibet is not the route for it.

Hence, his operational direction:

> I do not think there is any necessity at present for our Defence Ministry, or any part of it, to consider possible military repercussions on the Indo-Tibetan frontier. The event is remote and may not arise at all. Any present thought being given to it will affect the balance we are trying to create in India. It may also not remain a secret and that would be unfortunate.[3]

Soon enough, reports start arriving that the Chinese are concentrating their forces for invading Tibet. Panditji writes to the finance minister, John Mathai, on 10 September 1949: China may invade Tibet in a year or so, he writes. The Tibetans will not be able to resist the invasion. Many may even join the invading Chinese. This will bring China to the borders of India. Hence, we must build roads along our borders. Do not cut this programme for economizing expenditure, he writes, only to add, characteristically, I hate to add, *'At present we can proceed relatively slowly, as we have some time.'*[4]

But in Lhasa, even though they are preoccupied with rituals, diversions and protocol, the functionaries around the child Dalai Lama are worried. From the moment the communists take power, they have begun proclaiming that they will 'liberate' Tibet. They hear of Chinese troops gathering for an assault. A delegation of the Tibetan government waits to meet Panditji. But Panditji is busy with what he terms 'larger issues'; he is preoccupied in saving the world from crises that he believes are imminent. By now, both he and Panikkar are swept up by the history that is being forged in India, and in the new China. Panditji starts

---

3 *SWJN*, XII.410–11.

4 *SWJN*, XIII.260.

championing even more fervently the case for admitting communist China into the UN. He champions it in the UN, in the Commonwealth, everywhere.

From the first week of August, reports start arriving from Hong Kong that Chinese troops have begun moving towards Tibet. Panditji writes to Panikkar on 2 September 1950. You would have received copies of speeches I have been making in Parliament on foreign policy, he writes. 'On the whole, I created an impression on most people,' he notes. 'There are, of course, some who just cannot understand anything but a crude lining up with this or that Power.'

He can well understand Chinese feelings in regard to Tibet and Formosa, he says, 'but I am convinced that it is to their advantage as well as to the advantage of the world that *they should bide their time a little and not give cause to their enemies to say that China has aggressive and expansionist ideas.* 'On the whole, opinion is veering round to China's side and the chances of its admission to the U.N. have improved. Aggressive action at this stage "however justified" will injure these. *'Time is very much in favour of China and I do not see why they should not take advantage of this fact.'*[5]

It is after months of waiting that the Tibetan delegation is able to meet him on 8 September 1950. Panditji counsels them to proceed to Peking, and strive to secure assurances from the Chinese that their autonomy will be honoured. India can help only by giving 'friendly advice to China', and this it has already done 'by asking China that the problem of Tibet should be settled in a peaceful manner'. Put this alongside of the advice he has actually asked Panikkar to convey to the Chinese: bide your time a little longer!

The Tibetan delegation pleads that he urge at least that the talks be held in India as they are apprehensive that, if these are held in China, the Chinese communists will completely overawe them. No, we can't do that, Panditji

---

[5] *SWJN,* XV.I.432–33.

says. 'This would mean that India had a dominant position over China and Tibet.' 'In a peaceful settlement we can give Tibet diplomatic support,' he says—what kind of 'diplomatic support' he is actually prepared to give will become apparent soon—'but we cannot give any help in the event of an invasion. Nor can any other country.' 'It is for the Tibetans to make their choice between war and a peaceful settlement but in doing so they should clearly understand the consequences of their choice.' The Tibetans are disconsolate.[6]

Panikkar in Peking and Panditji in Delhi continue to maintain that an invasion of Tibet is highly unlikely. For one thing, the Chinese would not like to do anything that would give a handle to those who are opposed to the UN seat being given over to them, they maintain. They would not want to give a handle to 'warmongers' everywhere who are already trying their fervent best to undermine the new China's image.

Advice—in whose interest?

Around 7 October 1950 as many as 40,000 Chinese troops invade eastern Tibet. They seize Chamdo, the capital. Several thousand Tibetans are massacred—Tibetan sources put the dead at over 4,000. On 19 October 1950 Panditji cables Panikkar to convey his counsel to the Chinese rulers. We are not entering into the merits of the Chinese or Tibetans' claims in regard to the status of Tibet vis-à-vis China, he says. 'It is quite clear to us that any invasion of Tibet by Chinese troops will have serious consequences in regard to their position in the United Nations. It will strengthen the hands of the enemies of China and weaken those who are supporting their cause there.'

How profoundly he errs in his assessment of the Chinese

[6] *SWJN*, XV.I.434–36.

leaders in assuming that they care as much about what the world thinks of them as he does!

And Tibet can be taken by the Chinese for the asking. Why jeopardize your international reputation for what you can take at any time?

> Easy success in Tibet, *which can be had at any time later,* will not counterbalance loss in international sphere.

And he is defensive to boot:

> We have no ulterior considerations in this matter as we have pointed out. Our primary consideration is maintenance of world peace and reducing tensions so that all questions can be considered in a more normal atmosphere. Recent developments in Korea have not strengthened China's position which will be further weakened by any aggressive action in Tibet.

They should see our restraint: 'We are convinced that Goa and Pondicherry must come to us and it is easy for us to seize them by military means,' he tells Panikkar. 'But we have deliberately refrained from doing so because of larger considerations.' And so his perplexity:

> We do not understand the occasion for urgency and immediate military action in Tibet, when international situation is so delicate and no harm can result by delay in an attempt to seek settlement by negotiation.

Reports are not very definite, he says. However, reports from Lhasa suggest that 'Chamdo is not yet in Chinese hands, but threatened, though Chinese troops are reported to have entered what, according to our maps, is Tibetan territory.' Our position should be clarified to the Chinese, he says. And see the reasons in his mind:

> We cannot afford to have our world policy injuriously

> affected without at least trying our best to inform the Chinese Government in a friendly way of what we think is right and what is wrong. That world policy is based, apart from preservation of peace, on friendly relations between China and India as well as between China and other countries and United Nations.[7]

Would the Chinese rulers be caring for 'our world policy'? Why was the burden of keeping world peace to be borne specially by us? Should we have been so concerned about ensuring good relations between China and other countries and the United Nations? Notice also that the interests of Tibetans, to whom he has promised 'diplomatic support', do not figure in the enumeration at all.

A week has not passed, and on 25 October 1950 Panditji sends another long communication to Panikkar. The imperative need is to develop friendly and cooperative relations between China and India, he tells Panikkar. The future of Asia 'and to some extent of other parts of the world' depends on these... 'Your reports and communications have helped us greatly and *I think it may well be said that what we have done has, to some extent, even affected world policy. It is conceivable that but for India world war would have been much nearer.*'

Panikkar had been sending messages that were the American forces to cross the 38th parallel, a conflict with China would ensue. These assessments were conveyed by us to the governments of the UK and the USA, Panditji tells Panikkar. They said that China is bluffing. We told them that it appears to be dead serious. American forces crossed the 38th parallel. China did not act up to its threat, Panditji notes, 'and the U.K. and the U.S.A. took some pleasure in informing us that they had been right when they considered China's warning as mere bluff.'

'I am glad that China did not intervene at that stage

[7] *SWJN*, XV.I.436–37.

and thus prevented the Korean War from assuming huge dimensions,' Panditji said, adding, however:

> Still I must confess that this episode has weakened China's prestige to some extent and made people think that she indulges in empty threats. This is not a good thing; when a like crisis arises again, her warning might not be seriously taken.

How much more solicitous can one get?

Given what he has assumed should be the goals that China's new rulers ought to be pursuing, about the way to attain which he has been sending them friendly and disinterested advice, Panditji's perplexity rises to the point of incomprehensibility:

> China's attitude to Tibet again becomes more and more incomprehensible to me. I know Chinese feelings in the matter of Tibet... Nevertheless if military operations are started in the near future, it is quite clear to me that *they will injure China's interests considerably*. It is easy enough for China to overrun Tibet, *Tibet is hers for the asking at any time almost. When she is in such a favourable position, the need for military action seems to he very remote*. In the context of the world today any such action is bound to create a great deal of prejudice against China. It will put an end to our efforts to bring her into the United Nations. It will give a tremendous handle to her enemies, and Korea and Formosa will be affected. If China is aiming at a big conflict, then of course it does not matter much, but if she aims at the preservation of peace with honour, then this does matter. It is no good saying that China does not attach much importance to international opinion. No country, however great or big it might be, can afford to think so.

The Chinese had started issuing the customary statements—about conspiracies being executed by foreigners in Tibet: in fact, apart from a wireless operator and two or three other sundry persons, there were no foreigners in Tibet at all at the time. They even alleged that Nepal of all countries, a Nepal which at that very time was in the throes of an internal convulsion, was planning to intervene militarily in Tibet. The allegation that the British and Americans are intriguing in Tibet 'has no foundation in fact', Panditji tells Panikkar. The allegation about Nepal 'is even more fantastic'—the Nepalese government is encoiled in internal troubles.

With all the efforts that Panditji has been making on behalf of China, the moment he demurs in regard to China's plans in regard to Tibet, they denounce his 'friendly and disinterested advice' as having been instigated by the British and American imperialists! Panditji is touched to the quick:

> If the Chinese Government distrust India and think that we are intriguing against it with Western Powers, then all I can say is that they are less intelligent than I thought them to be.

But could it not be the other way? That they know exactly what will work with him? That all they have to do is to hurl an accusation at the liberal in Panditji, at the Panditji so conscious of what others think of him, and he will strain even harder to earn their approval? 'The whole corner-stone of our policy during the past few months,' Panditji explains, 'has been friendly relations with China and we have almost fallen out with other countries because of this policy that we have pursued.' But he is concerned with the 'larger issues'—world peace and the like. And, of course, about China's best interests: 'There is the danger of China feeling isolated and convinced of war and, therefore, plunging into all kinds of warlike adventures. This is too grave a risk for any great nation to take.' 'North Korea has been smashed,' he writes, again from the point of view of what is best in China's interests and reputation, 'and at this stage for China to help her directly, or to start an invasion of Formosa, would be foolish in the extreme from a military or political point of view...'

How good is his strategic assessment is shown up within the month: in the latter half of October, Chinese soldiers start entering Korea. Precisely a month after Panditji had pronounced that the move would be 'foolish in the extreme', on 26 November Chinese troops cross into Korea in massive waves. By 16 December the American army has got back to the 38th parallel. Trudging through frozen mountains, they at last reach Hungnan, from where they are evacuated by US ships. But to get back to Panditji's communication.

At last Panditji turns his thoughts to Tibet. 'About Tibet, our position is first of all that our frontiers with Tibet, that is, the McMahon Line, must stand as they are. There is no room for controversy over that issue.' As for the future of Tibet, 'In course of time, Tibet will certainly come nearer to China'—notice the delicate words he uses! 'A military invasion would not result in such a process of integration and foreign reactions will certainly be most unfavourable.'

He wants Panikkar to assure the Chinese that 'whether it is Tibet or any other place our activities can only be diplomatic.' 'There is no reason why we should be apologetic about our policy,' he says. 'By what we have done for China, we have earned the right to be frank. Our point of view should, therefore, be put before the Chinese Government fully whenever an occasion arises. If they disagree, we cannot help it, but it should not be said that we did not make our position clear.'

The Americans were hailing him as 'the great leader of Asia', he tells Panikkar. But because of the independent policy that he has been pursuing in regard to China and Korea, they have decided to 'debunk' him. Of course, in his assessment, he is not one to be moved by such trifles:

> All this, of course, does not affect our policy in the slightest. It only confirms it, and shows the immaturity of American

> judgement and also the lack of stability in it. I am informing you of this as it will help you to realize what the reactions of our policy are in the rest of the world. I am supposed to have 'sold out' to Mao through your bad influence. Panikkar is said to be 'Panicky'. It really is amazing how great nations are governed by very small people.[8]

That letter is sent on 25 October 1950. From the other side, Panikkar has sent a cable: Chinese see the possibility of large-scale war, they are preparing themselves for it. Panditji is upset: why are the Chinese getting themselves into this? He is impatient with them for not seeing elementary facts, in spite of his advice, repeatedly given. 'It is difficult for us to understand, how any intelligent person can consider Chinese security to be threatened along Tibetan frontier, whatever might happen, including world conflict,' Panditji tells the ambassador. The reference to intrigues by Nepal 'is equally absurd'. 'If Chinese Government distrust and disbelieve us, in spite of all that we have said and done, then there is nothing further that we can say. To us, any apprehensions of danger to Chinese security from side of Tibet which adjoins our frontiers are utterly devoid of foundation and cannot in our view, be a justification of military action; nor do we appreciate how, even in event of world war, such military action against Tibet can be of help to China.'[9]

That cable is sent on 25 October 1950.

The very next morning, on 26 October 1950, newspapers carry an official handout from Peking: the Chinese army has been ordered to advance into and 'liberate' Tibet! Panditji cables Panikkar. He tells Panikkar of his 'great regret' at this development, which, he says, 'we deeply deplore...' And he chastises Panikkar: there has been no information from you even of this official announcement, he tells the ambassador.

---

[8] *SWJN,* XV.I.438–43.

[9] *SWJN,* XV.I.444.

And he asks him to hand over a message to Chou En-lai. The Government of India expresses 'great regret' at this decision, he tells Chou. It is 'most surprising and regrettable'. The Tibetan delegation has left for Peking just yesterday. The delay in their departure was not because of any foreign influence… 'Deplorable… deep regret…' The decision is not in China's interest, he informs the Chinese premier. 'The Government of India can only express their deep regret that, *in spite of friendly and disinterested advice repeatedly tendered by them,* the Chinese Government should have decided to seek a solution of the problems of their relations with Tibet by force instead of by the slower and more enduring method of peaceful approach.'[10] What Chou and his colleagues think of Panditji giving such 'friendly and disinterested advice' will soon become evident. And, having conquered China through force, believing as they do in violence of the most extreme kind, are they the ones to think that the 'peaceful approach' is the one that yields more enduring solutions?

Minimizing the avalanche

By the next day, Panditji is scolding Panikkar. There was no information from you of Chinese troops advancing into Tibet. We were embarrassed to receive the official announcement of the Chinese government from the British government. Your representation to the Chinese government 'was weak and apologetic', Panditji tells Panikkar. Our views were 'evidently' not conveyed. 'The Chinese Government's action has jeopardized our interests in Tibet and our commitments to Tibet,' he says—remember these words when you read how he will minimize these interests and commitments in the coming months. Moreover, the action jeopardizes 'our persistent efforts to secure the recognition of China in the interests of world peace have suffered a serious setback.'[11]

[10] *SWJN,* XV.II.331–32.

[11] *SWJN,* XV.II.332–33.

But in public, even as he says that India 'greatly regrets' the decision of the Chinese, Panditji minimizes the invasion. What the Chinese have executed is a full-scale invasion, but, from what he tells Reuters on 29 October 1950, it would seem that all that the Chinese government is trying to do is to exercise the rights it had been given to certain disputed areas in eastern Tibet. He strives also to minimize the likely consequences of the invasion, even for Tibet. Tibet's autonomy is liable to be preserved, he says, by the terrain itself:

> Lhasa is situated far to the east of Tibet, and I doubt whether, even if China occupies the Tibetan capital, this will necessarily profoundly affect the situation in the western areas of the country.

An odd assessment, to say the least. The Chinese have declared that they will 'liberate' all of Tibet: why will they stop at Lhasa? And what is one to make of the 'necessarily profoundly'?

But Panditji does more. He advances grounds for exculpating the Chinese. The Chinese apprehensions that the US is out to undermine their regime may be right or wrong, he says, but they are real. Moreover, the Chinese do not have independent information about the world. Most of their information comes from the Soviets. They may have been propelled into their decision by the Soviet line about Anglo-American 'intrigues' in Tibet.[12]

Two days later he is giving an interview to I.F. Stone.

---

[12] It turns out that, in fact, Panikkar has told him that, while China was assured of Soviet support, 'there was no evidence that the Soviet Union was encouraging her to adopt a more hostile attitude towards the United States... China's foreign policy might approximate to what the U.S.S.R desired to be pursued in Asia, but it was based on an appreciation of her own national interests.' *SWJN*, XV.II.333–34; and the Editor's note at *SWJN*, XV.I.440.

'India has neither the resources nor the inclination to send armed assistance to Tibet...,' he says. But he is hurt. And why? *'We feel India has been ill-repaid for her diplomatic friendliness toward Peking.'* We do not dispute China's suzerainty over Tibet, he tells Stone, but Tibet's autonomy is as valid as China's 'pre-eminent domain in Tibet'. 'Sending an army is a poor way to maintain autonomy and come to a settlement.' What is 'disturbing more than anything else' is that Peking promised to negotiate differences with Tibet peacefully.[13] Should this modus operandi, of promising to negotiate a settlement peacefully and instead sending troops to settle the matter, not have remained in Panditji's mind when it came to our own borders?

'Difficult to say the Chinese have deliberately deceived us... We may have deceived ourselves...'

Across the board in India, people and leaders are upset by China's invasion. They have the gravest apprehensions about what the consequences will be for India itself in the years to come.

Rajaji writes to Panditji expressing concern at the invasion of Tibet. He points out that China seems to have gone back on its pledged word. He writes of the rights and position India has had in Lhasa, and expresses apprehensions about the implications for India. Panditji's response is characteristic. It contains several of the traits that will exact a heavy cost from him and the country in the coming years.

He tells Rajaji that he has been through the record—the telegrams and other papers in regard to Tibet. 'Legally our position seems to be a weak one in regard to Tibet. *Morally I find it difficult to say that the Chinese Government has deliberately deceived us at any stage. We may have deceived ourselves,* and they may have done wrong in the action they

---

[13] *SWJN*, XV.II.335–36.

took, as I think they did.' Having been unable or unwilling to do anything to prevent the aggressor, the liberal starts speaking up for the aggressor. Does this 'morally and legally' business square with the cables he has sent Panikkar in the preceding days?

'For the last year they have been talking about 'liberating' Tibet as a part of the Chinese fatherland,' he reminds Rajaji. But surely that is precisely the point: when for an entire year they have been declaring that they *will* invade Tibet, what has Panditji been doing? 'From the 15th of July of this year there has been a great deal of talk of this, and even some Chinese troops' movements were reported to us on the Tibetan border of China. Early in August the Chinese government issued the text of a proclamation by the Head of their Southern Command, who was "assigned to liberate Tibet". This proclamation stated that the People's Liberation Army will soon march towards Tibet.'

The question naturally arises, 'With all this information coming your way, what did you do?' Panditji recounts the telegrams that have been sent to Peking and the advice that has been given! 'At no stage did the Chinese Government say to us that they would not take military steps,' Panditji says, countering the charge that China has gone back on its pledged word. 'I think that the Chinese Government have taken a very wrong step, but I do not see how they can be accused of deception. They have been perfectly clear from the beginning.'

The more Panditji tries to exculpate the Chinese, the more he raises the question as to why he has himself not taken seriously their repeated proclamations.

But Panditji is not done. He goes on to set out reasons for the Chinese action. 'We have to remember also that the Chinese Government and people are living in constant fear of attack by the U.S.A. That fear may not be justified but it is not wholly groundless.' If we put ourselves in China's position, and see the demands of prominent men in the U.S.

that China be attacked; if we remember Chiang Kai-shek with his 'powerful army sitting nearby'; 'then we can perhaps appreciate the temper and apprehension of the Chinese Government and people.'

'Of course, all this does not justify military operations against Tibet,' he adds characteristically, 'but it does explain many things.' He is setting all this out, he tells Rajaji, 'to point out certain considerations which have to be borne in mind to understand why the Chinese Government may have developed a state of mind bordering on fear of what is going to happen, and fear leads to wrong action'—a plea of insanity?! Even the Chinese could scarcely have thought of that.[14]

Things speed up. Panditji is plugging the dykes everywhere. The Tibetans approach him to request that India move a resolution in the United Nations about what has happened. No, he rules. We shall not do so. If a resolution does come up, we shall support it on the general ground that the matter should be settled peacefully through negotiations.

B.C. Roy, the chief minister of West Bengal, sends him a press report about happenings on the border. The press reports are dramatized; Panditji writes back on 15 November 1950. 'But the fact remains that the approach of a Great Power like China to our frontier makes a great difference and we have to make our arrangements accordingly. We have in fact been considering this matter carefully with our Defence people.' B.C. Roy writes again enclosing this time an intelligence report. 'As I have already written to you, we are giving full consideration to this matter. Your report will be considered in that connection,' Panditji says. He concedes the point, only to put it down. 'It is, of course, necessary that we should keep a close watch on our border and ensure it against any possible incident that might happen,' adding, 'There appears to me, however, a tendency among our officers to get greatly excited

[14] *SWJN*, XV.II.336–38.

and take an alarmist view of all kinds of dangers, some real, others imaginary.'[15]

We come next to one of the most important documents in this entire, sorry sequence. K.M. Munshi recalls a meeting of the Cabinet on events in Tibet. 'All of us acquiesced in what Jawaharlal Nehru had already done,' he writes, 'only one or two venturing to voice feeble criticism. Among them was Sri N.V. Gadgil for whom there was a snub: "Don't you realize that the Himalayas are there?" I timidly ventured to say that in the seventh century Tibetans had crossed the Himalayas and invaded Kanauj.'[16] A few days after the Cabinet meeting, Munshi records, Sardar Patel wrote a detailed letter to Panditji.

The letter is one of the most important and prophetic documents in recent Indian history. The Sardar spells out almost to the dot what is going to happen in the coming years. He sets out steps that need to be taken, and suggests that a special meeting be held to determine the course of action. 'To my knowledge the meeting suggested by Sardar did not take place,' Munshi writes after reproducing the communication. 'Comment is hardly necessary,' he concludes.[17] Not only was the meeting never held, Panditji did not reply to the Sardar at all.

The Sardar's warning

He has carefully gone through the correspondence between the Ministry of External Affairs and our ambassador and through him the Chinese government, Sardar Patel writes, and he has tried to read it 'as favourably to our Ambassador and the Chinese Government as possible, but I regret to

---

[15] *SWJN*, XV.II.341–42.

[16] K.M. Munshi, *Pilgrimage to Freedom*, Bharatiya Vidya Bhavan, Bombay, 1967, Volume I, p. 175.

[17] Ibid., p. 181.

say that neither of them comes out well as a result of this study.' While concentrating their forces for an onslaught, the Chinese 'managed to instill into our Ambassador a false sense of confidence in their so-called desire to settle the Tibetan problem by peaceful means.' 'The final action of the Chinese, in my judgement, is little short of perfidy,' Sardar Patel says. 'The tragedy of it is that the Tibetans put their faith in us; they chose to be guided by us; and we have been unable to get them out of the meshes of Chinese diplomacy or Chinese malevolence.'

'Our Ambassador has been at great pains to find an explanation or justification for Chinese policy and actions,' the Sardar writes. 'There was a lack of firmness and unnecessary apology in one or two representations he made to the Chinese Government on our behalf.'

Referring to the reasons that the ambassador has been advancing to explain the Chinese invasion—reasons that, as we have seen, Panditji has himself been repeating—the Sardar says, 'It is impossible to imagine any sensible person believing in the so-called threat to China from Anglo-American machinations in Tibet.' And from that he draws a devastating conclusion: 'Therefore, if the Chinese put faith in this, *they must have distrusted us so completely as to have taken us as tools or stooges of Anglo-American diplomacy or strategy.*' And from that a further inference: 'This feeling, if genuinely entertained by the Chinese in spite of your direct approaches to them, indicates that, *even though we regard ourselves as the friends of China, the Chinese do not regard us as their friends.* With the Communist mentality of "whoever is not with them is against them", this is a significant pointer, of which we have to take due note.'

During the preceding months, the Sardar notes, 'outside the Russian camp, we have practically been alone in championing the cause of Chinese entry into the U.N.O. and in securing American assurances on the question of Formosa... In spite of this, China is not convinced of our disinterestedness; it continues to regard us with suspicion...' This in spite of the fact that in Peking we have an ambassador 'who is eminently suitable for putting across the friendly point of view'. Their last telegram was discourteous, and now comes 'the wild insinuation that our attitude is determined by foreign influences'. *'It looks as though it is not a friend speaking in that language but a potential enemy.'*

The invasion has brought China 'almost up to our gates', the Sardar notes. And this will have a host of consequences. First, 'The Chinese interpretation of suzerainty is different' from the one we seem to have in mind. 'We can, therefore, safely assume that *very soon they will disown all the stipulations which Tibet has entered into with us in the past. That throws into the melting pot all frontier and commercial settlements with Tibet on which we have been functioning and acting during the last half century.'* This is particularly ominous as China is now strong and united.

Second, on our side of the border, our people are 'ethnologically and culturally' similar to the Tibetans and the people of Mongolia. Third, roads and communications are poor, and in many stretches administration is barely present. Moreover, as 'continuous defensive lines do not exist', there is 'almost an unlimited scope for infiltration' of men and arms.

Finally, and this too must have pricked Panditji,

> Recent and bitter history also tells us that Communism is no shield against imperialism and that Communists are as good or as bad Imperialists as any other. *Chinese ambitions in this respect not only cover the Himalayan slopes on our side but also include important parts of Assam.*[18] They have their ambitions in Burma also...

In fact, the Sardar points out,

---

[18] At that time Assam and NEFA, the North East Frontier Agency, were the only two administrative units in our north-east.

> Chinese irredentism and Communist imperialism are different from the expansionism or imperialism of the Western powers. *The former has a cloak of ideology which makes it ten times more dangerous. In the guise of ideological expansion lie concealed racial, national and historical claims.* The danger from the north and north-east becomes both communist and imperialist.

And thus for the first time, after centuries, India has to be defended across two fronts. Pakistan in the west, and in the north and northeast *'a Communist China which has definite ambitions and aims and which does not, in any way, seem friendly disposed towards us'*.

The Sardar goes on to describe the situation in north Bengal, Sikkim, Bhutan, Nepal, the Naga Hills, swathes of Assam, and observes, 'I am sure the Chinese and their source of inspiration, Soviet Russia, would not miss any opportunity of exploiting these weak spots, partly in support of their ideology and partly in support of their ambitions.'

In a word, 'In these circumstances, to make people alive to the new danger or to make them defensively strong is a very difficult task indeed, and that difficulty can be got over only by enlightened firmness, strength and a clear line of policy... In my judgement, therefore, the situation is one in which we cannot afford either to be complacent or to be vacillating. We must have a clear idea of what we wish to achieve and also of the methods by which we should achieve it. Any faltering or lack of decisiveness in formulating our objectives or pursuing our policy to attain those objectives is bound to weaken us and increase the threats which are so evident.'

The Sardar goes on to list a series of steps that need to be taken: military and intelligence appreciation of the threat that China posed; an examination of our military capabilities and the disposition of our forces; a long-term evaluation of our defence needs; a reappraisal of our policy of going on advocating the Chinese case in the United Nations; methods to strengthen administration, policing, roads and communication across the Himalayan frontier; developing closer relations with Burma... He urges that a meeting be held early to consider all these matters.

The meeting is never held. Panditji does not so much as reply to the Sardar's letter. A month has hardly gone by and the Sardar passes away.

4

The policy is set

Panditji does not respond to the Sardar's detailed note. What he does instead is to send a long note on 18 November 1950 to the officials of the Ministry of External Affairs. In this he spells out the policy that the government is to follow in regard to Tibet and China.

Preceding this note, two messages have been exchanged with China. As the editor of the *Selected Works* records, the Indian government had sent a note on 1 November 1950. It said that the Indian agent in Lhasa as well as the trade agencies in Gyantse and Yatung should continue, and so should the P&T officers and the military escort along the trade route. The Chinese replied on 16 November. The Chinese said that India had all along been saying that it accepts Chinese sovereignty over Tibet,

> However, when the Chinese Government actually exercised its sovereignty rights, and began to liberate the Tibetan people and drive out foreign forces and influences to ensure that the Tibetan people will be free from aggression and will realize regional autonomy and religious freedom, the Indian Government attempted to influence and obstruct the exercise of its sovereign rights in Tibet by the Chinese Government.

Panditji must have seen where his unilateral pronouncements about Chinese suzerainty had led. But he had been making a point of using the expression 'suzerainty' and *not* 'sovereignty'. What had happened? It transpires that in transmitting a note sent from Delhi on 26 August 1950, Panikkar has substituted the word 'sovereignty' for 'suzerainty'. On 17 November, when the implications at last dawn on the busy prime minister and his ministry, Panikkar is told 'to draw attention immediately of the Chinese Foreign Office to the use by oversight' of the word 'sovereignty', and to point out that the correct expression, 'suzerainty', has been used in the subsequent message of 1 November.[1] The Chinese know what to ignore and what to build on.

Panditji begins with the sorry consequence: 'Stress is laid in China's note on Chinese sovereignty over Tibet, which, we are reminded, we have acknowledged, on Tibet being an integral part of China's territory and therefore a domestic problem.' He notes that the Chinese government has again repeated the allegation that outside influences have been obstructing China from completing its mission of liberating the people of Tibet, and that 'no foreign intervention will be permitted and that the Chinese Army will proceed.'

He can't fault the Chinese, for he acknowledges, 'It is true that in one of our messages to the Chinese government we used "sovereignty" of China in relation to Tibet. In our last message we used the word, "suzerainty". After receipt of China's last note, we have pointed out to our Ambassador that "suzerainty" was the right word and that "sovereignty" had been used by error'—remember this fine distinction as we proceed. We will have occasion to see, soon enough, how Panditji himself confounds the two concepts, and makes out that they mean more or less the same thing.

He says that it is easy enough to draft a reply to the Chinese note, but that we should remember that China is going to be our neighbour; that we have 'a tremendously long common frontier'; that the communist government is

---

[1] *SWJN*, XV.II.343, Editor's notes 4 and 5.

not going to collapse. 'Therefore, it is important to pursue a policy which will be in keeping with this long-term view.'

Now, this is a favourite phrase of Panditji—'the long-term view'—as is 'the larger considerations'. Whenever he deploys the former, you can be sure that he is preparing the case for ceding ground. Whenever he deploys the latter, you can be sure that he is preparing the case for ceding specifically the country's interest.

Gone is that earlier distinction between occupying Lhasa and western Tibet remaining unaffected. He now is as certain of the opposite: 'I think it may be taken for granted that China will take possession, in a political sense at least, of the whole of Tibet. There is no likelihood whatever of Tibet being able to resist this or stop it. It is equally unlikely that any foreign Power can prevent it. We cannot do so.'

'The Chinese note has repeated that they wish the Tibetan people to have, what they call, "regional autonomy and religious freedom",' he notes. He expects less from the promise now than he was suggesting a few weeks earlier: 'This autonomy can obviously not be anything like the autonomy, verging on independence, which Tibet has enjoyed during the last forty years or so.' And yet he keeps up a delusion:

> But it is reasonable to assume from the very nature of Tibetan geography, terrain and climate, that a large measure of autonomy is almost inevitable.

Hence, the object of Indian policy is to maintain Tibetan autonomy. We needn't now do anything about it as it is 'almost inevitable' that it will survive because of geography, terrain and climate. And it may also not be the case that the Chinese seek to control Tibet directly: 'It may of course be that this autonomous Tibet is controlled by communist elements in Tibet. I imagine however that it is, on the whole, more likely that what will be attempted will be a pro-communist China administration rather than a communist one.'

Tibet gone, the question is: what effect does China's takeover of Tibet spell for India's security? Panditji's first alibi for not being specific, and indeed for doing little is the old one—the prospect of a world war:

> If world war comes, then all kinds of difficult and intricate problems arise and each one of these problems will be interrelated with others. Even the question of defence of India assumes a different shape and cannot be isolated from other world factors.

But no one has said that the invasion is going to trigger a world war. Nor is it evident that any reaction from India, or by India in concert with others, will trigger a world war. But the strawman having been set up and knocked down, Panditji moves to an operational conclusion of the greatest significance:

> I think that it is exceedingly unlikely that we may have to face any real military invasion from the Chinese side, whether in peace or in war, in the foreseeable future.

First notice that what Panditji is ruling out is a full-scale invasion. But, surely, that is not the only option before China—then or in 'the foreseeable future'. Second, what makes an assault on India 'exceedingly unlikely'? The same, ethereal 'world factors' of which he has special understanding:

I base this conclusion on a consideration of various world factors.

How come?

> In peace, such an invasion would undoubtedly lead to world war. China, though internally big, is in a way amorphous and easily capable of being attacked, on its seacoasts and by air. In such a war, China would have its main front in the south and east and it will be fighting for its very existence against

> powerful enemies. It is, inconceivable that it should divert its forces and its strength across the inhospitable terrain of Tibet and undertake a wild adventure across the Himalayas. Any such attempt will greatly weaken its capacity to meet its real enemies on other fronts. Thus I rule out any major attack on India by China.

How costly it is for leaders, especially for leaders who are so exalted that no one is liable to question their assessment, to play strategist! For, this strategic assessment leads to an immediate practical conclusion, one that is set to be fatal in the coming years:

> I think these considerations should be borne in mind, because there is far too much loose talk about China attacking and overrunning India. If we lose our sense of perspective and world strategy and give way to unreasoning fears, then any policy that we might have is likely to fail.

Characteristically, Panditji sees the lesser evil only, as we shall see, to do little about his own apprehension:

> While there is, in my opinion, practically no chance of a major attack on India by China, there are certainly chances of gradual infiltration across our border and possibly of entering and taking possession of disputed territory, if there is no obstruction to this happening. We must therefore take all necessary precautions and those that might be necessary to meet a real attack.

He goes to some length to buttress this stance of preparing for limited preparedness, so to say:

> If we really feared an attack and had to make full provision for it, this would cast an intolerable burden on us, financial and otherwise, and it would weaken our general defence position. There are limits beyond which we cannot go at least for some years, and a spreading out of our army

> in distant frontiers would be bad from every military or strategic point of view.

Our major possible enemy is Pakistan, Panditji notes. If we start preparing for defending ourselves on both fronts, the burden would be unbearable. Moreover, if we fall out with China, Pakistan would undoubtedly take advantage of this.

He turns next to what Sardar Patel has said about communists being as good or as bad imperialists as others. To start off, he exaggerates the Sardar's point so as to be able, all that much more easily, to knock it down as 'naïve':

> The idea that communism *inevitably* means expansion and war, or, to put it more precisely, that Chinese communism means *inevitably* an expansion towards India, is rather naïve.

Had Sardar Patel said 'inevitably'? But, writing as he is a secret note to his captive officials, Panditji can exaggerate-to-knock-down at will:

> It may mean that in certain circumstances. Those circumstances would depend upon many factors, which I need not go into here. The danger really is not from military invasion but from infiltration of men and ideas. The ideas are there already and can only be countered by other ideas. Communism is an important element in the situation. But, by our attaching too great importance to it in this context, we are likely to misjudge of the situation from other and more important angles.

The sentence that follows is breathtaking:

> In a long-term view, India and China are two of the biggest countries of Asia bordering on each other and *both with certain expansive tendencies, because of their vitality.*

China is the one that has invaded and taken over Tibet.

India has done nothing of the kind. But, to justify not doing anything about the Chinese invasion, Panditji implies that we are the same kind; hence, why be so upset at what China has done?

He is back to his standard argument for giving in: friendship of China and India is important for the two countries, for Asia and for world peace. That is why the powers don't want to see us as friends:

> It is interesting to note that both the U.K. and the U.S.A. appear to be anxious to add to the unfriendliness of India and China towards each other. It is also interesting to find that the U.S.S.R. does not view with favour any friendly relations between India and China.

In a word, the policy of being friends with China, and by inference doing what is necessary to be friends of China, has the added virtue of being opposed by the great powers—that surely establishes that our policy is right! QED.

Time to draw the operational conclusion:

> The arguments lead to the conclusion that while we should be prepared, to the best of our ability, for all contingencies, *the real protection that we should seek is some kind of understanding of China.* If we have not got that, then both our present and our future are imperiled and no distant Power can save us.

He fortifies this with another conjecture for which there is no basis, indeed that is refuted by the event at hand, namely the invasion of Tibet and the brutal suppression of its people:

> I think on the whole that China desires this too for obvious reasons. If this is so, then we should fashion our present policy accordingly.

Acquiescing in the invasion of Tibet, therefore, is the prudent policy. *And it is in Tibet's interest that we acquiesce in its conquest by China:*

> We cannot save Tibet, as we should have liked to do, and *our very attempts to save it might well bring greater trouble to it.* It would be unfair to Tibet for us to bring this trouble upon her without having the capacity to help her effectively. It may be possible, however, that we might be able to help Tibet to retain a large measure of her autonomy. That would be good for Tibet and good for India. As far as I can see, this can only be done on the diplomatic level and by avoidance of making the present tension between India and China worse.

It so happens that there is an immediate opportunity at the 'diplomatic level'. The issue is liable to come up in the United Nations. A draft appeal has been circulated. Panditji proceeds to scotch this prospect also—in three steps.

> We have said that we are not going to sponsor this appeal, but if it comes up, we shall state our viewpoint. This viewpoint cannot be one of full support of the Tibetan appeal, because that goes far and claims full independence. We may say that whatever might have been acknowledged in the past about China's sovereignty or suzerainty, recent events have deprived China of the right to claim that.

But even this we should actually *not do,* and that too in the interest of Tibet itself!

> There may be some moral basis for this argument. But it will not take us or Tibet very far. It will only hasten the downfall of Tibet. No outsider will be able to help her and China, suspicious and apprehensive of these tactics, will make sure of much speedier and fuller possession of Tibet than she might otherwise have done. We shall thus not only fail in our endeavour but at the same time have really a hostile China on our doorstep.

The third step is predictable: we should not sponsor the appeal; next, we should not state our position on an appeal if it comes up; third, we should work to ensure that the appeal is not discussed at all—and this too in the interest of Tibet!

> I think that in no event should we sponsor Tibet's appeal. I would personally think that it would be a good thing if that appeal is not heard in the Security Council or the General Assembly. If it is considered there, there is bound to be a great deal of bitter speaking and accusation, which will worsen the situation as regards Tibet, as well as the possibility of widespread war, without helping it in the least. It must be remembered that neither the U.K. nor the U.S.A., nor indeed any other Power, is particularly interested in Tibet or the future of that country. What they are interested in is embarrassing China. Our interest, on the other hand, is Tibet, and if we cannot serve that interest, we fail.
>
> Therefore, it will be better not to discuss Tibet's appeal in the U.N. Suppose, however, that it comes up for discussion, in spite of our not wishing this, what then? I would suggest that our representative should state our case as moderately as possible and ask the Security Council or the Assembly to give expression to their desire that the Sino-Tibetan question should be settled peacefully and that Tibet's autonomy should be respected and maintained.[2]

Accordingly, instructions are sent all round: cables to Sir B.N. Rau, India's representative at the United Nations, to Panikkar, and others. Other countries maintain that as India is the major country that is affected, they will go by what India decides. The record shows that as India conveyed its view that the resolution should *not* be discussed, it is never put on the Agenda.[3]

Recall, what he had told the Tibetans—that India would help diplomatically. That help now has come to mean that India will keep China in good humour even as it crushes Tibet, so that it may not crush Tibet more swiftly.

---

[2] *SWJN*, XV.II.342–47.

[3] *SWJN*, XV.II.347–52.

A typical debate

As the weeks go by, anxiety mounts. Leader after leader of the Opposition expresses doubts about the way Panditji has let go of our interests in Tibet; of the way the poor Tibetans have been sacrificed for fanciful notions of saving the world from war; of the way our own security has been imperiled at the altar of 'larger considerations' of world peace and the rest.

Panditji initiates a debate on 'The International Situation' in the Lok Sabha on 6 December 1950.

As the world situation is delicately poised and as events are moving at a rapid pace, he wants 'the fullest understanding to exist between the Government and this House'. Hence, the debate. However, 'I find some difficulty in speaking about this matter,' he tells the House, 'because I wish to avoid saying any word which might hurt any country or any people.' The issue can be described in just one sentence, or two or three words, he says: *'The issue is: peace or war. And not war in a particular corner of the world, but an overwhelming and all enveloping war, which may well bring uttermost destruction to this world and which may well ruin the proud structure of our present day civilization.'*

This is typical of the way Panditji poses the alternatives: either world war or peace; as our choice is peace, we must do everything for peace; in particular, we must not ruffle China in any way; especially as it is already labouring under fear, and, therefore, is liable to act irrationally. In his speech, Panditji addresses himself mainly to the situation in the Far East, and what he has been doing to restore peace. He turns to Nepal—the convulsions in that country; our links with it; the barrier that protects us lying on the other side of Nepal, and, hence, 'we are not going to tolerate any person coming over that barrier.' 'Therefore, much as we appreciate the independence of Nepal, we cannot risk our own security for anything going wrong in Nepal which permits either that barrier to be crossed or otherwise weakens our frontier.'

On Tibet, his tone is very different. He recalls how the government has been communicating to China that 'we earnestly hoped that this matter would be settled peacefully by China and Tibet.' 'We told them that we had no territorial or political ambitions in regard to Tibet,' just that in view of our long trade and cultural relations, we hoped that Tibet would 'maintain her autonomy which she had had for the last forty or fifty years at least. We did not challenge or deny the suzerainty of China over Tibet.'

The Chinese kept saying that they too would want to settle the matter peacefully, Panditji tells the House, 'but in any event that they would liberate Tibet.' 'It is not quite clear from whom they were going to liberate it,' Panditji remarked—many acolytes must have nudged each other at the great man's wit. 'Their replies made us to understand that a peaceful solution would be found...'

Pause a moment. One thing that stands out in such statements, of course, is that throughout this period Panditji reads what he wants to read into what the Chinese are saying. The second thing is what Panditji has in mind when he talks of a peaceful solution being found. As will be evident from what he has been writing to his officers, the solution he has come to accept from the beginning is that China will swallow and digest Tibet—albeit, gradually, without creating a fuss.

Panditji continues: 'though I must add that they gave no assurance or guarantee about it to us.' 'They always put the two together: "We are prepared for a peaceful solution; but anyhow we are going to liberate."' 'So that, when we heard about their armies marching into Tibet,' Panditji tells the House, as if the inference he has drawn is elementary logic, 'it did come as a surprise to us and a shock.' Given the information that has been coming across for months and months, should he have been 'surprised' and 'shocked'? If he is indeed taken by surprise, is it not because of his great faith in his own counsel to them? Is it not because he has led himself to believe that the new rulers of China, isolated as they are, knowing as little about international affairs as in his estimate they do, will go by his 'friendly and disinterested advice, repeatedly given'?

And there is another reason he has thought that the matter will be settled peacefully: '...indeed, one can hardly think about war between China and Tibet,' he tells the Lok Sabha. 'Tibet is not in a position to carry on a war. There is no threat from Tibet to China, obviously. They say, there might be foreign intrigues; I do not know.'

Pause again. Is the fact that Tibet is in no position to fight China a reason why China will *not* invade Tibet? Or a reason why it *will* invade Tibet? Second, notice how he is putting that Chinese claim about foreign intrigues: 'I do not know.' Does this square with what he has been saying in cable after cable to Panikkar? 'Something which has no foundation in fact', 'still more fantastic', 'it is difficult for us to understand how any intelligent person can consider Chinese security threatened along Tibetan frontier...,' 'utterly devoid of foundation'... And here, 'I do not know.' This is a characteristic that we will encounter again and again: he says whatever he wants, and with that is able to put down the interlocutor.

'Anyhow, there was no immediate threat,' Panditji continues. 'Violence might perhaps be justified in the modern world; but naturally, one should not indulge in it unless there is no other way.' Notice the two sentences that follow: 'Well there was a way in Tibet as we had pointed out. So it was a surprise.' That certainly points to an inordinate notion of one's advice—that because we have pointed out another way to them, the Chinese are liable to follow it!

Even now, he says, we hope the advance will be halted. And then he implies without exactly saying so that the advance has in fact come to a halt—another reason not to do anything:

> As a matter of fact, there can be no doubt that for the last several weeks the main advance has been halted. But I cannot definitely say what they intend doing or whether *some small groups* have not gone in various directions or advanced in various directions. So far as we know, towards Lhasa there has been no advance and conditions in Lhasa at present are still normal. That, of course, does not solve the problem. All I can say is that I earnestly hope that even now, the Government of China will try to settle the matter peacefully.

We can see the operational conclusion that flows from such reasoning. As the main advance has halted, there is nothing that we need to do. When the main advance resumes, the full picture is not clear. When it is completed, and the place is subjugated, there is nothing for us to do as, by then, the place has already been subjugated. For us to do or say anything will only enrage the occupiers, and bring even greater hardship on the poor Tibetans!

Leader after leader in the Opposition rises to express deep dissatisfaction with what Panditji has said. Professor N.G. Ranga asks, why is the government not seeing who the new rulers of China are? Are they not the ones who just the other day insinuated that India is the foreign power that is interfering in the affairs of Tibet? We keep saying that we recognize the sovereignty of China over Tibet. But in the mind of the new rulers of China 'sovereignty makes no other meaning than expansion of their own control, political, economic and social over other peoples.' By going on saying that we recognize the sovereignty of China over Tibet, 'are we not giving a blank cheque to be signed on our behalf by somebody else in order to spread their own imperialist tentacles?' Would such rulers not take aim at India tomorrow? Yet, to his surprise, Professor Ranga tells the House, here is the government going on chanting that we have friendship for not just the people of China, not just for their government but also for Chinese sovereignty over Tibet! 'This beats anybody and everybody.'

Dr Shyama Prasad Mookherjee recalls the doggedness with which the prime minister has been advocating the case of China in the United Nations, and asks, 'How has China reciprocated?' He recalls the messages that the prime minister has been sending China about Tibet, and what has been China's reply? 'The reply that China has sent has shocked, surprised and has given sorrow to the Government of India.' Have that shock, surprise, sorrow had any effect on the policy China is pursuing? What is our definite policy regarding Tibet? he asks. 'The Prime Minister just glossed over it. He said: We have sent another request asking them to be peaceful, but has it made any difference? ....we sent frantic appeals to China asking her not to be violent but did China listen?' The boundary between Tibet and India is undefined. The prime minister keeps saying that we stand by the McMahon Line, 'but the maps of China which are in circulation even now include portions of Assam, Ladakh and Leh and territories in which India is vitally interested.' The reply that China has sent regarding Tibet 'definitely indicates that China will do everything necessary for the purpose of keeping intact what it considers to be China's border, it includes Tibet as well and the undefined boundary of Tibet so far as it touches the Indian border.' Dr Mookherjee charges Panditji with following 'a surrendering policy' in regard to Tibet, and warns of the day when the Himalayas will themselves become the route for infiltrating personnel into India.[4]

---

[4] Shyama Prasad Mookherjee also drew attention to the loud declamations of the prime minister in regard to the discrimination against blacks in South Africa and his conspicuous silence about the cruelties that were being heaped on the Hindus in East Pakistan—a contrast that has continued to this day. Referring to Panditji, Mookherjee said, 'He knows much better than even myself the life of misery, shame and humiliation which these millions of Hindus in East Bengal are being forced to live.

Acharya Kripalani draws attention to the alacrity and fervour with which the government has gone about, first, recognizing the new Government of China, and then urging other countries to recognize it and hand over the UN seat to it. And how has China reciprocated? When we advocated its membership in the United Nations, 'at that time China did not remember that we were inspired by some other nation but when it came to the question of Tibet they tell us that we are inspired by some other nation.'

M.R. Masani is the most scathing, and, it turns out, the most prophetic. The anxiety that the prime minister has expressed about the possibility of a world war should be supplemented, Masani says, with the anxiety 'against the possibility of another Far-Eastern Munich'. The prime minister stated that the issue is 'peace or war'. 'May I suggest that there is also the other issue of peace or appeasement leading to war?'

We have been acting out our friendship for China for a year, Masani tells the House. By now, we can judge what the character of the new rulers of China is: 'in three different directions the Chinese Communist regime has shown its aggressive character: in Korea it is at war with United Nations forces, which are seeking to establish a free and united Korea; in Indo-China, where they have armed and sent Communist guerillas across the frontier as was done in Greece some years ago; and our own neighbours of Tibet are now having an invasion of their country.'

He recalls the message that Mao had sent to the general

He said in the course of his speech that whatever happens, India will never agree to any discrimination being made in reference to South Africa, whether it is based on race or religion. When people who had their loyalty fixed upon undivided India, who made Indian freedom possible, and today also naturally look to India for protection and help in emergency, are forced to live in an atmosphere of insecurity and misery and humiliation, then, what is India's policy in respect of them? Are we so weak as to merely watch and appeal?'

secretary of the Communist Party of India: a message with wishes 'for the liberation of India' and the hope that India would go the Chinese way soon. Masani recalls the statement that has just been put out in the New China News Agency to the effect that 'the Anglo-American imperialists and their running dog, Pandit Nehru, were plotting a coup in Lhasa for the annexation of Tibet.' 'If this is the reward that comes to this country from one year's friendship and advocacy, surely the least we can do is to reconsider our estimate of the Chinese Communist regime... While we might maintain diplomatic relations with the Chinese Government on a basis of reciprocity, there can be no longer any illusions about friendship, about cordiality and about comradeship in Asia.' Masani goes on to say:

> By the one act of attacking Tibet and deceiving the Indian Government after their assurances given repeatedly, they have shown their utter contempt for the idea that we embraced, namely, of a free and united Asia. They have cut Asia into two—Communist and non-Communist Asia. Those of us who are not prepared to go all the way with them must fall on the other side of the fence. In that setting and in the face of this remark which comes from the New China News Agency in the last few weeks, that 'the Chinese People's Liberation Army will hoist the Red Flag over the Himalayas,' what are we to think of the friendship we may expect from them?

Do not rely on the Himalayas as an impregnable wall, Masani warns. They may turn out to be no stronger a defence than the Maginot Line turned out to be for France...[5]

Panditji replies at length the next day. That is, he speaks at length. He speaks about the course of history being affected by oceanic factors. He speaks about defence being a matter not just of armies and guns, but basically about

[5] *Lok Sabha Debates,* 6 December 1950, cols. 1257–312.

a country's economic strength, its capacity to feed itself, about the people's capacity and willingness to put up with some hardships. He speaks about our inner fibre slackening. He speaks about the lack of a sense of urgency among members as well as in the country as a whole. He speaks about the need for balance between what resources we devote to defence and what we devote to strengthening the economic structures on which defence must rest. He speaks about the rapid pace at which the world is changing, and how policies have to keep up with the changes. He speaks about realism, and what it really means in formulating policies. He speaks about idealism, and how idealism is the realism of tomorrow. He talks about democracy, and about the danger that it may not survive. He speaks about the futility of our liking or not liking systems—communism and the rest—and powers and their policies, about how one has to deal with the world as it is, about how great countries are not going to change their policies just because we do not like them or just because we condemn them. He speaks about war and peace. He speaks about power blocs, and about the futility of thinking in their terms. He speaks about how our policy is an independent one. He speaks about the 'tremendous ferment of change' in Asia. He speaks about coarsening of civilizations. And, of course, he speaks about members not keeping up with the times, of their not keeping in mind the larger considerations, of their remaining stuck in grooves. He speaks about members who talk of realism and being practical—of how such persons 'normally know nothing about realism or about the state of affairs that they have to meet or the question that they have to answer'. He speaks about members who have talked 'in a most unrealistic fashion'. He speaks of their arguments being 'completely out-of-date'. He speaks about a person who has advanced such arguments being 'yesterday's man, he is last year's person'.

He speaks at length, that is, but scarcely touches on any of the specific matters that members had raised. China comes in for reference indirectly—great nations, China being one of them, are not going to change their policies just because we do not like them. At the fag end of his speech, Panditji refers to the criticism that has been levelled about his going on declaring that we accept China's suzerainty over Tibet. That has always been recognized by India, he says. He then adds two sentences. In the first of these, he affirms an important distinction, a distinction that he has been assiduously making—recall his admonition to Panikkar at having conflated the two words. In the next, he nudges us further down the slope. He says,

> About China, about Tibet more particularly, Professor Ranga was somewhat displeased at my referring occasionally to the Chinese suzerainty over Tibet. *Please note that I used the word suzerainty not sovereignty.*

So far so good. But then the next sentence:

> *There is a slight difference, not much.*

He repeats, and he says that he has no hesitation in telling the Chinese this, that 'it is not right for any country to talk about its sovereignty or suzerainty over any area outside its own immediate range. That is to say, if Tibet is different from China, it should ultimately be the wishes of the people of Tibet that should prevail and not any legal or constitutional arguments.'

One other observation can be taken to apply by inference to his decision to discourage the UN from discussing the resolution on China's invasion of Tibet. Once we associate with such resolutions, he said, our capacity to help, to convey the point of view of one side to the other is reduced. Apart from this objective of performing a useful function, 'there was this general approach we had in this matter. Either you are aiming at conflict or at peace and settlement. If one is aiming at peace and settlement, one should adopt ways that lead to peace and not ways that lead to war.'[6]

[6] *Lok Sabha Debates,* 7 December 1950, cols. 1370–85.

5

Anxieties are brushed aside

13 March 1951: Panditji is addressing a press conference in Delhi. The Chinese have by now crushed Tibet under an avalanche of troops. Several thousand, have been killed. Panditji has been sending his notes and offering his 'friendly and disinterested advice'. The Chinese haven't cared a whit for it. 'Regarding Tibet, have the Chinese Government shown any change in their attitude in recent times?' a correspondent asks. 'Change from what?' Panditji snaps back. The correspondent explains: from the attitude they took up in their notes to India. Panditji goes into a rigmarole, and concludes, 'So broadly speaking, the attitude has been the same. But it has varied I suppose from time to time...'

The correspondent persists: by change in attitude I meant that, while the Dalai Lama was prepared for talks, they sent troops, from that attitude. Read Panditji's reply, and reflect on the impression he is trying to create:

> I don't know about any change in particular attitude but the Chinese troops, to begin with, came in just a very small distance in Eastern Tibet. I cannot speak of individuals straying further. I replied to a question in Parliament yesterday about some Chinese soldiers coming into India. As a matter of fact, one unfortunate Chinese soldier lost his track and penetrated into Indian territory by mistake. That was exaggerated as some kind of Chinese forces coming in.

> But, in fact, for the last six months, I forget the period, to our knowledge there has been no movement of Chinese troops at all except that initial movement that took place, and there they have been. And whatever other methods they have adopted, they have not been military methods.[1]

How he confounds the matter—as if the advance of Chinese troops into Tibet is comparable to that solitary soldier straying into India.

'What is the strength of the Chinese troops in Tibet?' he is asked. 'The Chinese troops who came into Tibet were relatively small in number,' he says.

11 June 1951: Panditji is addressing another press conference. 'Will the presence of Chinese troops in Tibet hinder preservation of India's interests?' he is asked. 'The facts are rather vague about the presence of forces, etc., and to what extent they might or might not hinder is also therefore not clear to me...'[2]

The Dalai Lama has had to flee Lhasa. He takes shelter in the Chumbi Valley near the Indian border. He decides to return to Lhasa—not surprisingly, given what has become evident about India's attitude. Panditji is relieved. We had advised the Tibetan delegation that they should try to come to a peaceful settlement preserving their autonomy, he recalls. 'This advice was largely based on the fact that it seemed to us that Tibet was incapable of offering any effective resistance, and any attempt at ineffective resistance would probably lead to far greater control of China. It was quite impossible for us to give any assistance and therefore it was not proper for us to raise any hopes in this direction.' But we still can help, and will: 'When occasion arises we can certainly put in a good word on the diplomatic plane to China. For the rest, the only policy we can adopt is to remain quiet observers.'[3]

---

1 *SWJN,* XVL.I.443–44.

2 *SWJN,* XVI.I.446.

3 *SWJN,* XVI.II.647.

3 November 1951: Panditji is addressing the press again. A correspondent asks about differences that are outstanding with China about boundary trade and the Indian mission in Lhasa. Panditji is again dismissive, but by now people are beginning to worry about the consequences that the invasion of Tibet is going to have for our boundary, and that seeps into Panditji's response also:

> They are outstanding only in the sense that they are there. Our boundaries are there and we are having no trouble with our boundary. So far as our Mission is concerned, our Mission is there and our trade continues. It is true that it is desirable to remove any doubt if there is any. In course of time that will be done by friendly talks with the Government of China. They are not coming in the way of anything.

'About maps,' he says, referring to Chinese maps that are showing large chunks of India to be part of China and to which Sardar Patel had tried and others have been trying to draw his attention,

> I may tell you something that I have not told you before, and that is this. All the maps used in China at present are very old maps and in fact, we were told by the Chinese Government not to pay the slightest attention to these maps. They are their old maps and they have no time to print them anew; they are simply carrying on with them because they are too busy with other things.[4]

What would Mao—with his maxim, 'Shout in the East, strike in the West'—have thought of a rival so gullible?

Panditji is so confident about his assessments of China, and of his eyes and ears, Panikkar, that he sends the latter to the West. 'Panikkar's visit to the West may help somewhat in making people in the West realize the significance of what is happening in China,' he tells B.N. Rau, the Indian

[4] *SWJN*, XVII.507.

permanent representative at the UN. 'I confess I do not have a very high opinion of the collective wisdom of the delegates to the U.N. They function in their own little world and repeat the same jargon without even trying to understand what is happening about them. Still it is possible some glimmering of understanding might come to them...'—a typical observation.[5] As we shall see when we come to the conversations that Panditji has with Chou En-lai and later with Mao, there is hardly a person who measures up to much in his eyes. Anyone who remembers what Lenin and Mao had written about intellectuals and the like would have little difficulty in imagining the inference that Mao and Chou En-lai would have drawn from such expressions of loftiness.

Panditji is unrelenting in his advocacy of China's inclusion in the UN. The Soviet Union puts up a motion for the inclusion of communist China. B.N. Rau cables Panditji saying the motion is liable to be defeated, and asks for instructions. Panditji is definite: even though the proposal may be defeated, we must vote for it.[6]

Two years have gone by since the Chinese invaded Tibet. They have crushed the people mercilessly. Monasteries have been ransacked. The lamas, beaten and tortured.

28 February 1952: Panditji is asked at a press conference, 'Has there been any infiltration of Chinese troops in Tibet?' 'Not that I am aware of,' replies Panditji.[7]

Panditji busies himself trying to improve relations between the US and China. He talks to the American ambassador in Delhi about this. He talks to Mrs Eleanor Roosevelt about this. The Chinese charge that American planes have been flying over Manchuria as part of a campaign of germ warfare. He exerts to tell both sides how each should handle

---

[5] *SWJN*, XVII.509.

[6] *SWJN*, XVII.510.

[7] *SWJN*, XVII.510.

the matter. He is keen, he tells Panikkar, that the Chinese government realizes how he feels in the matter. Three days later, he again tells Panikkar that 'I think it is desirable for you to convey to him [Chou En-lai] my own deep interest in the matter...'And yet again before he closes the cable, 'Your approach to Chou En-lai should be informal but I think it is desirable that you should indicate to him how I feel in the matter.'[8] What would Chou En-lai have thought of someone so anxious to show him the way?

Panikkar meets Chou En-lai within the month, and gets a taste of what is to come. He reports to Panditji. 'We are surprised to learn of Chou En-lai's apparent reluctance to discuss general problem of our interests in Tibet,' Panditji cables Panikkar. Chou En-lai himself had suggested that the question of our interests in Tibet and of our boundary 'was one for discussion and settlement'. We said we were ready for this. Hence, 'Chou En-lai's present excuse that the Chinese have been in Tibet only for a short time and have not yet studied problem thoroughly does not carry conviction.'[9]

Should this not have alerted Panditji to the Chinese mode? That they go on postponing discussion till they have completely consolidated their position on the ground, and once that work has been completed, all that is to be discussed is how their adversary should reconcile himself to the new reality. Nor is it just that Panditji should have been alerted by what he terms the 'present excuse'; are our rulers *today* alert to the Chinese way of handling a dispute—of going on dodging discussion till they have already 'settled' the matter?

Feeding the enemy

The cable to Panikkar gives us another glimpse also. In their meeting on 5 April 1952, Chou En-lai has told Panikkar that

[8] *SWJN*, XVII.513–14.

[9] *SWJN*, XVIII.471.

for some years China will have to depend on India for the 'daily necessities' in Tibet, in particular foodgrains. Won't India like to help get rice into Tibet? Panikkar is all for the proposal—to consolidate relations between the two countries in which history is being made! Panditji demurs: the proposal raises 'very difficult problems of transport', he tells Panikkar. 'We are prepared to examine this matter,' he continues, 'but this would be a concession which we should retain as a bargaining counter for negotiations for an overall settlement between China and us. It is not advantageous for us to accept such proposals piecemeal and yet have no general settlement.' Not just that, Panditji clearly sees what this request amounts to. He tells Panikkar, 'Presumably these food supplies are meant for Chinese army in Tibet which, from all accounts, is in great need of them. We are not particularly anxious to facilitate movement and retention of large numbers of Chinese troops in Tibet.'[10]

This is what Panditji says in his cable on 12 April 1952.

Later in the month, he visits Kalimpong, a place that has a large concentration of Tibetans who have had to flee from the Chinese forces. He addresses a public meeting. 'Nobody need get upset over the recent developments in Tibet,' he tells the gathering. 'I would like to repeat that one of the foremost interests of India is cultivation of friendly relations with her neighbours, especially China and Tibet.' A public meeting is, of course, not the place in which to explain how he is going to square that circle—of being friends simultaneously with Tibet and China—and so he doesn't![11]

By 24 May, however, he has changed his mind. Panikkar has been inquiring about the shipment of foodgrains to Tibet. Panditji agrees to send 500 tons of grain, with a target of 3,500 tons. He repeats his general view: 'We have told you

---

[10] *SWJN,* XVIII.472.

[11] *SWJN,* XVIII.472–73.

that any permanent or semi-permanent arrangements can be discussed only as part of general settlement of our interests in Tibet.' And he adds in parentheses,

> (These interests, as you know, are not confined to trade relations but involve political interests such as affirmation of the Frontier.)

The border has started creeping into the dispatches. And then, characteristically, Panditji adds another caveat:

> It would be preferable not to mention this in your proposed note. We had really intended this for your information only.[12]

On 21 June Panditji is asked at a press conference about the rice that has been sent to Tibet. 'Not in big quantities,' Panditji says. 'We did allow a small quantity, as an exceptional case. You know, it is a very difficult route... mule tracks, difficult mountain terrain and the rest of it. It is not an easy matter, but because of their great need, we have allowed some rice to get through.' And China has also made a 'generous gesture'—in spite of their own difficult food situation, they have exported one lakh tons of rice to us. Their army is in 'great need', and we, who want it out of Tibet, help it to remain!

Is the arrangement on an ad hoc basis? 'Yes, completely,' Panditji replies.[13]

We are in April 1953. N. Raghavan has replaced Panikkar as our ambassador. He reports that although the Chinese have not been abusing us, their attitude 'still continues to be cold'. Panditji is convinced to the contrary: no, it has 'become friendly'. In the course of a note to Raghavan, Panditji reverts to this question of supplying rice to the Chinese in Tibet. He is firm, or so it would seem till his next note on the subject:

---

12 *SWJN*, XVIII.473.

13 *SWJN*, XVIII.476–77.

> As we have told you, we are prepared to allow the 1,000 tons of Chinese rice which are already in India to be sent to Tibet, subject to transport arrangements. But, it must not be taken for granted that this is normal procedure. This transport business gives us a lot of trouble. In regard to other goods also, we are prepared to consider what we can supply to Tibet within reason.[14]

By the next year, of course, he is well on the way to becoming the emblem of *Hindi-Chini bhai bhai.* And so, having himself been the one who has been citing the difficulties in regard to transport, in a note of 1 July 1954 to the Secretary General of the Ministry of External Affairs, Panditji lays down the new line:

> We have stated previously that we cannot allow much trade on the ground of transport difficulties. That seems to me to be a wrong way to put it. We should allow as much trade as possible. If transport difficulties come in the way, they will limit the trade. It is not for us to plead transport difficulties and refuse permission for trade...

He now sanctions petrol, diesel, etc., also—items that are going to be used by Chinese forces alone: in any case, the quantities will be small, he says.[15]

Three weeks later, he is even more categorical. He tells the foreign secretary,

> I am clearly of opinion that we should agree to sell rice to China almost in any quantity. We have got large stocks... If the Chinese want to send rice to Tibet, we should not object to it... Our selling rice to China... will indicate our healthy food position and that of China in this respect...[16]

It is quite a sight, one which we shall see again and again—

[14] *SWJN*, XXII.354–55.

[15] *SWJN*, XXVI.483.

[16] *SWJN*, XXVI.488, Editor's note.

the felicity with which Panditji is able to think up ever-new arguments for whatever he wants to do, as well as for whatever he wants *not* to do. But we have run ahead of the story.

An anxiety creeps in

We saw how China's shifting attitude in regard to the border had begun to foment some uneasiness in Panditji's mind—'We are surprised to learn of Chou En-lai's apparent reluctance to discuss general problem of our interests in Tibet...' he had told Panikkar in his cable on 12 April 1952. At the same time, Panditji was eager *not* to be the one to mention the matter to the Chinese: recall his cable to Panikkar of 24 May 1952, in which he said that what we had to aim at was a general settlement which had to include the 'affirmation of the Frontier', but added, 'It would be preferable not to mention this in your proposed note.'

Panikkar meets Chou En-lai on 14 June 1952. 'The question of boundary was not touched and no allusion was made to any political problems,' he informs Panditji by cable. Indeed, anyone reading the dispatch would have noticed the change in Chou En-lai's tone: he told Panikkar that he was sure India would not want to retain any 'special privileges' in Tibet which were the result of unequal treaties that had been imposed by British imperialists. That put paid to many subliminal hopes of the government but it isn't something anyone would talk about—after all, Panditji is handling the matter himself.

But even Panditji is by now nonplussed, to put it at the least. 'We think it is rather odd,' he cables Panikkar in return, 'that in discussing Tibet with you Chou En-lai did not refer at all to our Frontier. For our part, we attach more importance to this than to other matters.' 'We are interested, as you know, not only in our direct Frontier but also in Frontiers of Nepal, Bhutan and Sikkim, and we have made it perfectly clear in Parliament that these Frontiers must remain,' he goes on to observe, only to repeat that fatal operational direction:

> There is perhaps some advantage in our not ourselves raising this issue.

'On the other hand,' Panditji tells Panikkar, 'I do not quite like Chou En-lai's silence about it when discussing even minor matters.' Why should Chou En-lai not have been proceeding on the same assumption—that 'There is perhaps some advantage in our not ourselves raising this issue?' Especially so, as, in his case, he would have added 'till we have consolidated our hold over the areas we want.'

Panditji tells Panikkar again that he wants a 'comprehensive settlement which includes Frontier'. He fortified his operational direction of not raising the matter with an absolutely incomprehensible, and fatal assumption. He tells Panikkar,

> In our instructions to you dated 25th January, you were asked to specify our interests including those on the Frontier. We presume you have done so. *If so, we can presume that Chou En-lai's silence means some kind of acquiescence.* It is not for us to suggest any reconsideration. At the same time I should like to be assured on this point.

The Chinese do not just deflect the matter. They tie up Indian expectations and claims with British imperialism, and thereby reject them. In a 'clarification' of what Chou En-lai had told Panikkar, the Chinese Foreign Office states that what Chou had said was as follows:

> Chinese Government would like to state a principle at the same time solving problems and then follow this up with successive solution of other specific problems... The existing situation of Sino-Indian relationship in Tibetan China was scar left by Britain in course of their past aggression against

> China. For this Government of India was not responsible... Relations between new China and new Government of India in Tibet should be built anew through negotiations.[17]

Everything, therefore, was to be thrown into the melting pot. Everything, including the border, was to be negotiated anew. And if India stuck to what had been agreed upon during the British period then it was trying to take advantage of what had been wrested from China by imperialists, and thus thwarting Sino-Indian relations from blossoming anew! A classic communist bind.

That was patent. Panditji and his acolytes also must have seen it. But they chose to swallow the ruse. Not just that. As we shall see as we proceed, they internalized this reasoning, and started repeating the very words.

By early September 1952, Panditji is instructing the foreign secretary, 'On reconsideration, I accept Shri Panikkar's advice that we should not make specific mention about the frontiers...'[18]

'The larger world point of view'

In early September 1952, the Indian Mission in Lhasa reports that there is unrest, that several groups of Tibetans have emerged, that one of them has asked for assistance, a mere two lakh rupees. Panditji comes down as a thunderbolt. 'We do not wish to interfere in internal affairs of Tibet,' he cables the mission, 'and we can certainly be no parties to any secret or other activities against the Chinese. That would be both practically and morally wrong. It is for Tibetans and Chinese to settle their problems...' Our objective 'is proper maintenance of our frontier line', he says, and adds, 'This we have made quite clear to the Chinese Government'—have we? Has it not been his direction, repeated again and again

---

[17] *SWJN*, XVIII.474–75.

[18] *SWJN*, XIX.651.

that we should *not* raise the boundary question with the Chinese? 'And on that there can be no yielding'—if only strong words on file and in cables could secure frontiers!

And then, predictably, that infernal 'larger world point of view' compounded by the continuing reliance on geography—a reliance that exempts us from doing anything:

> We have to judge these matters [the request for Rs. two lakh] from larger world point of view which probably our Tibetan friends have no means of appreciating...
>
> Our own appraisal is that owing to geography and climate and other factors, it is difficult for Chinese Government to exercise full control over Tibet. But if any challenge to their authority takes place, they will easily crush it ruthlessly and this will result in ending such autonomy as Tibet might otherwise have.[19]

So, not only must we not do anything—because of the 'larger world point of view' that we alone can appreciate; not only need we do nothing as geography will safeguard Tibetan autonomy from the Chinese; the Tibetans should do nothing—lest they lose what they might otherwise retain.

On 10 December 1952, Panditji sends a cable to N. Raghavan, who has replaced Panikkar as our ambassador in Peking. 'Our attitude towards Chinese Government should always be a combination of friendliness and firmness,' Panditji instructs him. 'If we show weakness, advantage will be taken of this immediately.' What he has in mind is immediately apparent. 'This applies to any development that might take place or in reference to our frontier problems between Tibet and Nepal, Bhutan, Sikkim, Ladakh and rest of India,' he tells Raghavan. 'In regard to this entire frontier we have to maintain an attitude of firmness. Indeed, there is nothing to discuss there and we have made that previously clear to the

---

[19] *SWJN*, XIX.651–52.

Chinese Government... The old McMahon Line is considered to be our frontier and we shall adhere to it.'[20]

Carpers 'pushed aside by the advance of history'

We come next to a communication that holds multiple lessons. An officer, S. Sinha, has been in charge of our mission in Tibet in 1950. He has come back, having seen first-hand what the Chinese have been doing. He is now officer on special duty in the Ministry of External Affairs—which Panditji heads. He puts up a note about the Chinese in Tibet, and what this spells for India. Apart from what Panditji says in his response, the way he comes down on the note and the hapless man is precisely the way a person of his position and eminence must not. Which officer will furnish frank counsel when such is the treatment that may be meted out to him?

'It is clear that we should remain wide-awake about our North-Eastern frontier situation from Ladakh right up to Bhutan and Assam,' Panditji begins. 'Mr. Sinha's note is helpful in drawing our attention to various present and possible dangers'—with Panditji that sort of compliment is always an ominous opening.

Sure enough, as night follows day, the sentence that follows is true to form. 'But I find Mr. Sinha's approach to be coloured very much by certain ideas and conceptions which prevent him from taking an objective view of the situation,' Panditji records on file. 'The note starts by reference to the lust for conquest of the Chinese and is throughout based on this. Mr. Sinha looks back with a certain nostalgia to the past when the British exercised a good deal of control over Tibet and he would have liked very much for India to take the place of the British of those days.' Could it not be that the officer was moved not by nostalgia for the past but by foreboding for the future?

[20] *SWJN*, XX.488–89.

Panditji turns the argument on its head, and introduces words that he is going to use time and again in the future to justify inaction: it isn't just that the position we had in Tibet, the access and influence, could not be defended, it wasn't right to defend them. 'As a matter of fact, *the weakness of our position in Tibet has been that we are successors, to some extent, of an imperial power which had pushed its way into Tibet.* When that imperial power has ceased to have any strength to function in the old way, it is patent that we cannot do so, even if we so wished. We do not, in fact, wish to do so in that particular way. What we are really interested in is our own security and the maintenance of our frontiers intact.'

'It serves little purpose to think regretfully of past days and past ways,' Panditji declares. Notice how he is using characterization to condemn an argument: 'That is only done by people who have been pushed aside by the advance of history and who can only think of the past when they played an important role in the historic process.' Panditji is by contrast the man in tune with the future. He is the one who recognizes the tides of history: 'The biggest event since the last War is the rise of Communist China. It is totally immaterial whether we like it or dislike it. It is a fact.'

What has happened in Tibet is but natural: 'It followed naturally that a strong Chinese Government would assert its claim on Tibet, which every previous Chinese Government had done with more or less success.' And from that follows another inevitability: 'It followed also that there was no power, however big, which could resist that claim in Tibet. Certainly we could not do so. To take up an attitude of resistance without the strength to follow it up would have been political folly of the first magnitude. Therefore, we had to accept the changes that took place.' And that is not the end of the chain of inevitabilities: 'We shall have to accept any other changes internal to Tibet.' Yet, inevitability must be stopped at our borders: 'But one thing we are not prepared to accept is any modification of or intrusion across our frontiers. Therefore, we must concentrate on that and not think vaguely of other matters.'

That counsel would be credible if he himself were thinking less than 'vaguely' about the one thing that he says concerns us.

'While there is much in Mr. Sinha's report that has a basis of truth, this is put forward in such an exaggerated and emotional way that it loses force. I am sorry that a representative of ours should allow his objective analysis to be affected in this way. That does not help in understanding a situation'—dress down an officer on file like this, and that too when you occupy as exalted a position as Panditji did at the time, and see who comes up with honest counsel in future.

'We live in a revolutionary period when the whole of Asia is in a state of turmoil and change,' Panditji records. 'We have to keep up with that change and not merely regret the days of pre-change.' Precisely: we have to be awake to the turmoil that that 'biggest event since the last War, the rise of Communist China' will spell for us. Panditji turns to what has to be done in practice: 'In the ultimate analysis we have to build up our strength. That strength means not so much frontier outposts and the like but internal strength—political and economic. One of the biggest things in Asia today and in the future is the rate of progress of India and China. If India makes good, more especially on the economic front, in the course of the next five to ten years, then India's future is not only assured but is very promising. If we fail internally, then of course anything can happen on our frontiers or elsewhere.' The issue of what is to be done on the ground has slipped away.

But not entirely. 'We have, of course, to be alert and vigilant on our borders,' Panditji concedes, and immediately goes off into the intangible. 'This is not so much from the point of view of resisting any major incursion but rather to make clear to China and the world that we are going to stick to our frontier. Any challenge to our frontiers will have to be met. In fact, it means a challenge to the whole of India, and not merely to the frontiers.' But will it be met merely by recording strong words on files?

'As Mr Kapur[21] says, and many other reasons can be advanced also, *no major challenge to these frontiers is likely in the near future.* If we are alert, no challenge will take place within a reasonable time and possibly even later.'

He repeats his standard reason for not doing much: 'It must always be remembered that the strength of our position lies in certain geographical factors which cannot easily be changed or overcome—not so much to Himalayan mountains but the added and inhospitable land of Tibet on the other side which cannot support or logistically provide for any large forces.' Next, he repeats the point Sardar Patel had emphasized and to which at the time he had not responded: 'The weakness of our position on those borders lies in the fact that Bhutanese, etc., are closely allied culturally and socially to the Tibetans and naturally look towards Tibet from that point of view.'

'The weakest parts of the frontier are those lying between Bhutan and Sikkim,' he continues. 'In a sense there is graver danger in Nepal, if that country goes to pieces... The general policy we should pursue is: (i) Strengthen our communication system with the border areas and have well-equipped check-posts there, (ii) Strengthen our Intelligence system, (iii) Develop these border areas economically and otherwise and thus bring them more and more within the orbit of India's economic and national life by making them feel that they are integral parts of India and profit by it'—not very different from what Sardar Patel had urged two-and-a-half years earlier, and about which little has been done.

And not just Sardar Patel. As the subsequent paragraph in Panditji's own note shows, others also had been drawing

---

[21] B.K. Kapur, India's political officer in Gangtok, Sikkim. He will be coming in for the standard treatment soon.

attention to the need to urgently strengthen our borders, and had met with no greater success. Panditji's note continues:

> For the last year or possibly two years the U.P. Government has been writing to us about their border with Tibet and the difficulties of maintaining any check-post there because of lack of communications and accommodation. In spite of urgent reminders from the U.P. Government, the matter has got stuck up either in the Home Ministry here or in the Finance Ministry. This should be looked into, as this is important.

What did the situation nine years later—in 1962—show? That this important matter had received the attention it deserved? This is one of the lessons that comes through: when the prime minister is so busy saving the world, when he has taken so many things upon himself within the country as Panditji had, the truly important things will get neglected. He will, of course, keep ordering on files and in meetings that such and thus be immediately done, but as, the next moment, his attention moves elsewhere, so will that of the machinery of administration.

Panditji turns to the uncertainties about the border with Tibet and China. Recall that he himself has started becoming a bit anxious by the ominous silence of Chou En-lai. But Panditji sticks to the 'hear no evil, speak no evil' formula. He records:

> When Sardar Panikkar was in Peking, the question arose of our settling our frontier with Tibet, that is the McMahon line, finally with the Chinese Government. Mr. Panikkar was of opinion that we had made our position clear to the Chinese Government and that it will serve no useful purpose to raise that question. But if occasion offers itself and especially if any challenge to that frontier is made, then we shall have to make this perfectly clear.[22]

---

[22] *SWJN*, XXI.555–58.

But why would the Chinese raise the matter in a form and at a time to suit our convenience? They were 'settling' the question—by the way they were consolidating their stranglehold over Tibet, by the roads and airfields that they were constructing; in a word, by altering the situation on the ground.

And who is to bear responsibility for what transpired later? It isn't just that Panditji was the prime minister. it isn't just that he was the external affairs minister. As Panditji records in the last paragraph of his note on Sinha's proposals: 'We have to deal directly in our Ministry with the Northeast Frontier Agency. That is our responsibility and we should keep the development of those areas constantly in mind'—the areas into which the Chinese were to ingress a few years hence were under the direct administrative charge of his ministry.[23]

Lest they take umbrage

We should catch up with another feature. While Panditji is recording stern notes on file from time to time, he strains to see that we say or do nothing that might discompose the Chinese in the slightest. Recall that during this entire period, Panditji is doing all he can to advocate the Chinese case in regard to the UN—at the United Nations, at the Colombo Prime Ministers' Conference, at the Commonwealth Prime Ministers' Conference, at press conferences the world over:

> That China is represented by Formosa is 'factually absurd', he tells the Prime Ministers at Colombo. Apart from being an embarrassment for China, it is an embarrassment for Asia...[24]
>
> There is no more vital or urgent issue than the admission of Communist China into the United Nations, he tells the

[23] *SWJN*, XX.558.

[24] *SWJN*, XXV.423–26.

> Commonwealth Prime Ministers in July, 1956. Had she been a member some years ago the course of history might well have been altered; for example, the Korean war might never have occurred.[25]

He is, as he himself puts it, presenting their point of view on matters like Formosa and Korea at conference after conference.

'I have explained China's attitude fairly fully,' he cables Raghavan, the Indian ambassador in Peking immediately after the Commonwealth Prime Ministers' Conference in February 1955, 'and I believe this has created some impression...' The next day, he again cables Raghavan and says again, '...Prime Ministers' Conference took no decisions on China problems but there was full exchange of views and consideration of possible developments. I stated China's position fully.'[26]

And he is always making it a point to ensure that Chou En-lai gets to know that he is advocating China's case:

> Please assure Chou En-lai of our deep concern and our anxiety to find solution, or the beginning of one, which will avert war and result in China obtaining her legitimate rights. As I have told you, we agree with legal and constitutional position taken up by China, but it is not enough for us to lay stress on that and do nothing more. We do not want China to give up any of her just claims or sacrifice any vital principle. But if we are to avert war, we must proceed with caution, step by step. We shall not relax our peaceful endeavours and we look to China to assist us.[27]

> Please tell Chou En-lai that I appreciate what he has written and we have made the Chinese position clear in our talks in London and with US Ambassador here. Krishna Menon has also done so in London, Ottawa and Washington. We

---

[25] *SWJN*, XXXIV.259.

[26] *SWJN*, XXVIII.167–68.

[27] *SWJN*, XXVIII.170.

> have not reached conclusive stage yet. These efforts will continue.[28]

On the other hand, whenever he takes a position that is even slightly at variance with the way they would like things to pan out, the Chinese denounce him roundly:

> India, in this case literally Panditji personally, is acting under foreign influence, they charge, when he expresses how dismayed he is at their invasion of Tibet. 'The Anglo-American imperialists and their running dog, Pandit Nehru, were plotting a coup in Lhasa for the annexation of Tibet,' the New China News Agency declares as justification for the invasion.

Later, Panditji has the Indian representative at the UN table a resolution on Korea, after, as he himself puts it to his friend U Nu, the premier of Burma, 'full reference to the Chinese Government'. When it is tabled, they reject it and, together with the Soviets, denounce it: 'At best, you are dreamers and idealists; at worst, instruments of horrible American policy,' the Soviet delegate says; Chou En-lai denounces the resolution as 'void, illegal, unfair and unreasonable'. Panditji is wounded: 'This has pained me greatly,' he tells U Nu, 'because for our part we have been trying to develop friendly relations with China, and had no desire to do anything against her wishes.' His only recourse is philosophic resignation: 'However, there it is,' he says. 'It is not always easy to understand the motives and springs of Communist behaviour.'[29]

What is the effect of this tactic—of keeping him on his toes? Of making him strain to come up to their expectations? Exactly what we would expect of liberals of the period: he tries harder. He strains to ensure that no one who can be even

[28] *SWJN*, XXIX.364.

[29] *SWJN*, XXI.446–48, also Editor's note, p. 447.

vaguely associated with him or India says or does anything that would meet with Chinese disapproval in the slightest.

- That Chinese forces have started advancing into Tibet is in the air. In an interview to Reuters, his comrade and acolyte, Krishna Menon, implies that India has been in touch with China on the issue, and has advised it 'in the direction of moderation irrespective of legal rights'. 'Tibet is a very ticklish issue,' Panditji tells Menon. 'We have to proceed rather cautiously in regard to it and we do not want it stated that we have been addressing the Chinese Government on this subject. They are sensitive and this itself might create an undesirable reaction in them...' He points to his own example: 'For some time past, I have been asked questions about Tibet at press conferences. I have answered them rather vaguely and tried to avoid any direct commitment... We do not intend to make any such clear declaration because whatever we say may be embarrassing either from a Chinese or a Tibetan point of view. Anything we say to the Chinese loses its effect to some extent if any public reference is made to it.'[30]
- As anger against the Chinese invasion mounts, leaders and citizens decide to observe a 'Tibet Day' in August 1953. Panditji shoots off a missive to the general secretary of the AICC. 'Obviously, no Congressman should join such committee or participate in the observance of "Tibet Day",' he lays down. 'This is an unfriendly act to China and is against the policy we have pursued during these years. There is absolutely no reason for observing such a day now. I really do not understand why Professor Ranga or the others should suddenly decide to observe this day.' 'I think we should inform members of the Party that they should keep aloof from this. If you will remind

---

[30] *SWJN*, XV.I.429.

me, I shall mention this at the Party meeting tomorrow.' A few days later, he notes on file that the joint secretary concerned 'was quite right in the answer he gave to the Counselor of the Chinese Embassy about the Tibet Day. He might have gone a little further and added that this particular note in the Press... was made by opposition splinter groups in Parliament who have no importance whatever. We disapprove entirely of this appeal by a few persons and we attach no importance to it.'[31]

The boundary question

Tibet has been consigned. On the boundary, Panditji is doing a Micawber. He has convinced himself that by not taking up the question with the Chinese, it will remain undisputed. In September 1953, however, in a message to Chou En-lai, he mentions the question in passing. 'It has been a matter of deep satisfaction to me to note the growing cooperation between our great countries in international affairs,' he says. 'I am convinced that this cooperation and friendship will not only be to our mutual advantage, but will also be a strong pillar for peace in Asia and the world. I hope that our two countries will maintain full contact and cooperate with each other in dealing with problems of mutual interest. That has been Your Excellency's wish and I reciprocate it fully...'

'Your Excellency informed our Ambassador last year that there is no difference of point of view in regard to Tibet between India and China and that your Government is anxious in every way to safeguard Indian interests in Tibet,' he continues. 'You added that there is no territorial dispute or controversy between India and China in this matter and that "we are not desirous of abruptly bringing to an end existing institutions and arrangements, as such a course would create a vacuum".' He tells Chou En-lai that the Indian

---

[31] *SWJN*, XXIII.482–83, also Editor's note, p. 483.

government 'have been anxious to come to a final settlement about pending matters so as to avoid any misunderstanding and friction at any time...' He turns to what in hindsight are matters of the second order of smalls.[32] One can take either view—that, as Chou has himself said that there is no difference of opinion about the border, there is no reason for Panditji to propose further discussions on the matter: in which case, the lesson is that Chou was deceiving him so that the Chinese hold over Tibet would become complete and its infrastructure along our borders would become far superior to anything we had; or that Panditji should not have taken Chou En-lai's verbal statement at face value and pressed for a formal settlement about the border as he had been saying in his cables: recall, for instance, his initial reactions to the request for providing rice for Chinese troops in Tibet, and his admonition that we should not do things piecemeal, and instead seek a comprehensive settlement including on our border. In any case, Chou is to disabuse him soon enough.

On 16 October 1953, Chou En-lai replies to Panditji's message. Where Panditji has recalled him as having affirmed that there are no differences of opinion between China and India in regard either to Tibet or the border, Chou En-lai puts a taint on how matters had been and are. He says that 'the existing situation of Sino-Indian relations in the Tibetan region of China *were the vestiges of the process of the past British aggression against China.*' 'For all of these, the Government of India was not responsible'—this had but one meaning: we are not blaming today's India for the way things have been, correspondingly today's India can claim no rights or facilities that arise from the way things have been till now. 'Special rights which arose from the unequal treaties between the British Government and the old Chinese Government were no longer in existence,' Chou says. He is doing *exactly* what Sardar Patel had forecast China would do. Had the Sardar

---

[32] *SWJN*, XXIII.485–86.

not pointed out in his letter to Panditji that 'The Chinese interpretation of suzerainty is different' from what we take it to mean? Had he then not pointed to the consequence that would follow? *'We can, therefore, safely assume that very soon they will disown all the stipulations which Tibet has entered into with us in the past. That throws into the melting pot all frontier and commercial settlements with Tibet on which we have been functioning and acting during the last half century.'*

'Therefore,' Chou En-lai continues, 'the relations between new China and the Government of India in the Tibetan region of China should be built up anew through negotiation.' Would 'relations' not include the boundary?

Panditji is clearly taken aback, but, as usual, he postpones taking the matter up. He sends a reply that circumvents every single implication that leaps up from Chou En-lai's message. The apprehensions he has, he consigns in a postscript to Raghavan. He tells the ambassador, 'Chou En-lai's message to me raises some controversial points and there are a number of inaccuracies in it. However, I have not discussed these in my reply, *as they are relatively matters of detail.*'[33]

'Matters of detail'? Chou En-lai is saying as plainly as can be that the 'relations'—manifestly, the entire gamut of relations—have to be negotiated anew, and we are taking comfort in 'inaccuracies' regarding 'matters of detail'?

Taking 'the balanced view'

S. Sinha puts up another note. Entitled 'Chinese Designs on the North East Frontier of India', it enumerates dangers that flow ineluctably from the steps that China is taking in Tibet, and right along our borders. The predictable dodge is adopted. The note is sent to the selfsame Panikkar for his comments. Panikkar says that 'the issue is not one of Chinese, or Chinese-inspired military adventure against the borders

---

[33] *SWJN*, XXIV.595–96, also Editor's note, p. 596.

of India.' The issue is of developing the areas on our side of the border, of strengthening administration, etc., of making the people of these regions feel that they are Indians and have a valued place in India. Would showing them what the Chinese are doing to the Tibetans not help? Why is one set of measures a substitute of the other? Is it not the case that we should do both? Open our eyes to what China's moves imply for our security and prepare for that on the one hand, and at the same time develop our border areas?

Fortified with the comments of Panikkar, Panditji comes down on Sinha. 'For Mr. Sinha to talk about China's designs itself indicates that he is not taking quite an objective view of the situation but has started with certain presumptions,' he begins. 'I do not rule out the possibility of such developments in Tibet, on our border or elsewhere. But we must take a balanced view.' The view that he disapproves is always unbalanced; or stuck in the past; or stuck in the cold war mould; or subjective and emotional...

Panditji has by now come down firmly *against* the order in Tibet: it isn't just that we cannot support Tibet. His position now is that we *must not* support Tibet. The reason is his progressive view of history! The Tibetan order is feudal. And how can we be supporting feudalism? 'We cannot support feudal elements in Tibet,' he records, 'indeed we cannot interfere in Tibet.' And from this base, one has to be only logical: 'Having come to that conclusion, we should abide by it and not pine for a different policy, which anyhow is totally outside our reach.'

Yes, we should develop our border areas, but here too we must not interfere with the way of life of the people. We should gently encourage liberal forces and develop communications.

Next, his oft-repeated position: we must not talk about the border for that will imply that there is something to talk about. 'As for our frontier,' he writes, 'it is our well-declared policy that the line is a settled one and not open to argument or discussion, except perhaps with regard to minor tracts here and there which might be doubtful.'

And then his strategic assessment: 'I cannot go into people's minds, much less into the Chinese mind, but I can judge from circumstances. It is completely impracticable for the Chinese Government to think of anything in the nature of invasion of India.' The proposition illustrates one of many flaws: *Panditji is always positing only two options for the Chinese*—negotiated settlement or a full-scale invasion of India by China. He has little difficulty in dismissing this possibility. And from that dismissal, he comes to the operational conclusion: as a full-scale invasion is not possible, we can take our time about things.

His judgement of 'circumstances' renders a full-scale invasion 'completely impracticable'. 'Therefore I rule it out,' he rules. He allows another possibility, though, 'It is not impossible for some infiltration [sic] to create local trouble,' only to prescribe a general prescription, 'We must guard against that.'

'There is danger in Nepal, but this too is due to internal chaotic conditions than to outside interference,' he writes. And even here, the hand we have to be alert towards is not that of China—'As a matter of fact, the outside interference that is troubling us is American and not Chinese.'

Generalizations—each unexceptionable in itself—follow. 'We must realize fully that our policy in regard to China is one of friendliness and co-existence, allied with firmness in regard to any interference with our basic rights'—the problem is that the margin where firmness must begin keeps shifting, and what is 'basic' keeps getting defined down. 'Ultimately the basic right is the perseveration of the frontier'—true, but as 1962 is to show, ringing declarations on file are not enough; preserving the frontier requires strength on the ground, and how much is done in the coming nine years for that becomes evident in that fateful year. Dilutions follow, as always: 'There are also some other rights and customs which are not very controversial. We shall not give up any basic right. For the rest we shall deal with the Chinese in a friendly manner.' *That*, and not carping about possible dangers, is the right, balanced perspective: 'It is important today, and even more so in the long future that India and China should have friendly relations and not have a dangerous frontier. The best way to ensure this on our side is to develop the border regions on this side not only in the sense of roads, etc. but in the sense of winning people there to the conception of India.' Unexceptional, but just as ethereal.

But how can Panditji close the note without reference to the 'wider picture'? Without putting the officer down? So, before concluding, Panditji observes:

> It is perfectly true that the post of Political Officer in Sikkim is of importance. That officer must clearly understand our policy not only in the region of the frontier and in Tibet but in its wider aspect all over the world.
>
> It appears that Mr. Sinha does not appreciate our policy fully. He should be enlightened.[34]

Weeks pass. Talks are to be held in Peking. A note is put up to Panditji about the main points that are liable to arise. Leading these is, 'the question of India's frontier with Tibet. Panditji issues instructions to the Secretary General of the Ministry of External Affairs:

> I agree about the attitude we should take up in regard to the frontier, we should not raise this question. If the Chinese raise it, we should express our surprise and point out that this is a settled issue. Further that during the last two years or so, when reference was frequently made about Indo-Chinese or Indo-Tibetan problems, there has never been any reference to this frontier issue and it is surprising that this should be brought up now. Our delegation cannot discuss it.

---

[34] *SWJN*, XXIV.596–98, also Editor's note, p. 597.

If only this doggedness in *not* letting the matter be raised had been accompanied by consolidating our position on the ground! This time, even Panikkar is for some firmness: he suggests that, if the Chinese insist on raising this issue, our delegation should walk out and end the negotiations. Panditji rules, 'We should avoid walking out unless the Chinese insist on taking up this question.' But he keeps the possibility open, deferring the decision: 'If such an eventuality occurs, the matter will no doubt be referred to us.'[35]

If only 'principles' on paper could shield countries

Panditji couldn't be busier saving the world than he is in the coming months. Indo-China, Formosa, the irresponsible pronouncements of Dulles, hydrogen bomb, racialism, colonialism, the Colombo Conference... In between, we sign the agreement with China about trade with Tibet. Panditji asks that the text be circulated to governments of the Commonwealth. We have given up all facilities and rights. But the preamble has the poetry from which much satisfaction is derived in the coming months—it states that the agreement is based on the principles of 'mutual respect for each other's territorial integrity and sovereignty; mutual non-aggression; mutual non-interference in each other's internal affairs, equality and mutual benefit and peaceful co-existence'—the 'principles' are to become a mantra in the coming years. Panditji will soon be advising Chou En-lai to sign a declaration with Burma enumerating the same principles. They will soon become the scaffolding for the declaration at Bandung. For the moment, Panditji sets out the points to be made in the note that is to accompany the text of the agreement when it is sent to governments of the Commonwealth: the need for a new agreement because of the 'recent changes in Tibet'; the 'petty difficulties' that had

[35] *SWJN*, XXIV.598.

arisen; the prolonged discussions... And, of course, the wider perspective: 'This Agreement not only settles these various points in regard to Tibet which have been troubling us during the last two years or so'—the agreement 'settles' these in the sense that India recognizes Tibet as 'the Tibet region of China'—'but also, we hope will have a stabilizing effect over this region, as well as, we think, to some extent, in Asian affairs...'[36]

He also hands down a set of instructions about the future. Among these, he lists instructions about the border:

> I agree also that we should establish check-posts at all disputed points, wherever they might be, and our administration should be right up to these borders. This matter has been delayed and we should try to expedite it. Thus, the U.P. Government has written to us frequently about their problems on the Tibet border and, more especially, about the development of communications to that frontier. We should find out how matters stand and try to do something to expedite decisions and action.[37]

Two points should be noted in passing. First, Panditji is repeating the directions that he has been giving for over two years. The position is still such that he has to direct his ministry, 'We should find out how matters stand and try to do something to expedite decisions and action.' The second point to note is the counsel that the army gave at the time. Merely setting up 'check-posts' will be worse than having none, its leading officers said. They must be backed up with forces that can defend them. Otherwise, they will be overrun in one fell sweep... The officers who give these warnings shall come to a sorry end.

The sequence now takes a complete turn. It takes off, so to say. A conference has been going on in Geneva about

---

[36] *SWJN*, XXV.468–69.

[37] *SWJN*, XXV.469–70.

the fighting in Indo-China. Panditji is deeply involved in it. Krishna Menon has been representing him and India. A budding joint secretary proposes that an informal suggestion may be made to Chou En-lai that he stop over in India on his way back from Geneva to China. Panditji immediately warms to the prospect. 'I rather like the idea of Mr. Chou En-lai being invited to go *via* India from Geneva to China.' He says that Krishna Menon who is in Geneva may put the suggestion to Chou informally.[38]

[38] *SWJN*, XXV.469–70.

6

A satisfying tutorial

Krishna Menon meets Chou En-lai from time to time on the sidelines of the Geneva Conference. He conveys Panditji's invitation to Chou En-lai that the latter visit India. Chou accepts. Krishna Menon cables Panditji. 'He is a fine and I believe a great and able man,' Menon says. 'I do not believe that the Chinese have expansionist ideas... I found little difficulty in getting near him. He was never evasive with me even on difficult matters after the second day. He is extremely shrewd and observant, very Chinese but modern.'[1]

Chou En-lai visits India. Panditji has five rounds of discussions with him on 25, 26 and 27 June 1954. The verbatim record of the conversations covers forty pages of the *Selected Works.* Tibet is not mentioned at all. Uncertainties about our boundary that Panditji has been growing more and more anxious about are not mentioned at all.

The first round is devoted to what has been happening in Geneva. Panditji inquires. Chou fills him in. After this round, Chou En-lai speaks little, just a sentence or two at a time. Panditji talks most of the time. In fact, Chou does more, he does what many in the years to come will come to see as his special skill—he flatters Panditji off the ground.

Knowing Panditji's view of himself—as the one concerned with saving the world from the foolishness of lesser men, as

---

[1] *SWJN,* XXVI.365, Editor's note.

the one who has deeper knowledge about the world and its affairs—Chou En-lai sets himself up as the eager student.

'On this question of peace in Southeast Asia and peace in Asia, I would like to exchange views and to hear whatever views Your Excellency holds,' he tells Panditji. '...If on this point Your Excellency thinks that we should do something further, we shall only be too pleased to do so,' he says as Panditji dilates on his idea of converting South-east Asia into an 'area of peace'. Panditji moves to Pakistan, and gives an equally full disquisition about it.

As Panditji finishes, Chou asks, 'What about Ceylon?' Panditji starts an exposition: 'About Ceylon, there is not much to say. It is a small island. They have not had much to do with international affairs. Her independence was an accident which followed India's struggle for independence... It has a rich soil which produces a lot without much effort...'

The next day, the discussion starts with Indo-China, and the responsibilities that India may have to assume as chairman of the commission that is being contemplated.

Knowing Panditji's partiality for them, Chou steers the conversation to the principles that have been alluded to in the trade agreement between China and India—a sort of draft for what will become the *Panchsheel*. 'As to how to extend this relationship which exists between India and China and how to apply it to other States,' Chou says, 'I would like to hear Your Excellency as Your Excellency knows these States and their Governments much better.' Panditji advises Chou to start with Burma, and what Chou should suggest to U Nu. 'I thank Your Excellency for your advice,' Chou responds. 'We shall consider it...' Panditji elaborates on the sequence that Chou should follow in approaching U Nu. 'Yes,' says Chou, 'What Your Excellency suggests is a very good idea. I shall study Your Excellency's suggestion.'

Chou asks about SEATO, about Anthony Eden's proposal for an eastern Locarno. Panditji launches on another exposition.

'I hope we shall have a chance to continue discussion tomorrow,' Chou says as they come to the end of the round. 'I am very glad to have had such a rare chance of exchanging views with Your Excellency so frankly and fully.'

'I had a message from Moscow today,' Panditji opens as they meet the next day. He turns to the problem of how much he must tell other countries of the Colombo Conference about their conversations... 'Yes,' Chou En-lai says, 'Your Excellency has to decide what should be sent to these countries.' 'One has to exercise one's discretion,' Panditji says of the great dilemma he has to reflect on.

'I am very anxious to know Your Excellency's views on the present situation in Asia,' Chou begins, laying out the widest possible canvas for Panditji to traverse.

'About three weeks ago, I had the Foreign Minister of Australia, Mr. Casey, with me,' Panditji commences. 'Did Your Excellency meet him?' And then follows the elucidation: 'Australia and New Zealand are, on the one hand, very intimately connected with England...'

He turns his gaze in the direction Chou has not looked, westward: 'The countries of West Asia are very backward—every one of them,' he informs Chou En-lai. 'They are small and very much under the influence of those who supply them with money and arms...'

'When Your Excellency said that Israel is strong enough to deal with the Arab countries put together, did you mean militarily strong enough?' Chou asks, keeping up the eager-student part.

Panditji explains patiently. 'I was in Egypt last year,' he starts and proceeds to elaborate. 'Is the new Government in Egypt fairly established?' Chou inquires. 'It is firm at the moment,' Panditji explains, 'but at its head are young military officers. They are in earnest, but with no experience or political knowledge. They are nationalistic, but with no roots in the people except that they are popular because they kicked out the King.' He elaborates this assessment.

'Your Excellency said that the national and popular movements in West Asia are not mature,' Chou remarks. 'Does that mean that there is a lack of mature leaders in these States?'

'Is the present situation that the United States is gradually replacing Britain and US influence is increasing?'...

'The living conditions of the people in this area are still very bad?'...

'Afghanistan has very good relations with India. Is it different from other West Asian States?'...

'In this area the population is not much?'... 'It is a desert area. The total population of the Arab countries is less than thirty million and more than half of this is in Egypt,' Panditji explains.

'Is Afghanistan included in this?'

'No, Afghanistan is not Arab.'

'Iran and Afghanistan are also Islamic countries?'... Panditji explains Islamic resurgence, and how the Iranians belong to a different sect...

'Is it impossible for India to get Thailand into the South-east Asian countries...?'

Panditji takes off on Thailand: '...There is a small group of people on top and the rest of the people are lazy, as they do not need to work.'

'Do they export much rice?... They export large quantities of rice?' Chou inquires innocently.

'What is the policy of UK and USA toward Thailand?'

Panditji introduces what Chou En-lai has forgotten to ask: 'A rather interesting development in Africa,' he tells his pretend-student, 'is the coming of Sudan as a new country. We sent an expert to conduct the elections there.'

Chou takes the hint: 'What will happen after the elections?' he asks. 'Will it be independent or associated with Egypt?'

'What is the relationship of India to Japan?'... How do they undercut your textiles?...

'This morning I asked Your Excellency many questions

and have learnt a lot from Your Excellency...' Chou says as they break for lunch.

They resume. Panditji: 'As Your Excellency was going away this morning you said you had one or two questions to ask me. I have also many questions to ask Your Excellency. Perhaps you would ask me first. Of course, there is no lack of questions.'

'All right. I shall start,' says Chou settling into the role he has adopted. What should be done to further cooperation between our two countries in the economic, cultural and political sphere?...

Panditji ranges far and wide—the fear among smaller countries of bigger ones; the way hostile forces take advantage of this; how fear distorts perception; how, having himself been through struggle and suffering, 'I do not find any difficulty in understanding and appreciating the background of China, the recent developments during the last ten or twenty years,' adding, 'Unfortunately I have not been there and I want to go there...'; the influence Gandhiji has exerted; India's role in the Commonwealth—'In the Commonwealth, India's influence has become more and more and we have influenced the policy of the Commonwealth considerably'; the US—'It is a powerful country and yet it is afraid, and it is more afraid than any country in Europe...'; 'I cannot influence American thought very much although I get a large number of letters from ordinary people from America against American policy at present and appreciating Indian policy...'; how Revolution cannot be exported; the communists of India...

And then on to another country and people about whom Chou has forgotten to ask: 'Does Your Excellency know about the Burmese people?' Panditji asks Chou. 'I had no chance to know them,' Chou replies helpfully. 'They are a friendly people, rather childlike. They are calm and composed. They are very proud, and, therefore, sometimes take offence very easily. But they are a very nice people and hospitable and friendly...'

Panditji asks his one question: 'Tomorrow when Your Excellency goes to Agra, we shall try to draft a statement... What should be the contents of this statement?'

Chou is not to be deflected from his role: 'Your Excellency has more knowledge about the world and Asia than I have. I am not being modest...'

The two meet for the final session on 27 June. 'Did Your Excellency see the draft statement?' Panditji begins.

'Yes. I saw it a few minutes before I went to see the picture,' Chou says—he has been taken to see Sohrab Modi's *Jhansi ki Rani*. 'It is a good picture. It is in technicolour.'

Panditji is now the film critic: 'The story is not so good,' he pronounces.

Chou En-lai is polite: 'It is quite good and represents resistance against foreigners.'

Panditji will not allow dilution of progressive touchstones: 'It was a resistance by the feudal elements against foreigners.'

'Yes,' says Chou, more generously, 'Resistance always starts from the upper classes...'

Again the conversation traverses the whole globe—except Tibet, our border, Chinese activities and plans around these parts. Panditji thinks little of the US and its system: 'Excellency must remember that the US Constitution has many things bad in it... No one can speak with authority in America—not even the President, because the Congress may pull him up.' Panditji elaborates.

Chou interjects only to let Panditji be even more expansive: 'I agree with the last point Your Excellency has made... I wonder if we can constantly exchange views in the future, as that would be a great force for peace.'

'Of course,' Panditji says, 'I hope so'—and resumes his exposition about the Americans: 'There is one corollary that follows from what I said before. The American people are terribly frustrated as no one is following them, and one never knows what a frustrated person may do.'

Another exposition follows—why and how China should establish relations with the UK... Frustration of the US... Geneva Conference.

'Yes,' Chou intervenes. 'I wish to come back now to another question regarding relations between India and China.'

'But I should like to say just one thing more,' Panditji says, brushing aside the interruption. The UK, Australia... how they say things opposing US policy in private but dare not say them in public... 'Now, Your Excellency must have seen what has happened in Guatemala...' And then, without so much as a breath in between, 'One small thing about Burma. U Nu is an ardent Buddhist and spends several hours in prayers and does his rosary. He often says he is becoming a monk, but I do not think he is going to do it—not in the near future—because there is no one else to take his place...'

At last Chou gets in a word: 'I come back to the relations between our two countries,' he says. 'We wonder if Your Excellency can visit our country before the end of this year...'

Panditji accepts readily. But he is not done with his tutorial, nor does Chou give up his well-practised act. 'At today's press conference, with quite a number of correspondents, I will not be able to answer any questions,' Chou remarks. 'I did not hold any press conference in Geneva.'

'I myself have not held any press conference for some time and have refused to see press correspondents,' Panditji says, adding, 'although they have come especially from abroad for this purpose and gone back.'

'Yes, exactly,' Chou remarks. 'May I say that in deference to Your Excellency's wishes, I agreed only to meet the press?'

Panditji can't resist another helpful hint to polish up his student: 'Yes. Your Excellency knows it of course that the best way to deal with the Press, if you do not want to answer a question, is to be humorous...'[2]

---

[2] *SWJN*, XXVI.366–96, 398–406.

What would the shrewd, cosmopolitan Chou have thought of the man? That he knew a lot about the world? Or that he was anxious to show him that he knew a lot about the world? That leaders from all over the world were in daily touch with him? Or that he was anxious to show him that leaders from all over the world were in daily touch with him? That he was a really helpful person keen to educate him on how to conduct himself? Or that he was presumptuous in wanting to teach him how to do so?

He 'is receptive to ideas'

We don't know. But we do know that Panditji is full of the way the tutorial has gone. 'He (Chou En-lai) strikes one as a frank and forthright person, which is rather unusual in the average Communist leader,' Panditji writes to U Nu later the same day, 27 June 1954. 'He speaks with some authority and is receptive to ideas. He thinks a good deal in terms of Asia and even more so in terms of Southeast Asia...' 'Chou En-lai does not know much about Burma. He asked me many questions'—at least not about Burma, Chou did not ask; Panditji asked him, 'Does Your Excellency know about the Burmese people?' before giving him the instruction—'and I tried to answer them. His whole approach was a friendly one desiring to understand.'[3]

Two years would not have gone by when Chinese troops would have entered Burma. And a somewhat annoyed Panditji will be advising U Nu on how to deal with Chou En-lai, and advising Chou En-lai on what China should be doing about Burma![4]

But that is two years away in the future. For the moment, Panditji is content with the way the pupil has received the instruction. 'Our talks covered a wide field and have been

---

[3] *SWJN*, XXVI. 407–10.

[4] *SWJN*, XXXIV.385–87; XXXV.506–12.

very helpful,' he writes to Krishna Menon after midnight on the same day. 'Chou En-lai is, I think, impressed by much he saw here and we have got to know each other fairly well. He is now very Asia-conscious and is anxious to understand other Asian countries about which he knows little. Repeatedly talked about India being economically and industrially more advanced than China...'[5]

Panditji leaves for Mashobra near Simla. From there, on 1 July 1954, he dictates a detailed letter to the chief ministers. The letter covers over twenty printed pages. His satisfaction beams through. 'The visit of Mr. Chou En-lai... an historic event of significance... The coming together of India and China... a major event for Asia and, perhaps, even for the world... It is clear that the future course of events in Asia, not to mention the world, would be powerfully affected by the future relationship of India and China...'

Then follows a long explanation of why the government has decided not to aid Tibet, an explanation to which I shall return. For the moment we follow him on Chou En-lai:

> He told me that he was not well-acquainted with most of the Asian countries... and would like me to tell him about them. He also said more than once that India was economically and industrially more advanced than China. I mention this to show that he took up no superior attitude at all in any matter. He was exceedingly receptive and wanted to know about India and other countries... All this indicated to me his extreme desire to develop friendly relations with these various countries and to remove all apprehensions from their minds. All this can, of course, be clever strategy looking to the distant future. No one can judge inner motives. But it seemed to me that Chou En-lai was quite honest about what he said. His mind was concentrated on developing his own country industrially and otherwise not getting entangled in any difficulties. In particular, he was always thinking of Asia and China's and India's responsibility to Asia.

---

[5] *SWJN*, XXVI.410.

Talk of deluding oneself! By now, the Chinese have almost certainly begun initial preparations for the road cutting off Aksai Chin.

'I have indicated a number of subjects which I discussed with him,' Panditji tells the chief ministers. 'As our conversations proceeded, they became more friendly and uninhibited and so I brought in other subjects also.' Panditji goes on to elaborate these other subjects... 'I have given above a fairly detailed account of my talks with Chou En-lai because I am anxious that you should be in full possession of this background. *We are playing, almost against our will, an important part in international affairs and, to some extent, the maintenance of peace in future might well depend on us...*' 'But, sometimes, there is what appears to me to be very unintelligent criticism. It is necessary, therefore, to be clear in our minds...'[6]

---

[6] Jawaharlal Nehru, *Letters to Chief Ministers, 1947–1964,* Volume 3, 1952–54, G. Parthasarathi, General Editor, Government of India, Delhi, 1987, pp. 580–601.

7

Carried away

That letter of 1 July 1954 to the chief ministers is as good a place to resume the story as any. Clearly conscious of the strong misgivings all over the country about what has happened in Tibet, and the danger it spells for us, Panditji is at pains to explain the reasons behind his persistent inaction.

Our ambassador had got on well with the new communist rulers, he begins, referring to K.M. Panikkar's tenure, '*but there was always some uncertainty in my mind as to what the Chinese Government might do*'— contrast this with the warm words he has been using to and about Panikkar, and with the way he has been plummeting for the latter's advice over that of others. And see the next sentence: 'It was clear that China would establish its sovereignty over Tibet.' Any uncertainty there? And notice the word, not 'suzerainty' that he has been using saying it is different from 'sovereignty', but sovereignty itself. 'This had been China's policy for hundreds of years, and, now that a strong Chinese State had been formed, this policy would inevitably be given effect to. We could not stop it in any way, nor indeed had we any legal justification for trying to do so. All we could hope for was that a measure of autonomy would be left to Tibet under Chinese sovereignty.'

And there have been reasons for this outcome, as solid as they have been valid. To start with, our position in Tibet was a relic of imperialist Britain: 'In effect, therefore, we were successors to certain expansionist policies of the old British Government. It was not possible for us to hold on to all these privileges because no independent country would accept the position.' Of course, the factor of far greater consequence had been the 'real influence of India... insubstantial but important'. This arose from the fact that the Tibetans looked up to us for guidance. But 'this tendency was a relic from the old days of British dominance and partly because they were afraid of China coming more firmly into the picture.' But all we could do was through diplomacy. And 'We did that as tactfully as we could, knowing that we could not make very much difference.' '*I think, however, that our efforts had some influence and somewhat delayed the Chinese invasion of Tibet'*—something you wouldn't have guessed from his cables of two years earlier!

It is patent, he tells the chief ministers, that to resist China's power in Tibet 'was wholly outside the range of practical politics'. And also that things have not turned out that badly either: 'They [the Chinese] have taken care... not to interfere with the domestic set-up much and have not interfered at all with their social conditions, *although these are feudal'*— that last phrase, as we have noticed, has begun figuring more and more in Panditji's dispatches: we couldn't have been defending a feudal set-up, he begins saying again and again in justification. Of course, the Chinese have begun building roads, airfields, etc., but that too is natural 'because communications in Tibet were very bad.'

'There has been much talk of Chinese troops' concentration on our frontier with Tibet,' Panditji tells the chief ministers. 'There is not much truth in this except that some Chinese troops are present on the frontier and in various parts of Tibet. The total numbers are not great and are spread out.'

But haven't B.C. Roy, the chief minister of Bengal, and others been sending him information about these troops? Panditji has the answer for that also: 'We get news often from Kalimpong about these Chinese military preparations in Tibet,' he explains. 'It must be remembered that Kalimpong is a nest of all kinds of spies and the information these people gather is utterly unreliable. It usually comes from émigrés who leave Tibet.'

He returns to his faith in geography: 'Indeed, the chief defence of Tibet is its very difficult terrain and the inhospitable nature of the climate. It is no easy matter for very large numbers from outside to live there.'

Being clear in our minds, instead of getting lost in what we could not help, he says, 'we concentrated on one matter which was important to us. This was our frontier with Tibet.' '...On this matter we were not prepared to parley with anyone, and I declared publicly in Parliament and elsewhere that this frontier, including the McMahon Line was a firm one and was not open to discussion.' 'Indeed, I went further,' he continues, explaining how very firm he has been, 'and said that, from the defence point of view, we considered the Nepal frontier with Tibet also our defence line.' He did this for a reason, he explains: 'I said all this deliberately so that the Chinese Government might have no doubts about our attitude.' But then why shy away from clarifying the matter directly to the Chinese? Panditji has the answer: 'I did not think it necessary to address the Chinese Government on this question because that itself would have shown some doubt on our part.'

The string of presumptions becomes longer. Panditji turns to the agreement about trade with Tibet that has just been concluded with China—the agreement, signed in Peking on 29 April 1954, is the first one, as we have noted above, in which India signed on to the Chinese description of Tibet as 'the Tibet region of China' and, in effect, gave up all the facilities and rights it had enjoyed in Tibet till then. 'As a matter of fact, we have given up nothing,' Panditji says, qualifying the 'nothing' with 'nothing *which we held or could hold.*' 'Obviously we cannot function within Tibet as if

Tibet was under our influence. We have recognized certain obvious facts of the situation and come to understandings about trade, pilgrimage routes between India and Tibet, etc. There is no giving in at all.' In fact, there is accomplishment: 'Two important aspects of this Agreement are: (1) that *indirectly the question of our long frontier is settled;* and (2) the principles of non-aggression and non-interference, etc., are laid down.'[1] How wishes have taken over! 'The question of our long frontier is settled'? That 'the principles of non-aggression and non-interference, etc., are laid down' in the agreement is any protection?

Chou En-lai stops over in Burma. U Nu writes to Panditji about the talks he has had with Chou En-lai. During these, Chou has said that the question of the boundary between China and Burma has never been settled in the past. U Nu has told Chou that in due course, Burma will take up this matter with the Chinese government through its ambassador in Peking. Panditji writes back on 9 July 1954. The communication covers several subjects. On the boundary question, he reiterates his stance:

> So far as the border questions are concerned, we have, on our part, no matter to raise with them [the Chinese Government]. Our border is quite clear. Since we were clear about this ourselves and have stated so quite openly, there was no point in my raising this question with him. In your case, however, there is a difference and so it is as well that you raise this matter clearly.[2]

'All this prevents intelligent thought'

It is now the turn of a few other officers to be put down. B.K. Kapur is India's political officer in Sikkim. He sends notes

---

[1] *Letters to Chief Ministers,* op. cit., Volume 3, in particular pp. 584–87.

[2] *SWJN,* XXVI.412–14.

and a letter. He expresses apprehensions about the designs of China's communist rulers, and suggests what we must do to prepare for eventualities. He recommends that we should not close our options in regard to Tibet. He warns that the Chinese will not be deterred by pledges of non-aggression, non-interference in internal affairs, etc., of the kind contained in the preamble to the Sino-Indian Agreement on Tibet.

The questions Mr Kapur has raised, Panditji begins, 'are important not only in themselves, but because they are concerned with much larger issues. Indeed, they are concerned with our wider policy towards China and our general world policy.'

'Naturally, the Tibetans have our sympathy,' Panditji says. 'But that sympathy does not take us far and cannot be allowed to interfere with a realistic understanding of the situation and of our policy. I have an impression that Mr. Kapur has not fully appreciated this wider policy of ours. It is necessary, therefore, that he and others concerned should understand it and should realize that this policy is the only one which might be helpful to the Tibetans, not in the measure perhaps that they desire but to some extent.' Our policy—it is a policy of doing nothing, actually, apart, of course, from putting in a friendly word with the Chinese, and that also at some future date when an occasion may arise—is not only in our interest, it is in the interests of the Tibetans themselves. 'Any other policy of encouraging the Tibetans to oppose Chinese over-lordship over Tibet would be raising false hopes in the Tibetans which we cannot fulfill and is likely to react unfavorably on the Tibetans,' Panditji explains. And now there is a new reason also: 'It would, of course, be opposed to the principles we have laid down in our recent Agreement with China.'

'Mr. Kapur talks that the Chinese Government is not likely to be influenced by considerations of non-interference, etc. At the same time he hints that we should also not be influenced by any such considerations, except in so far as that we should not do anything which might create obvious difficulties for us.' 'That is neither a moral nor a practical proposition,' Panditji pronounces. Assume for a moment that the officer is correct in his assessment that the Chinese will not be deterred by words in preambles. What would be moral for us to do to safeguard our interests?

Panditji allows a point, only to deflect it. 'No country can ultimately rely upon the permanent goodwill or *bona fides* of another country, even though they might be in close friendship with each other,' he begins. China and the Soviet Union are friends today, they may fall out. In a word, anything is possible. 'Therefore, we have always to keep in mind the possibility of a change and not be taken unawares. Adequate precautions have to be taken.' True, no agreement is a permanent guarantee of security. Not a possible agreement in Geneva over Indo-China, and so also not the Sino-Indian Agreement on Tibet.

Notice what is being done: the point that the officer is making about China is being brushed aside with the shrug, 'Yes, of course, that is possible, but then *everything* is possible.'

Panditji isn't done. He *can't* be done till he has nailed the officer for being stuck in old-thinking. Panditji says,

> The Americans and others can only think in terms of Communist aggression and villainy, of international communism trying to dominate over the world. And so on. All this prevents intelligent thought. If we wish to discuss these matters helpfully, we must avoid certain terms which create powerful reactions in the mind, such as imperialists, communists and the like. I do not like Mr. Kapur talking about Chinese communists, although they are communists. He should talk about the Chinese Government. In the same way, I do not like people talking about the Iron Curtain. The mere mention of these words confuses thought and shows that we are not considering a matter objectively.

Recall that Panditji himself again and again talks in terms of communists, and their ways! Recall what he wrote to his friend, U Nu, when the Chinese denounced the resolution on Korea that he has had tabled after 'full reference' to them. He says how unfair their denunciation is. 'However, there it is,' he says. 'It is not always easy to understand the motives and springs of communist behaviour.'[3] But here, 'I do not like Mr. Kapur talking about Chinese communists, although they are communists. He should talk about the Chinese Government...'

'Of course, both the Soviet Union and China are expansive,' Panditji continues. 'They are expansive for evils other than Communism, although Communism may be made a tool for the purpose. Chinese expansionism has been evident during various periods of Asian history for a thousand years or so. We are perhaps facing a new period of such expansionism. Let us consider that and fashion our policy to prevent it coming in the way of our interests or other interests that we consider important.'

A liberal's felicity

'I can quite understand that many people in Tibet have been disappointed at the agreement between us in China over Tibet,' he says. 'This must be partly because of the colour put on it by the Chinese in Tibet. That agreement however, was quite inevitable. It was a recognition of a certain factual situation which we could not possibly change. We have, in fact, at least got some advantage out of that agreement in other respects. If we had not had that agreement, the position would have been no better for us in Tibet and a little worse for the Tibetans. It certainly would have been worse for us from a wider point of view.' Of course, he does not have to spell out how this would have been the case. Anyone who has

[3] *SWJN,* XXI.446–48, also Editor's note, p. 447.

acquaintance with 'the larger picture', anyone who has 'the wider point of view', anyone who is keeping up with the tides of history, would know.

And in any case, such interests as we had in Tibet were things that *ought* to have been shed. 'We must remember that our so-called interests in Tibet'—you wouldn't have missed the new description, our interests in Tibet have become 'our *so-called* interests in Tibet'—'derive largely from our inheriting certain British interests which they succeeded in establishing in the days of British expansionism.'

How can we clutch such filthy things? But then, what are we to do when the Chinese reject the McMahon Line on that precise ground? That it too is the result of 'British expansionism'?

But Panditji is not to be deflected. 'We became the inheritors of British imperialism to a slight extent,' he says. 'We were popular with the ruling classes of Tibet at this stage because they thought we would come in the way of Chinese expansionism. We could not do so in Tibet and we could not possibly hang on to privileges which had no meaning in the present state of affairs.'

Why fret over things that 'had no meaning in the present state of affairs'? Why bother about the dismay among Tibetans when it is only those among 'the ruling classes of Tibet' who wished *only* that we be useful to them?

And we must be clear. 'Mr. Kapur says something about our not throwing cold water on various movements in Tibet against the Chinese, though we should not associate ourselves with them, that we should allow them to simmer and not die out. Let us be clear about this. Whatever happens in Tibet proper is beyond our reach. We can neither help nor hinder it. The question is what we do in our own territory. Do we encourage this or not? It is clear that we cannot encourage it. At best we can tolerate it, provided it is not too obvious or aggressive. A very delicate balance will have to be kept up.' On this reasoning, Panditji says that, as we tolerate all kinds in Kalimpong—'a nest of intrigues and spies'—we can as well tolerate a few Tibetans. He adds, however, 'I am sure that the Tibetan émigrés in Kalimpong, etc., are in close touch with the Americans, White Russians, etc., and are being encouraged by them with money and in other ways. In fact, I heard that there was a question of their collecting arms also. All this seems to me childish and totally unrealistic.' The 'delicate balance' will come to lean more and more towards Chinese sensibilities as the years go by.

'Even one of the major and much advertised efforts of the Americans to bring down the People's Government of China through Formosa is now recognized to be futile,' he notes, and asks, 'Is it then in the slightest degree conceivable that some petty violent effort organized by Tibetans and others on our border would produce results in Tibet?' We can allow some activities by them but only if these are 'peaceful and unobtrusive'. We should explain this to the Tibetans so that they do not misunderstand us, but 'It is clear that if they indulge in any aggressive action and the Chinese Government complains to us, we shall have no alternative left but to take some steps against them, at any rate to curb them.'

But all is not lost. The old friends, terrain and altitude return. 'The real argument in favour of Tibetan freedom or autonomy is the nature of the country,' Panditji writes. 'It is most inhospitable to others, it cannot maintain large numbers of foreigners and the like. If the Tibetans are stout enough to keep up a spirit of freedom, they will maintain a large measure of autonomy and the Chinese will not interfere. If the Tibetans actively rebel, they will be ruthlessly put down by the Chinese and even their autonomy will go. They are between the Soviet Union and China and one or other of these two powers will have a dominating political influence there. We in India cannot exercise it for geographical as well as other reasons. As a friendly Power to China we can be helpful occasionally in the diplomatic field.' Another repetition of another reason not to do anything—and in what way he will 'be helpful occasionally in the diplomatic field', we have seen: by preventing even a discussion in the UN of repression by the Chinese, and thereby saving the Tibetans from greater repression!

Panditji reiterates the other reasons for neither acting nor regretting the fact of not acting:

> We must remember that Tibet has been cut off from the world for a long time and, socially speaking, is very backward and feudal. Changes are bound to come there to the disadvantage of the small ruling class and the big monasteries. Religion may continue to be a powerful force to hold the Tibetans together, but social forces are also powerful. Thus far the Chinese have been careful not to interfere with social customs, religion, etc. So far as I know they have not even interfered with the land system which is feudal. I can very well understand these feudal chiefs being annoyed with the new order. We can hardly stand up as defenders of feudalism.

In a word,

- The system in Tibet has been and is feudal;
- The ones who are upset are the feudal chiefs;
- We can hardly be the defenders of feudalism;
- Moreover, the terrain and altitude of Tibet will save its autonomy;
- In any case, why this inordinate concern? The Chinese have been careful not to interfere with the religion and social customs, not even with the land system.

One can only marvel at the capacity of a liberal to rationalize playing possum.

Panditji's note proceeds to deliver instructions on other matters, and concludes:

> Our general position as contained in this note should be explained to Mr. Kapur.
>
> Mr. Mullik, the DIB,[4] should also be made to understand it. I shall be seeing him also...[5]

Old maps, no contingents

The Indian delegation at the negotiations in Peking is led by N. Raghavan, our ambassador there. His adviser, K. Gopalachari, sends a report on the discussions. Panditji dictates a long note of instructions. It has all the ingredients with which we have become familiar: putting others down, the intellectual superiority; the string of unwarranted assumptions—'our border is settled and firm because our policy is that it is settled and firm'; the half-measures—check-posts must be set up forthwith but no contingents need be provided to defend them.

Just as he had come down on Kapur for using the word 'communists' while referring to the Chinese, Panditji now says that the line to which he has himself been referring as the 'McMahon Line' should not be referred to as that:

> In future, we should give up references, except in some historical context, to the McMahon Line or to any other frontier line by date or otherwise. We should simply refer to our frontier. Indeed, the use of the name McMahon is unfortunate and takes us back to the British days of expansion.

What is this? A device to deflect the charge of Chou En-lai that our relations with Tibet and China are all the product of British expansionism, and that we have to negotiate them anew? Even that would be something. But the fact that Panditji himself continues to use the expression 'McMahon

---

[4] B.N. Mullik, Director of the Intelligence Bureau.

[5] *SWJN*, XXVI.476–80.

Line' in the coming years would lead one to infer that this is just another one of those flashes of fastidiousness with which an intellectual puts others down—the way some 'pretender-to-aristocracy' may put others down for not knowing the proper order in which to use the array of forks and knives around the plate at dinner.

But it isn't just that we have been using the wrong expression, we have been using the wrong maps. Hence, Panditji instructs the Secretary General and foreign secretary:

> All our old maps dealing with this frontier should be carefully examined and, where necessary, withdrawn. New maps should be printed showing our Northern and North Eastern frontier without any reference to any 'line'. These new maps should also not state there is any undemarcated territory. The new maps should be sent to our Embassies abroad and should be introduced to the public generally and be used in our schools, colleges, etc.

And then his thesis about why our border is a done issue:

> Both as flowing from our policy and as a consequence of our Agreement with China, this frontier should be considered a firm and definite one which is not open to discussion with anybody. There may be very minor points of discussion. Even these should not be raised by us.

He returns to this theme as he concludes his instructions:

> As I have said above, we need not raise the question of our frontier. But, if we find that the Chinese maps continue to indicate that part of our territory is on their side, then we shall have to point this out to the Chinese Government. We need not do this immediately, but we should not put up with this for long and the matter will have to be taken up.

The Chinese continue to print the maps. At every turn,

Panditji finds some new reason not to take up the matter with them. On this occasion, Panditji's new reason for his assumption—that the border is sealed and settled—is the recent Sino-Indian Agreement over Tibet:

> Our frontier has been finalized not only by implication in this Agreement but the specific passes mentioned are direct recognitions [sic] of our frontier there.

He lays down the 'forward policy' which is to cost the country so dearly—the 'policy' of putting stakes in the ground with nothing to back them, the policy which the army generals are warning him will prove disastrous, and which does prove disastrous in just a few years. But as he has ruled that this is what the 'policy' will be, that is what it will be:

> It is necessary that the system of check-posts should be spread along this entire frontier. More especially, we should have check-posts in such places as might be considered disputed areas.
>
> Check-posts are necessary not only to control traffic, prevent unauthorized infiltration but as symbols of India's frontier. As Demchok is considered by the Chinese as a disputed territory, we should locate a check-post there. So also at Tsang Chokla... In particular, we should have proper check-posts along the UP-Tibet border and on the passes, etc., leading to Joshi Math, Badrinath, etc.

He puts his foot down on the proposal to back these check-posts with the only kind of force that will make them viable:

> The Joint Secretary in his note has mentioned the possibility of our increasing the strength of our garrisons at some of our border-towns such as Gangtok, Leh, Simla, Almora, etc. I do not think this is necessary from the point of view of guarding this North Eastern frontier. In Leh, we have adequate forces. Round about Simla in the Punjab, we have quite adequate forces. But, apart from this, I do not consider

> it at all necessary to keep large contingents of our forces near this border area. Apart from check-posts, we should have some kind of border militia. I like the idea that this Border Militia should be raised locally and used for the construction of roads, etc. This will not only give a sensation of security to the people there but also add to their self-respect.[6]

'Old maps'

Panditji has told Chou En-lai how he would want to visit China. He is duly invited. The visit in October 1954 is to sweep him off his feet. From now on he will just not brook any suggestion that more be done about our border with China. He will henceforth have another string of reasons to persist in his policy. But two exchanges occur which are important for the record—they also hold a vital lesson: that far from taking the silence of the Chinese as acquiescence as Panditji has done in the case of Chou En-lai's conversations with Panikkar, one must not take even explicit remarks by a person like him and a regime like that of China as an assurance against an assault. Not words they speak or do not speak, but actual strength on the ground is the only thing that matters. The Chinese could have read the lesson to him out of Sun Tzu:

> The art of war teaches us to rely not on the likelihood of the enemy's not coming, but on our readiness to receive him; not on the chance of his not attacking, but rather on the fact that we have made our position unassailable.

Alas! That was the one thing Panditji thought was unnecessary.

During this visit Panditji has talks with Mao Tse-tung and Chou En-lai. The exchanges with Mao float over many generalities at what may be called the 'philosophical level'. As

---

[6] *SWJN*, XXVI.481–84.

happened during the five rounds of talks in Delhi, the talks between Chou En-lai and Panditji range over a vast field. In some respects, they are similar. Chou again strikes the pose of the eager student: 'What is the situation in Indonesia?' he asks; 'Are there any foreign factors in Indonesian troubles?' he asks; 'What about Ceylon?' he asks; 'What about Siam?' he asks; 'What about the three States in Indo-China?' he asks. In reply to each query, Panditji gives a longish exposition—this to the person directing a country that is initiating operations in many of these countries! But there is a difference also from the sessions in Delhi. Chou En-lai also talks at length. He is more confident, and more open.

On two points Panditji's strategy of indirection seems to pay off. Chou makes statements that are of significance as far as the record is concerned.

Recall that in their earlier discussions, Panditji has mentioned at length how several countries are propelled by fear—he has dramatized the point by his description of what accounts for the policy of the US. He has also emphasized more than once that several of the countries in South-east Asia are afraid of the large countries in the region, and how it is necessary to assuage this apprehension. He takes up this theme again with Mao[7] and the next day with Chou. In passing, Panditji mentions as examples the apprehensions about the loyalties of overseas Chinese, he mentions the maps that the Chinese government continues to publish and which show large chunks of other countries—like Burma—to be parts of China. Chou En-lai gets what Panditji is driving at. On infiltration and assistance to insurrectionist groups within other countries, matters that are of concern to India also, Chou says,

> As regards the question of infiltration, this is entirely a matter for the people of various countries. You referred to it in Delhi and you said that decisions were made by the

[7] *SWJN*, XXVII.6–11.

> people of each country and, therefore, no interference was permissible from outside. As far as we are concerned, we will make greater efforts to implement the Five Principles. We can build greater confidence and show to the world an example that not only can we strictly abide by the principles but we can do it well. We can do it by specific examples and during your visit here we can talk more about some more specific questions.[8]

A little later, Chou En-lai turns to the question of maps. He says,

> Maps: It is a historical question and we have been mostly printing old maps. We have made no survey of the borders and not consulted with our neighboring countries and we have no basis for fixing the boundary lines. We made our maps and revised them from the maps of other countries. At least we do not have any deliberate intentions of changing the boundaries as KMT had. The whole thing is ridiculous. The question of boundaries between China and Burma was not settled even in Manchu regime and you will find differences even in our boundaries with the Soviet Union and Mongolia. We can further discuss the matter with U Nu but we want time for preparation.[9]

This, of course, is an important statement. Panditji takes it to apply to the Sino-Indian border also. He is to place great reliance on it, as we shall see. For the moment, he comes back to what Chou has said, just to make sure that Chou will not go back on his statement. Panditji tells Chou En-lai,

> As regards maps, I just casually mentioned to you some of the anxieties of our neighbors. We are not worried on this point. Our frontiers are clear but I mention it in the case of Burma because questions of this kind become a handle in the hands of enemy [sic] Supposing we publish a map

---

[8] *SWJN*, XXVII.18.

[9] *SWJN*, XXVII.19.

> showing Tibet as a part of India, how would China feel about it? But as I said, I am sure, the maps were old maps and you did not mean it.[10]

Although Panditji is to place much reliance on these assurances in the coming years, and to refer to them on several occasions[11] the Chinese will disregard them with accustomed ease—and Panditji will have occasion to acknowledge that the Chinese statements had ominous nuances to them. The factor that will prove of far greater consequence, and will become a set of blinkers is the reception that the Chinese orchestrate for Panditji.

'I would have been less than human if I had not been influenced by all this'

There is a vast volume of literature that records how fellow travellers and even sceptical visitors were bamboozled by

---

[10] *SWJN*, XXVII.20.

[11] For instance, in the account he sends to the chief ministers upon his return to India, Panditji recalls this exchange as follows:

> I referred to Chinese maps which still showed portions of Burma and even of India as if they were within Chinese territory. So far as India was concerned, I added, we were not much concerned about this matter because our boundaries were quite clear and were not a matter for argument. But many people took advantage of these old maps and argued that China had an aggressive intent, or else why continue to use these maps. In Burma also this caused apprehension. Premier Chou replied that these maps were old ones and China had not done any surveying to draw new maps. Their boundaries even with Mongolia and the Soviet Union were still not clearly demarcated and there were discrepancies. I pointed out that this might be so. So far as India was concerned, I repeated, there was no doubt about our boundaries and I was not worried about them. But I wondered how China would feel if a part of Tibet had been shown as part of India in our maps.

Jawaharlal Nehru, *Letters* to *Chief Ministers, 1947–1964,* Volume 4, G. Parthasarathi (ed.), Government of India, Delhi, 1988, pp. 76–89, at p. 82.

communist regimes over the decades. Panditji who had himself been taken in by the Soviets when he had accompanied his father on a visit to the Soviet Union in 1927 was well acquainted with much of this literature—the trumped-up trials of Stalin's time, the Potemkin villages, the reality behind Soviet claims of Stakhanovite workers and economic miracles, all these were the staple literature of his generation. So, it wasn't that Panditji was an innocent. And yet he was completely taken in, and this, even more than his general predilections about progressive regimes, was to lead him and, through him, India into 1962.

'Over a million people lined the twelve mile long route from the airport,' the editor's note records about the welcome in Peking, 'and for the first time the Chinese dispensed with the bullet proof cars and Nehru rode in an open car. Desmond Donnelly of the *Daily Mail* described the reception as a "Roman triumph".'[12]

In communication after communication, Panditji talks of the stupendous welcome he has received. As he prepares to leave China, he dictates a letter to Chou En-lai from Canton. He says,

> No words of mine can tell you how deeply impressed I have been with my visit to this new China and with the welcome that I have received both from the leaders and the Government of China and the people. That welcome was tremendous enough to have moved anyone. I have had a good deal of experience of mass gatherings and popular welcomes in my own country, as well as in other countries and I have grown receptive to not only what I see but what I feel. I have felt, during these ten days of my stay in China, something deeper than a popular welcome of an individual, whoever he might be. It has seemed to me that there was some emotion behind it, some conscious or subconscious awareness of the significance of my visit at this juncture of

---

[12] *SWJN*, XXVII.7, Editor's note.

the history of our two countries. Your visit to India had that significance also and the people of my country showed their awareness of it by the welcome they gave you, even though you came suddenly...

As is his wont, he sees history unfold:

My visit to China was in continuation of your visit to India and a further link in the chain that is binding our countries to each other. It was this feeling in the popular mind, whether in India or in China, that these two great countries, both with their tremendous past and their great promise for the future, are drawing closer to each other and are destined to cooperate in the building up of that future. That, I believe, influenced our peoples.

To some extent, even peoples of other countries have realised the significance of this new development in the relationship of India and China, and so, apart from individuals, these visits have become important events in a historic process...[13]

On returning to India, he writes to Edwina Mountbatten. 'My dear Edwina,...

This visit to China as well as the Indo-China countries has indeed been an event of some historic significance...

I had a welcome in China, such as I have in the big cities of India, and that is saying a great deal. *I do not think there was any precedent for it in China.* A week or two before I reached Peking, some of the big people of the Soviet Union were received there with all honour. But they had, what might be called, an official welcome. They were placed on the high seats and much praise was showered upon them. The welcome given to me was both official and popular. It is said, probably correctly, that a million people took part in it on the day of my arrival in Peking. They lined the twelve-mile route from the aerodrome and crowded

[13] *SWJN*, XXVII.51–53.

> the streets. There was perfect discipline and there were few policemen about, though no doubt there must have been plenty of other people to maintain this order. School boys and girls and college students and workers in factories had turned out with banners. And then there were others who joined them. I was taken in an open car with Chou En-lai and I was standing in it. That seemed somewhat odd in, what is called, a 'Police State'. Indeed, I was told that this was the first time Chou En-lai or anyone of his high position in China, had appeared in public in this way...

Nor was that all:

> It was not only the numbers but their obvious enthusiasm. *There appeared to be something emotional in it.* For once, official direction and public feeling completely coincided, though no doubt they do so to some extent often enough. *I had a feeling, and others confirmed it, that my going to Peking brought certain reactions on the Chinese people.* Thus far, they had dealt with or welcomed people from the Soviet Union or other communist countries. There was certainly more of fellow-feeling for them. *But my arrival there produced a somewhat different type of release.* They felt happy that a great country like India, which was not in the communist fold, was friendly to them. *Their outlook widened and their self-assurance increased.* A sense of Asian cooperation, apart from Communism and the like, produced this sense of relief and release. India became, in their eyes, a friend and her stock went up. As a representative of India, I became a symbol, which they honoured and cheered.
>
> There were many functions and I am surprised that I have survived all of them, especially the banquets which took place every day. You know Chinese banquets how long they are, how full of toasts. Most of these banquets had as many as 700 or 800 guests of all types—apart from the official hierarchy and the diplomats, there were scientists, medical men, professors in the colleges, etc., actors and actresses and specially honoured workers at the end. Even there, there was

> genuine enthusiasm. I would have been less than human if I had not been influenced by all this...[14]

He writes to the chief ministers in the same vein: 'I received an extraordinarily cordial welcome everywhere in China. This was not only an official welcome but a popular welcome also in which millions joined. I was greatly impressed by it. It was clear to me that this welcome represented something more than political exigency. *It was almost an emotional upheaval representing the basic urges of the people for friendship with India.*' 'Young men and girls and children were particularly in evidence,' he continues a few paragraphs later, 'and they were a pleasant-looking crowd, jolly and full of enthusiasm. Undoubtedly, there is a great deal of regimentation as it is called. Their discipline was remarkable.' But to Panditji this does not indicate any of the things we are later to associate with the Mao era. He continues, 'But I would say that the Chinese people have always been a more or less disciplined people.' He sees prosperity: 'The shops appeared full of goods. There were thousands of small privately owned shops. There were some big state-owned department stores. These were also full of various kinds of goods, though luxury articles were not in evidence. These department stores were crowded with literally thousands of persons... I did not sense the presence of any fear among the Chinese. They had plenty of self-confidence and self assurance.'[15] No fear in Mao's China as literally hundreds of thousands are being killed!

An 'emotional upheaval', a 'release'—and that too among 'millions'... Panditji is right: an individual who concludes that such release and upheaval have been caused by his moving among them, that the outlook of millions has been widened and their self-assurance increased, and, having come to this

---

[14] *SWJN*, XXVII.66–71, at pp. 67–68.

[15] *Letters to Chief Ministers*, op. cit., Volume 4, at pp. 86–87.

conclusion, is unmoved by the phenomena 'would be less than human'.

'China, entirely for its own sake, wants peace... '

Panditji now starts testifying to China's peaceful intentions with the authority of the eyewitness. 'I am convinced that China, entirely for its own sake, wants peace, wants time to develop its country and thinks in terms of at least three or four five years plans—fifteen or twenty years time to lay the foundations of a socialist State,' he tells the press. 'So all this question of aggression, internal or external, has to be seen in that context of their not desiring to get entangled.'[16] He tells the chief ministers: 'I have no doubt at all that the Government and people of China desire peace and want to concentrate on building up their country during the next decade or two.'[17] He tells the BBC,

> My own impression is that the Chinese People's Government have given many evidence [sic] of their peaceful intention during the past several months. They, of course, deny any desire to interfere; I am not aware of any interference recently anywhere. It is a little difficult of course to judge of internal activities in a country which may have nothing to do with the Chinese Government.

The BBC correspondent asks Panditji whether he has any evidence to that effect. Panditji replies,

> I have no such evidence anywhere, but I do know that the Chinese leaders are very anxious to have these peaceful relations, and those peaceful relations can only subsist on a basis of non-interference. They realize that and they said, 'we have no intention of interfering internally or externally.'

---

[16] *SWJN*, XXVII.73.

[17] *Letters to Chief Ministers,* op. cit., Volume 4, at p. 86.

The correspondent says that means that Panditji is accepting their word at face value. Panditji gives the sort of Marxist answer no Marxist would give! 'For my part I accept their word because that word fits in with objective conditions in Asia and their country and in the world,' he says. And not just that, there are the Chinese people, there is their innate nature:

> Apart from this I have seldom come across—I am judging from impressions of large crowds and I am used to large crowds—a people inclined to more friendliness and peaceful cooperation. I am talking about crowds now so that whatever information they may have had or misinformation, has not affected their friendly approach... The people everywhere are friendly and peaceful in the mass. Only I found—if I may use the word—a little more of it in China than I normally find anywhere else.[18]

In an interview with Agence France-Presse and Radio France in Saigon, Panditji is asked, 'Are they convinced about the possibility of coexistence between communist and non-communist countries?' Panditji, as he does frequently, first puts the questioner down: 'There is no question of their being convinced or not convinced because this is the only possible course to be adopted if war is to be avoided,' he says. 'If this possibility does not succeed at any stage, conflict will certainly arise; but most people in the world have expressed a wish to make all possible effort to avoid a war. As far as China is concerned, the Chinese authorities are, at the moment, very busy with their present Five Year Plan and also subsequent five year plans. They are very anxious to establish their economy on a firm footing and they are all the time thinking seriously in terms of economic rehabilitation and progress in general; the Chinese authorities naturally wish to avoid anything that will come in the way of their progress.' 'Did you

---

[18] *SWJN*, XXVII.87–90.

discuss the question of Chinese support to the revolutionary movements in other countries?' the journalists ask him. 'The Five Principles expressly refer to non-interference by one country in the internal affairs of another,' Panditji retorts, and that is the end of the matter.[19]

So, the Chinese dedication to peace and not to get entangled in the foreseeable future, is almost a historic inevitability! And on top of that, it has been sealed and set in the Panchsheel! This is Panditji's assessment of rulers who just three years earlier had hurled their forces on to two fronts simultaneously—Tibet and Korea. This is his assessment about rulers for whom 'power flows out of the barrel of a gun,' with whom exporting revolutions is an article of faith. But, then, Panditji has seen the truth for himself. He is the eyewitness.

Soon, he has discovered yet another benefit that has accrued from his overture to China. 'The Indian Government ha[s] been very successful in meeting the threat of Communism, largely because of the Indian Government's policy towards China, which ha[s] disconcerted and perplexed the Indian Communist Party,' he tells the Commonwealth prime ministers in London in February 1955. 'By recognizing the Peking Government and by agreeing with them certain principles on which they could live together, the communist will to create trouble in India ha[s] been undermined.' He proceeds to argue China's case on Formosa...[20]

True to his word to Chou En-lai, Panditji busies himself with preventing the outbreak of war over Formosa, and

---

[19] *SWJN,* XXVII.93–99, at pp. 97–98.

[20] *SWJN,* XXVIII. 165–66. It is about his exposition at this meeting that Panditji cables the Indian ambassador in Peking twice that he, Panditji, has explained the Chinese position fully to the Commonwealth prime ministers; that 'I believe this has created some impression;' that he should 'assure Chou En-lai of our deep concern and anxiety to find solution, or the beginning of one, which will avert war and result in China obtaining her legitimate rights...' [Ibid., pp. 167–70.]

seeing how China can acquire its legitimate asset. Soon, he is advising the US as well as China on how to lower the tensions that have erupted with the capture of four US airmen in China... And then, he is unweaving the tangles of Indo-China...

He visits the Soviet Union for a fortnight in June 1955. This time he gets convinced that the Soviet government and people are just as keen to ensure peace. In a letter to the American president, Dwight Eisenhower, Panditji says,

> I felt strongly that the Government of the Soviet Union desired peace and a settlement of the various problems that had led to so much tension in the past and in the present. The Far East problem, I believe that they are sincere in this matter. So far as the public in the Soviet Union was concerned, I witnessed amazing demonstrations of welcome and I have no doubt in my mind that there is a very strong feeling for peaceful settlements and the removal of present day tensions. I found great constructive work proceeding wherever I went in Russia or in the Asian Republics of the Soviet Union. New towns were being built as well as great public buildings and factories and numerous houses and apartments. All this constructive work also indicated to me a desire for peaceful progress.
>
> My general impression was that a marked change had come over Soviet policy and that this was not a mere temporary phase. This gave me hope for the future and indicated that, more than at any time in the past, there was substantial reason for hope as a result of peaceful approaches and settlements.[21]

[21] *SWJN*, XXIX.355–57.

8

'Two miles this side or two miles that side'

The countries of Indo-China continue to occupy his attention. Tensions in the Middle East intensify—he gets busy dousing them... Months follow months of total immersion in these troubles. Suddenly, there is a little knock: Chou's protestations notwithstanding, the Chinese continue to print the 'old maps' showing large parts of India to be Chinese territory; but now, Panditji learns that the Soviets have started reproducing the alignments in Chinese maps.

On 6 May 1956, Panditji sends a note to Krishna Menon. He recalls that Chinese maps have been showing a large part of Assam to be part of Tibet; he recalls what the Chinese have been saying about the maps being old and their not having had the time to carry out any surveys to check the maps' accuracy. He tells Menon that the government had decided not to raise the matter 'because, so far as we were concerned, there was no dispute. The Tibet frontier ran along the McMahon Line and we consider it a firm frontier. I stated that more than once in Parliament.'

'Even when I went to China,' he recalls, 'I casually mentioned Chinese maps to Chou En-lai and, so far as I remember, he said something about the maps being old and that we can settle frontier questions in a friendly way later.'

Recall that thus far Panditji's inference has been that such statements of Chou En-lai as well as his silence have meant that China has acquiesced in our understanding of the border. But suddenly, Panditji is a bit unsure about this inference, an inference he has been forcing everyone concerned to internalize. Panditji now tells Krishna Menon:

> *In effect, therefore, China never clearly accepted our frontier as it is. All that they have said is that the old maps are not reliable.* We have stated to them and in Parliament that our frontier is as given in our maps.

A shift of such enormous consequence, made as if in passing. The shift is reinforced in the next paragraph:

> At the time of the agreement with China about Tibetan questions, *it was taken for granted by us* that all pending questions between India and China had been settled. In some of our communications too, stress was laid on this. *But, China has never admitted this clearly, though they did not deny it either.*

Contrast what Panditji is saying now with what he has told the Secretary General of his ministry less than two years earlier. In the detailed note of instructions that we have encountered earlier, we see Panditji maintain, 'Our frontier has been finalized not only by implication in this Agreement [the Sino-Indian Agreement on Tibet] but the specific passes mentioned are direct recognitions [sic] of our frontier there.'[1]

And now this new problem:

> I find that the Russian maps (and we have good Soviet atlases which were given to us in Moscow) also reproduce the Chinese maps in regard to the Indian border and show a part of India as being in Tibet.

---

[1] *SWJN*, XXVI.481–84, at p. 482.

And things have started happening on the ground:

Every year, there are petty incidents on our UP-Tibet border. Some Chinese soldiers come across up to ten or fifteen miles or even more.

They come in 'up to ten or fifteen miles or even more', and they do so every year, and yet these are just 'petty incidents'? Panditji explains:

> There has been no actual conflict but there has been some friction. They have ultimately withdrawn.

Panditji formulates the dilemma he has not been able to resolve over the years:

> The question arises as to what we should do in these circumstances. When an actual incursion like this has taken place into our territory, we have, of course, protested in Peking. We did this only a few days ago. But, should we take any other action? That is, should we definitely raise the question of the frontier with the Chinese Government? This frontier is not clearly demarcated, and some doubt may arise about some point along it. The question is not, however, about some doubtful points but rather about a much wider territory which the Chinese maps show.

He turns to the build-up on the Tibetan side. Only to again reassure himself that the build-up is but natural and does not *necessarily* indicate any aggressive intention—the question really is 'does it indicate a greater *capacity* for aggression against us'? it is a question Panditji does not ask, not now, not in the future. Panditji writes,

> On the Tibetan side, roads and airports are being built. That is, I think, natural because the Chinese wish to develop Tibet and to improve communications. This does not necessarily mean any hostile or aggressive intention against India, but

> this, taken together with occasional petty raids and the maps which continue as they were, does produce a sense of disquiet.

He reverts to the accustomed stance:

> I mentioned this matter to our Ambassador in Peking when he was here recently. He seemed to think that we should bide our time and not take any active step.

But Panditji and, because of him, the government have been biding time for years. Have they done enough during this period to strengthen our position on the ground?

Panditji proposes that these questions be considered 'more fully among ourselves'.[2]

By now, Panditji is clearly getting worried. Within a week of his note to Krishna Menon, in May 1956, Panditji dictates another note—this time to the foreign secretary. 'The building of roads and air strips by the Chinese in Tibet appears to me to be a natural development from the Chinese point of view,' he says, still not wanting to face fully what they portend for our security. 'In order to hold and develop Tibet, they must have these communications.'

But he is immediately back in the phrases that he has been recording for long. He merely reiterates the 'set up check-posts' strategy. 'It is true that roads right up to our border and air strips near our border create a new situation for us, which we must bear in mind,' he allows, adding immediately, 'I rule out any kind of physical or aerial attack on India for a considerable time to come at least.' 'So far as infiltration, etc., are concerned, they have to be met by other means.' So, what is the upshot? What is to be done? 'Proper check-posts on the border and a certain vigilance right along the border, development of communications on our side and general economic and like development of our areas'—he

---

[2] *SWJN*, XXXIII.475–77.

lists these familiar desirables, but sees that they will make little difference to the immediate situation, and, therefore, adds 'which, of course, is rather a long term programme.'

He returns to the worry all this spells, though only 'a little'. 'What worries me a little is the persistence of the Chinese maps indicating parts of our territory as being in the Chinese State,' he says. That business about the maps being old ones which he has hitherto accepted and broadcast to others is clearly wearing thin. 'I think that we shall have to take up this matter some time or other. We can consider this separately. In this connection, however, I think that we should take up with the Soviet Government, their maps of this border area, which appear to be a copy of the Chinese maps.' So, the decision about taking up the matter with the Chinese is again deferred.

But shouldn't we be doing more to strengthen our forces on the border? In Panditji's assessment there isn't much we can do, except to go on doing what we have been doing, presumably at the pace at which we have been doing it. He records:

> From a military point of view, we can do little except
> (1) check-posts at all suitable points on the border;
> (2) giving efficient training to our men in mountain warfare; and
> (3) developing roads and other communications.

There has been a proposal to strengthen our air capabilities; someone has suggested long-range bombers, etc. Panditji rejects the suggestion. 'This is against our basic approach to the problem of defence. They are too costly and, if we get them, it means that we do not equip ourselves with more useful aircraft and delay, to some extent, our industrial development. The basic strength that India should aim at will only come through rapid industrial development. For the moment, this means fulfilling the Second Five Year Plan.' So, we are back to the things that are going to take even longer than the measures that he has himself just said constitute 'rather a long term programme'.

Before concluding, Panditji again comes down heavily on an officer. This time it is the turn of Apa Pant, the political officer in Sikkim and Bhutan. The officer has conveyed the information that he has received—he has been told that China now has one hundred twenty thousand troops in Tibet. Panditji says, 'I am astonished to see from the letter of Apa Pant, dated March 7th, that he estimates Chinese troops in various areas of Tibet as one hundred twenty thousand. Apart from this figure being much too big to be easily accepted, the difference between this figure and Menon's figure of forty-five thousand is very great. I think, we should ask Apa Pant on what basis he has suggested his figure.'[3]

A few weeks later, in July 1956, Panditji is at the Commonwealth Prime Ministers' Conference in London. He gives a long exposition on China. During this he tells the assembled prime ministers,

> The Chinese Government and people would be preoccupied for years to come with the agricultural and industrial development of their country. It was difficult to predict the future but it seemed unlikely that they would harbour aggressive intentions against any other country. India was confident that her policy of maintaining friendly relations with both Russia and China provided a sufficient guarantee for her own security, and she sought no additional protection.

Three days later, he is again arguing China's case for the seat in the UN. The minutes of the meeting record:

> Mr. Nehru said the problems concerning the international status of Communist China were so important that there

---

[3] *SWJN*, XXXIII.477–78.

> would be justifiable criticism if there was no reference to them in the final statement about the discussions at these Meetings. *There was, in his view, no more vital or urgent issue than the admission of Communist China into the United Nations.* Had she been a member some years ago the course of history might well have been altered; for example, the Korean war might never have occurred.[4]

A wake-up call

By the time he returns to Delhi, the papers are reporting large-scale incursions by Chinese troops into Burma. There has been no provocation. There is no occasion for them to do so. They just force their way in, occupy a thousand square miles of Burmese territory, and settle down.

We just *have* to do something, Panditji tells his officers. The Government of Burma has approached us. The incursions violate the Panchsheel. They can have a bearing on our own borders. After weighing alternatives, he suggests that an aide-memoire be prepared for being sent to China. He sets out the points to be made.

'This *aide memoire* will require very careful preparation and we shall have to decide what we should say and what we should not say,' he begins. He is still in a quandary about the question that most directly concerns India: 'I think that we should not raise directly the question of the Indian frontier with Tibet or China. But, indirectly, this may well come up in connection with the McMahon line and also because it is alleged that the Chinese have come across our frontier also somewhere near the Burmese frontier. (This has to be verified as soon as possible.)'

A point is worrying him specially. 'We are aware that the People's Government of China have claimed that they are not bound by previous treaties and agreements,' he notes, with the worry, no doubt, whether the Chinese could not

[4] *SWJN*, XXXIV.250–54 and 259.

take the position about all the agreements on which our border with them rests. '...but in international usage, no previous treaty or agreement can be denounced or altered unilaterally as other Governments are concerned with it. Also long use and possession, history, tradition, custom and natural geographical features are factors of considerable importance'—factors he will be compelled to invoke soon. 'In any event, no change can be made unilaterally,' he notes.

And then the aide-memoire should mention that, 'Apart from international usage and convention, any such unilateral action would be against both the spirit and the letter of the *Panchsheel* doctrine to which China, Burma, India and other countries have adhered.' Should the very fact that he has to remind China so soon after its signing up on these principles, so soon after Chou En-lai having told him that China will set an example of adherence to them, should this fact by itself not alert him to what we might have to face soon?

And then the point he has made to Mao and Chou En-lai during his conversations with them, and which seemed, at least then, to have registered with them: 'Some mention might be made of the apprehensions of some countries in South East Asia which fear Chinese expansion.'

Next, the customary argument: that foreign powers hostile to friendship between our countries will exploit such fears. 'Foreign agencies who do not approve of friendship between Burma and China exploit these differences and apprehensions, and other countries in South East Asia are also affected,' he says the aide-memoire should state. 'Thus, not only the friendly relations between Burma and China, but the larger interests of peace in Asia are concerned and every effort should be made not to give any cause for suspicion or apprehension to these countries of South East Asia...'[5]

A week or so later, on 4 September 1956, Panditji sends a

[5] *SWJN*, XXXIV.385–88.

telegraphic message to U Nu through the Indian ambassador in Rangoon. With Chinese forces in firm occupation of Burmese territory, Chou En-lai has invited U Nu to Peking for discussions about the border tensions. Panditji counsels U Nu that 'it would be advisable for you to accept this invitation and discuss these matters frankly and informally with Chou En-lai. This is a more helpful way than tackling them only at official and government level.' A contrast to the position he has set for himself! He follows this message up with a longer letter. 'I need not tell you that we have considerable interests in this matter,' Panditji writes, 'even apart from our concern in respect of Burma. This question affects India as well as Burma.' 'There is also the very important consideration which, no doubt, you have in mind...,' he says. 'The whole edifice of the Five Principles and coexistence may crack if this dispute between Burma and China is not approached in a friendly and peaceful way and satisfactorily settled. That would be most unfortunate and would have far-reaching consequences.' And so he is most anxious to help. But he does think, Panditji says, that the best course would be for U Nu to accept Chou En-lai's invitation to go to Peking. There he can discuss the matter with Chou directly. 'I might separately send a personal message to Chou En-lai at an appropriate moment.'[6]

That message is sent on 12 September 1956. Panditji emphasizes the harm the dispute can inflict on the edifice of Panchsheel. He mentions how it will be used by powers that are hostile to friendship among countries in this part of the world. He enunciates a principle that has direct relevance to the Indian position in regard to the Sino-Indian border: 'I would like also to mention that, by and large, in these sparsely inhabited frontier mountain areas, frontiers and positions which are based on previous agreements and have also been accepted by usage, custom and tradition for

[6] *SWJN*, XXXV.508–10.

appreciable periods, should not be disturbed or altered except by friendly agreements.'[7]

When the Chinese do, in fact, usurp these 'sparsely inhabited frontier mountain areas' in Ladakh, Panditji, as we shall soon see, says, 'Not a blade of grass grows there...' Mahavir Tyagi, the MP, I am told, remarked, 'Here, look at my head'—he was quite bald—'not a blade of grass grows here. To whom is Jawaharlal gifting my head?'

Ten days have not passed, on 20/21 September 1956, the wake-up alarm rings louder—Chinese troops cross a pass in Himachal, the Shipki La. The decision to cross deep into this border, is manifestly a deliberate one. The Chinese officer says that they have been ordered to patrol right up to Hupsang Khad, a spot 196 miles from Simla. It turns out that they have come in thrice in the preceding weeks. 'This is a serious matter,' Panditji records, 'we cannot accept this position.' We should, of course protest. But that will not be enough. Our guards must remain at their post 'even at the cost of conflict'.[8]

Soon, there is a cable from R.K. Nehru about the dates on which Chou En-lai proposes to visit India. Either for this reason or because he thought that police and not the army will be the appropriate force, by 8 October 1956, Panditji is taking a softer view. He emphatically turns down a proposal to send troops to Shipki La. 'In fact, even in the spring next year, I do not envisage the necessity of sending troops. The fate of Shipki La is not going to be decided by fighting or by large show of force... The main thing to do is to have a Police outpost there and that our personnel should be in physical possession of the Shipki La when the snows melt.' He does allow that it may be useful to send a few army men to reconnoitre the area.[9]

---

[7] *SWJN*, XXXV.511–12.

[8] *SWJN*, XXXV.515–16.

[9] *SWJN*, XXXV.518.

The Dalai Lama is in India at India's invitation. Panditji meets him on 26 and 28 November 1956. The Dalai Lama is distraught. Panditji jots down the points of their exchange. The Dalai Lama puts the figure of Chinese troops in Tibet at 120,000, the very figure for which Panditji had come down on Apa Pant. The foreign secretary inserts a paragraph in Panditji's notings about the talks: 'The Dalai Lama appealed to India for help. PM's reply was that, apart from other considerations, India was not in a position to give any effective help to Tibet; nor were other countries in a position to do so. Dalai Lama should not resist land reforms.' Instead of help, Panditji gives advice. He records the advice he gives: 'D.L. should become the leader of the reform. Best way we can help is by maintaining friendly relations with China, otherwise China would fear our designs in Tibet.' An excuse, and a presumptuous one—'otherwise China would fear our designs in Tibet.'[10]

Further talks with Chou En-lai

Chou En-lai arrives in Delhi on 28 November 1956. Panditji welcomes him at the airport. 'This new ideal of *Panchsheel* is reverberating in the world,' he says. 'Many countries are with us in this. There are grave dangers to the world and so it is more than ever necessary to put this goal before the world. This is how we can serve the cause of world peace.'[11]

There are four rounds of talks—one round at Bhakra-Nangal; one on the train back, this round in effect from 10.30 p.m. to 2.30 a.m.; and two rounds in Delhi.

The talks differ in two respects from the ones that were held when Chou first came to Delhi. Chou En-lai talks as much as Panditji. Second, while several subjects come up—

---

[10] *SWJN*, XXXV.520–22.

[11] *SWJN*, XXXV.522.

the crises in Suez and Hungary, for instance—the two have candid exchanges on Tibet and the Sino-Indian border.[12]

Chou En-lai introduces the subject of Tibet. It is well known that the Chinese have not been able to 'pacify' the Tibetans. Disturbances have continued to erupt. Distrust and hostility are pervasive. Chou En-lai gives his version of what is happening in Tibet at great length—the moderation of the Chinese authorities, a small clique in Lhasa which continues to instigate people, this clique is in touch with Tibetans in Kalimpong... Chou brings his thesis home: he puts the onus on India. Troubles in Tibet have risen because the Dalai Lama is away in India; the hub of the conspiracies and subversive activities is Kalimpong. The Dalai Lama's brother is involved. They are being aided and instigated by the Americans and the remnants of Kuomintang in Taiwan. The local government and the People's Liberation Army units are handling the matter within Tibet. 'So, for the time being, the matter is over,' Chou says, 'but, as long as Dalai Lama is away, something might happen. The Kalimpong people are thinking of keeping Dalai as long as possible so that his absence could be taken advantage of. This is chiefly instigated by the USA and Taiwan. *Since Dalai Lama is in India, if anything happens it will be unfortunate. We will, of course, take measures to put down any incident in Tibet, but still it is not good if something happens.*'

---

[12] On Hungary, Chou gives the standard communist, in fact the Soviet line: conspiracies, counter-revolution, etc. Panditji ranges between 'But can socialism succeed by force, without freedom?' and the lament of the 'progressive': 'The most unfortunate part of the Hungarian episode, it appears to me, is'—note, not the brutal suppression and mass-scale killing of the people, not the extinguishing of their freedom, but—'that it has harmed the cause of socialism in Europe and elsewhere and many of us who are friends of USSR are very much distressed and find it difficult to justify what has happened there. There is an unfortunate conflict between nationalism and socialism. Socialism has to be based on nationalism or otherwise it is weakened.' *SWJN*, XXXVI.590–92.

The conversation moves to the historical status of Tibet, and to the Tibet-India border, and we shall return to these in a moment. But soon, Chou returns to the theme—India has to ensure that Tibetans do not do anything that the Chinese government regards as anti-Chinese. He tells Panditji that, if the Dalai Lama goes to Kalimpong, attempts might be made to keep him there, or that if the Panchen Lama goes there, he may be treated 'discourteously'. 'If such incidents happen,' Chou states, 'Indian Government has power to intervene and check them, because such incidents, partake of the nature of anti-Chinese activities or activities designed to create an independent Tibet or espionage or encouragement to subversive activities. We are mentioning these possibilities to your Government in advance so that, if anything happens, the Government of India could take preventive measures.'

The message goes home. Panditji assures Chou En-lai, 'As regards the Dalai Lama, we do not want any incident to take place about Dalai Lama in Kalimpong or while he is in India. We will do as Your Excellency and Dalai Lama decide. What kind of incident does Your Excellency fear might happen? If you can give some specific idea about the trouble, we can prevent it.' The Dalai Lama does not go to Kalimpong. Tibetans there are put on notice. The Dalai Lama returns to Tibet.

Tibet and the border

Chou tells Panditji that the latter knows a lot about Tibet. That Tibet has always been a part of China although it was not made a province of China in the past... Panditji takes him up on this. He says he does not quite understand what Chou meant when he said that Tibet in the past had not become a province of China. Chou's response is important. He says,

> That Tibet is part of China is a fact, but it [w]as never an

> administrative province of China but kept an autonomous character. Therefore, when we started negotiations for peaceful liberation of Tibet, we from the first recognized the autonomous character of the region.

He explains what he meant when he told Panditji that he knew more about Tibet than Chou himself:

> When I said that India knew more about Tibet, I meant about the past history. For example, I knew nothing about McMahon Line until recently when we came to study the border problem after liberation of China.

Panditji is gracious. He sidesteps his knowledge of history, and focuses on arguing the case for Tibet's autonomy. Panditji tells Chou,

> Historical knowledge is not important but is useful as background information. History is gone. My impression was that whatever it may be in theory, for all practical purposes Tibet has all along been autonomous. But at the same time, whatever government there might have been in China, Tibet has always been claimed by the Chinese government. The British tried to create some trouble on account of their fear of Czarist Russia but this is past history. We recognize that China has, in law and in fact, suzerainty over Tibet even though it may not have been exercised sometimes. As Your Excellency has said, Tibet has behaved in an autonomous way and was cut off from other countries. The criterion of an independent State is that the State should have independent foreign relations and Tibet had no foreign relations except with England.

On such criteria, hardly a country in Europe, to say nothing of North and South America, would be what it is today. Furthermore, once we accept that Tibet had no authority to conduct foreign relations, how will we defend the agreements it came to with India about the border? But Panditji seems to see no difficulty. He takes Chou up on his remark that he, Chou, knew nothing about the McMahon Line till recently:

> The McMahon Line was put forward in the 1913 Conference between the Chinese, the Tibetans and the British. That Conference decided not only the McMahon Line but also two other points. The Chinese Government raised objection only to the other two points.[13] Surely, the Chinese Government always knew about it (i.e. the McMahon Line).

The conversation goes back to handling the Tibetans in Kalimpong... Chou restates the Chinese version of Tibet's history. He contrasts the position of Tibet with that of Bhutan and Sikkim, of how the latter were never under China. He returns to the McMahon Line:

> McMahon Line—What I meant was that people like me never knew about it till recently. The then Chinese Government, namely, the warlords in Peking and the KMT naturally knew about it. Perhaps, U Nu might have told Your Excellency that we studied this question and although this Line was never recognized by us, still apparently there was a secret pact between Britain and Tibet and it was announced at the time of the Simla Conference. *And now that it is an accomplished fact, we should accept it.*

Chou, as is customary with him, immediately introduces a clause which can provide a ground for going back. Indeed, he now interjects the Tibetans as a wedge! He tells Panditji,

> But we have not consulted Tibet so far. In the last Agreement which we signed about Tibet, the Tibetans wanted us to reject this Line; but we told them that the question should

---

[13] The Chinese objections related to the demarcation of Inner and Outer Tibet.

> be temporarily put aside. I believe immediately after India's independence, the Tibetan Government had also written to the Government of India about this matter. But now we think that we should try to persuade and convince Tibetans to accept it. This question also is connected with Sino-Burmese border and the question will be decided after Dalai Lama's return to Lhasa. *So, although the question is still undecided and it is unfair to us, still we feel that there is no better way than to recognize this Line.*

In a word, Chou thrice repeats that the Chinese Government has concluded that, whatever the past and even though it is not altogether satisfied with it, the McMahon Line should be accepted now:

- 'And now that it is an accomplished fact, we should accept it.'
- 'But now we think that we should try to persuade and convince Tibetans to accept it.'
- 'So, although the question is still undecided and it is unfair to us, still we feel that there is no better way than to recognize this Line.'

Panditji advances that matter a step further. With the Line accepted, we should settle on some principles by which such minor adjustments that might have to be made can be made:

> The border is a high mountain border and sparsely populated. Apart from the major question, there are also small questions about two miles here and two miles there. But if we agree on some principle, namely the principle of previous normal-practice or the principle of watershed, we can also settle these other small points. Of course, this has nothing to do with the McMahon Line.

'Yes,' Chou En-lai responds, 'the question can be solved and we think it should be settled early.'

Two points should be borne in mind. First, Chou's statements on accepting the McMahon Line are unambiguous, they are repeated thrice. Yet the Chinese will have no difficulty in going back on them. Second, even as Chou is saying all this about the border in the east, the Chinese government has begun constructing roads that will hack off thousands of square miles of our territory in the west.

The conversation shifts back to Tibet. Panditji assures Chou En-lai that India's main interest in Tibet is religious—the Dalai Lama is a mythical figure here, Mansarovar and Kailash are pilgrimage centres. Panditji says that he recognizes that Tibet cannot remain cut off from the world, that he himself would want it to progress but he thinks it would be best if the Tibetans come to feel that they are themselves bringing about the changes...

Earlier, when he is dilating upon the situation in Tibet and on the policy of the Chinese government in regard to it, Chou has told Panditji,

> Tibet is divided into three parts...These three parts still have some distance (differences) among them. We have always advised unity. Our policy has always been to give them an autonomous government under the Central Government, enjoying a large measure of autonomous rights. The Central Government always consults them on all related matters and local matters are handled by themselves. We fully respect their religion; everyone lives in religion there and every family has to give one or two of its members to the temple. At present we do not talk of democratic reforms to them; but when other parts of China become economically better and if Tibetans feel the need and agree to it, then we can introduce them.

Chou now goes further and tells Panditji that, actually, the Chinese government wants Tibet to have and develop direct contacts with other Buddhist countries in Asia, except that one must guard against foreign powers conspiring to use such contacts. He reverts to what he has said earlier to put the onus on India and on Panditji personally to do more: 'But if there is foreign influence in it, then it becomes troublesome. Therefore, we maintain that religious contacts should be developed in Asian countries, but at the same time we should stop subversive activities. Espionage activities are carried out in the open in Kalimpong and we feel that the Government of India should intervene because these activities will interfere with religious contacts and exchange.'

As for the Chinese government, 'We respect religion,' Chou says. Even though the government may strive to involve the Tibetan people in the changes, that does not mean that there won't be trouble 'because there are some who are open to foreign influence and there are some who lack understanding'. Moreover, there are differences among Tibetans: 'Those who are progressive want quick reforms, but this makes the non-progressive ones suspicious of the progressive elements, and they feel that the latter are being influenced by the Hans.'

One can read either message into what Chou En-lai has told Panditji: that the Chinese will respect the autonomy of Tibet, in particular that they will respect the religion of the Tibetans; or that anyone who opposes them in the name of practising religion is either under foreign influence or is a regressive opposed to reform. Even more important from the point of view of lessons we must draw for the future, the two aspects of policy that are going to have the maximum effect on Tibetans and their religion are ones that Chou doesn't mention at all: that the Chinese government will swamp Tibet with the Han Chinese and reduce the Tibetans to a minority in their land; and that they will split the 'three parts', subsume two of them into adjacent provinces, and redefine 'Tibet' to be the truncated 'Tibet Autonomous Region'.

The conversation moves to Sino-US relations. Wanting as always to promote good relations among others, Panditji explains the point of view of the Americans... In the last round, the conversation turns to Nepal, and Chou is sensitive to India's interests and position in regard to the country.[14]

The last two rounds of exchanges take place in January 1957. Panditji is quite satisfied. His policy of not raising the question of the boundary seems to have at last paid off—Chou En-lai has accepted the border as defined by the McMahon Line.

Another surprise

Three months have not passed, and Panditji is in for a bit of a surprise. U Nu writes to him. China is creating difficulties in the talks on the Sino-Burmese border. He wants some help in excavating records from the archives. Panditji replies the very day he hears from U Nu.

'I am sorry that there has been some difficulty in your arriving at a settlement about border problems with the Chinese Government,' he writes. 'I confess that I do not very much like the attitude of Premier Chou En-lai in this matter. The impression created upon me is that he was not fully adhering to what he had told you or U Ba Swe[15] previously. But this is for you to judge.'

Panditji has earlier given an account of the talks with Chou En-lai to U Nu and S.W.R.D. Bandaranaike, among others. Given what has happened in the talks of Burma with China, he recounts what Chou En-lai told him in greater detail.

'In your letter you say that while Premier Chou En-lai was prepared to accept the McMahon Line in the north, he objected to the use of the name "McMahon Line" as this may produce "complications *vis a vis* India", and, therefore, he preferred to use the term "traditional Line".'

---

[14] *SWJN*, XXXVI.583–619, 623–30.

[15] The deputy prime minister and defence minister of Burma.

'When Chou En-lai was here last, we discussed many matters at great length,' Panditji recounts. 'He referred to his talks with you and U Ba Swe and indicated that while he was not convinced of the justice of our claim to the present Indian frontier with China (in Tibet), he was prepared to accept it. That is, he made it clear that he accepted the McMahon Line between India and China, chiefly because of his desire to settle outstanding matters with a friendly country like India and also because of usage, etc. I think, he added he did not like the name "McMahon Line".'

Panditji emphasizes that

> This statement that he made to me orally was important from our point of view and so I wanted to remove all doubts about it. I asked him again therefore and he repeated it quite clearly. I expressed my satisfaction at what he said. I added that there were two or three minor frontier matters pending between India and China on the Tibet border and the sooner these were settled, the better. He agreed.

Panditji says that he agrees that the expression 'McMahon Line' should be discarded—'It reminds one of British incursions and aggression.' The basic point is that 'our frontier with China, except for two or three very minor matters, was a fixed and well-known frontier and there was no dispute about it. We had never raised this question with China, but I had stated in Parliament here and also to Chou En-lai in Peking that there was nothing to discuss about our frontier as it was fixed and well-known. We have now our check-posts all along this frontier.'

'Thus, so far as we are concerned, this frontier (known previously as the McMahon Line) is not a matter in dispute at all and Chou En-lai has accepted it. It is true that his acceptance was oral, but it was quite clear and precise.'[16]

A meeting is to be held to discuss these two/three minor

---

[16] *SWJN*, XXXVII.507–09.

places about which alone, Panditji keeps telling everyone, there is some disagreement. He writes to Sampurnanand, the chief minister of UP. There are three places where we have had some trouble in the past, Panditji tells him. 'We were not greatly worried about these particular places,' he writes, 'and the actual territory involved was probably a few miles this way or that way.' The really important aspect relates to the whole border between India and China. 'As you know,' he tells the chief minister, 'this border was settled long ago by a tripartite meeting, and this border is often referred to as the McMahon Line.' Chinese maps have been showing large parts of India to be part of China. 'So far as we are concerned, we have made it repeatedly clear in Parliament and elsewhere that this border is a firm one, and there is nothing to discuss about it,' Panditji says. 'In fact, there was some slight attempt on the part of Chou En-lai to discuss this matter with me when I went to Peking. I told him there was nothing to discuss.'

That last phrase is something that Panditji is to repeat on several occasions. His premise perhaps was that had there been something to discuss, Chou En-lai would have pressed the subject. As the latter did not, we can take it that he accepted our position that the border was settled and firm. A costly premise, as he was to soon find out.

Even as he records this, Panditji is not entirely at ease. 'The fact, however, remained that this could not be treated as an agreed border, between India and China,' he writes immediately afterwards, 'and the question might be raised at any time by China. This would affect not a few miles of mountain territory, but quite a large area.'

Panditji goes on to recall that on his last visit to Delhi, Chou En-lai had talked about the China-Burma border, and stated in that context that China had accepted the McMahon Line in regard to the boundary between China and Burma. Furthermore, 'He [Chou En-lai] added that although the matter was by no means clear, as the British

Government of the day had been committing aggression in various places, nevertheless, as India and China were friends, he was prepared to accept this McMahon Line as the border between India and China also.' 'This was an important statement and admission from our point of view,' Panditji tells Sampurnanand, 'and I therefore had him repeat this quite clearly. I added then that quite apart from this long frontier about which there was no argument, there were two or three smaller border disputes, and the sooner we settled them, the better. This settlement should take place on the basis of usage and geographical features. He agreed.'

We are waiting for the Chinese representative to come to Delhi to discuss this, Panditji writes.

The reason he is writing, Panditji says, is that Sampurnanand should know what the position is, and should ensure that no misbehaviour by local persons vitiates the atmosphere of the forthcoming talks. 'But, broadly speaking,' he notes in conclusion, 'we should realize that these matters are being settled in conference and, what is more important, that the major border issue has already been settled for all practical purposes.'[17]

'Dispute is rather a big word'

Yet, beneath all this, there is growing unease—the public posture and the privately felt reality begin to diverge more and more.

The Chinese have stepped up oppression in Tibet. The Tibetans expect India to help. They send emissaries. Delhi does nothing: on the contrary, it maintains that were it to do anything, the Tibetans would be put to even greater suffering. *January 1958*: The former prime minister of Tibet calls on Panditji. Panditji is busy. The former prime minister 'read out a long story of the sufferings of the Tibetans and

17 *SWJN*, XXXVIII.689–90.

their wanting independence and India's help in obtaining it,' Panditji informs the foreign secretary, Subimal Dutt. 'This itself took a long time and I had no more time to spare.'

'I told him briefly that it was folly to think of defeating China by armed force,' Panditji records, 'that India could not supply any arms, that Tibet had become so backward that change had become imperative.' He continues, 'If the Tibetans did not change themselves, the change would come from outside. There was no possibility of putting the clock back and reverting to the previous State of Tibet remaining there. Briefly my advice was that the Tibetans should keep united and claim full autonomy. They should not challenge China's overall sovereignty. If they stood for autonomy and were united, they would be able to retain their way of life and at the same time they should try to introduce reforms.'[18]

Chinese aggressiveness continues. Chinese oppression of Tibetans intensifies. Chinese maps continue to show large chunks of India as parts of China. Panditji is for indirection. In a note that he dictates on 8 April 1958 to the foreign secretary, Panditji says that our High Commission in London should take up the matter with the Chinese embassy there, and that we might also express our regret at such maps to the Chinese embassy in Delhi, but 'On the whole, I am inclined to think that we need not at this stage ask our Embassy in Peking to take up this matter'. He explains the merit he sees in this indirect course: 'Thus, our present approach will not be too formal and at the same time the Chinese Government will know what we feel about the issue of such maps.' He has 'a vague idea,' Panditji adds, that a meeting is to take place about the border issues. We may mention the question of the maps to the Chinese representatives at the meeting also.[19]

Months pass. The Chinese continue to issue those maps. By August 1958, Panditji's assessment turns. 'I do not think

[18] *SWJN*, XLI.671

[19] *SWJN*, XLII.655.

that we should allow this matter to pass without some kind of protest,' he instructs the foreign secretary. 'To ignore this repetition of inaccurate maps showing large parts of India in China is, in a sense, to accept them. Anyhow it weakens our case to some extent.' Have the joint secretary meet the Chinese counsellor and hand him an aide-memoire or an informal note, he directs. 'In the course of the talk it should be mentioned that I referred to this matter to Premier Chou En-lai on more than one occasion,' Panditji writes, 'that is, when I visited China and also I think when Premier Chou En-lai came to India. His answer was that present maps were based on old maps and the Chinese Government had no time to correct them. As the People's Republic of China has now been functioning for many years and new maps have been repeatedly printed and published, it is surprising that these corrections have not been made. We hope that they will be made soon.'[20]

Parliament session commences. On 4 September 1958, questions about the maps showing large parts of the North-east including Assam as parts of China put by the Praja Socialist Party member from Assam, Hem Barua come up. When attention of the Chinese authorities was drawn to these maps, Panditji says, 'we were told that these were reproductions of old maps, coming down from the previous regime, when Marshal Chiang Kai-shek was in authority in China, and they had had no time to revise them. So they were carrying on.' That this was not an all together satisfactory explanation in Panditji's view was apparent: 'Evidently, the People's Government in China has revised many things since Chiang Kai-shek's regime, but this matter has been left over.' Panditji added, 'We have been privately assured on some occasions that they attach no importance to these maps and they will revise them in time. That is where the matter stands. We have drawn their attention again to it.'

---

[20] *SWJN*, XLIII.536.

Barua inquires about the boundary as a whole, about the Chinese position regarding the McMahon Line. Panditji says that 'So far as the broad boundary, the international frontier is concerned between India and the Chinese State including the Tibetan region, it is not a matter of dispute so far as we are concerned. It is a fixed thing. There is nothing to talk about.'

'But that has been violated,' Barua interjects.

'May I proceed?' Panditji exclaims, not saying whether the border has been violated or not. He recalls that when this matter was referred to in the House earlier, 'I said that we had nothing to discuss because it is an obviously known established frontier of ours. We saw no reason to ask for a discussion on a thing that required no discussion.' Yes, there are 'two or three specific cases of what might be called boundary disputes.' 'These are very small ones,' Panditji adds characteristically. 'Somewhere in the mountains, whether it is two miles this side or two miles that side, there has been an argument—dispute is rather a big word—between the two countries and it has been decided that the matter should be settled by talking with each other…' 'They are of no particular importance. The area concerned is very little and there is no other value… Honourable Members will remember that these places in high mountains are such that they are not easily accessible and in fact nobody can go there for six or seven months in the winter—only in summer months some people go for grazing purposes there.' These 'minor matters' are pending. They are being discussed. 'So far as the major matters are concerned, there is nothing to discuss.'

What is the total area of Indian territory that is shown as part of China in these maps? Barua asks. The map is on a very small scale, Panditji says. A mere line may cover 20 miles, 50 miles. 'May I know if it is 1,700 miles in total?' Barua asks. 'I can't say,' Panditji answers. 'I have no idea.'[21]

---

[21] *Lok Sabha Debates, Second Series,* Volume XIX, cols. 4629–32, 4 September 1958. Also *SWJN,* XLIV.567–69.

'Very small ones . . . Somewhere in the mountains, whether it is two miles this side or two miles that side… there has been an argument—dispute is rather a big word… They are of no particular importance. The area concerned is very little and there is no other value…'—from that to 'acne' in 2013, to 'a localized problem', one continuous line!

Two months have not passed, and a party of Indian surveyors is arrested by the Chinese at Shyok, south of the Karakoram Pass. For a month, there is no news of them. Upon inquiry, the Chinese tell our embassy in Peking that they had arrested the party a month earlier. The counsellor at our embassy in Peking does not realize the importance of the matter. Instead of informing Delhi by cable, he sends a letter. Panditji approves the proposal of the foreign secretary that a strong protest be lodged with Peking. But his note is ambiguous, it cuts both ways, and does not quite square with what he has been saying about the border being established, firm, settled, etc.: he is more on the way the Chinese have dealt with the surveyors' party and not told the Government of India anything about them or about what they have done; '…we might indicate that the fact of this particular area being in Indian or Chinese territory is a matter of dispute between the two countries. This question will be dealt with separately. But the fact that our surveying party went there in the ordinary course of their work cannot be said to be an intrusion in admittedly Chinese territory.'[22]

The incident and information coming in from Tibet have lent some urgency to the Ladakh portion of the border also. Panditji instructs the foreign secretary to bear in mind that, according to what he, Panditji, had been told, it is not just the boundary in the east that was settled by the McMahon Line, but in Ladakh also—the terminology was new at the time, and he was using the expression 'McMahon Line' as a generic expression for the agreements that had been arrived

---

[22] *SWJN*, XLV.697–98.

at from time to time; he was soon to be more specific in communications to Chou En-lai. Therefore, he says, 'If we touch the McMahon Line in one place, then there is no particular reason why it should not be varied elsewhere.' He reiterates what Chou En-lai had told him: that China was prepared to accept the McMahon Line because of friendly relations between India and China. 'He made this quite clear as will be patent from the note I wrote on that occasion,' Panditji records. 'Of course, we have nothing in writing from him. Still we might perhaps refer to this McMahon Line which settled our frontier and which has been accepted ever since then…'[23]

What is becoming patent is not just what Chou En-lai had said but also the imprudence of relying on what he had said. And even more so on the deduction that because Panditji had said that there was nothing to discuss and Chou En-lai had not pressed the matter, the latter had accepted the position that the border was settled, established, firm.

[23] *SWJN*, XLV.699.

9

'You didn't even know we were building a road...'

Things go on deteriorating. The Chinese now put a different construction on the maps being 'old maps'. Up till now they have been saying that these were old maps dating from the Kuomintang era, and that they had not had time to correct them. Now they leave out the last clause. These are old maps, in the sense that they are authentic in that they are based on maps that have been continuously published since the pre-liberation times!

A letter to Chou En-lai

Panditji sees the gravity of the change. He is compelled to address a formal letter to Chou En-lai on 14 December 1958—about the maps, of course, but also about the border question in general. At the time, 1954, when the Sino-Indian Agreement was negotiated, Panditji writes, a number of mountain passes were mentioned. 'No border questions were raised at that time and we were under the impression that there were no border disputes between our respective countries. In fact we thought that the Sino-Indian Agreement, which was happily concluded in 1954, had settled all outstanding problems between our two countries.'

Panditji recalls that the two of them had long discussions during his visit to China in October 1954. He had noted with pleasure, he says, that there was no dispute or problem affecting our relations.' He had briefly mentioned the matter of large parts of India being shown in China in the maps, he writes: 'I presumed that this was by some error and told you at the time that so far as India was concerned we were not much worried about the matter because our boundaries were quite clear and were not a matter of argument.' Panditji recalls, 'You were good enough to reply to me that these maps were really reproductions of old pre-liberation maps and that you had had no time to revise them,' adding, 'In view of the many and heavy preoccupations of your Government, I could understand that this revision had not taken place till then. I expressed the hope that the borderline would be corrected before long.'

And then you had visited India in October 1956, Panditji says. In the course of discussions during this visit, you had told me about your settling the border with Burma in accordance with the McMahon Line. 'You told me then that you had accepted this McMahon Line border with Burma and, whatever may have happened long ago, in view of the friendly relations which existed between China and India, you proposed to recognize this border with India also. You added that you proposed to consult the authorities of the Tibetan Region of China and you proposed to do so.' To reinforce the point, Panditji reproduces the note he had recorded of their talks immediately after the exchange. 'I remember discussing this matter with you at some considerable length. You were good enough to make this point quite clear,' Panditji writes. 'I then mentioned that', while there were no disputes between us on the frontier, there were 'certain very minor border problems which were pending settlement'. We decided that these should be settled amicably by representatives 'on the basis of established practice and custom as well as watersheds'. Your representative had come to Delhi. An agreement could not be finalized. 'I had thought then of writing to you on this subject, but I decided not to trouble you over such a petty matter.'

Panditji then turns to the question of those maps, and the fact that they continue to be reproduced in Chinese publications. Questions were raised about these in Parliament also, he writes. When attention of the Chinese government has now been drawn to these maps, and how they show large parts of India to be in China, we have been told that the map 'is drawn on the basis of maps published before the liberation'.

'I was puzzled by this reply,' Panditji tells Chou En-lai, 'because I thought that there was no major boundary dispute between China and India. There never has been such a dispute so far as we are concerned and in my talks with you in 1954 and subsequently, I stated this…'[1]

What Chou meant by what he said!

Chou En-lai writes back on 23 January 1959. Panditji must have felt the ground move from under his feet—Chou has opened up the entire question of the borders; every single premise on which Panditji's approach has been based, on which each of his public statements including those in Parliament has been based is out of the window.

'In your letter you have taken much space to discuss the question of Sino-Indian boundary and thus enabled us to understand better the Indian Government's stand on this question,' Chou writes. Accordingly he will set forth the views and stand of the Chinese Government, he says.

'First of all,' he says, 'I wish to point out that the Sino-Indian boundary has never been formally delimitated. Historically no treaty or agreement on the Sino-Indian boundary has ever been concluded between the Chinese Central Government and the Indian Government.' In the past few years, there have been some disagreements on the ground, he points out. 'The latest case concerns an area in the southern part of China's jurisdiction. Patrol duties have continually been carried out in that area by the border guards of the Chinese Government. And the Sinkiang-Tibet

[1] *SWJN*, XLV.702–06.

highway built by our country in 1956 runs through that area. Yet recently the Indian Government claimed that that area was Indian territory. All this shows that border disputes do exist between China and India.'

Hardly a sound argument, but a typical one: X barges into your house; you point out that it belongs to you; he exclaims, 'See, there is a dispute about it.'

In any event, that must have stung Panditji. For the passage pointed to a fatal oversight—one for which we pay to this day. Chou is saying that China built the road through Aksai Chin in 1956. For three full years, the Government of India did not say anything—it knew nothing about it. Three years having gone by, it has suddenly woken up, and is asserting that the area through which this area has been built belongs to it: that is what his statement says in effect. Years later, during his talks with Henry Kissinger, Chou En-lai is to make fun of Indian authorities on this very point. Chou recalls for Kissinger that China had built the road from Western Sinkiang to the Ali District of Tibet, and how, suddenly Pandit Nehru had raised the issue of this road. Chou tells Kissinger, 'I said, "You didn't even know we were building a road the last three years, and now you suddenly say that it is your territory." I remarked upon how strange this was...'[2]

To the point that Panditji had made about no issues relating to the boundaries between the two countries having been raised during the negotiations that preceded the 1954 Agreement, Chou has typical answer: we didn't raise the issue then because we did not think the conditions were ripe for a settlement of it and we had had no time to study the matter. But now...

As Chou En-lai puts it, 'It was true that the border

---

[2] For the record of the conversation, *Memorandum, The White House, Top Secret/Sensitive/Exclusive Eyes Only, Memorandum of Conversation,* Great Hall of the People, Peking, July 10 1971, 11.20 pm-11.50 pm, *www.gwu.ed/nsarchiv/NSAEBB/NSAEBB70/#11*

question was not raised in 1954 when negotiations were being held between the Chinese and Indian sides for the Agreement on Trade and Intercourse between the Tibet Region of China and India. This was because conditions were not yet ripe for its settlement and the Chinese side, on its part, had had no time to study the question. The Chinese Government has always held that the existence of the border question absolutely should not affect the development of Sino-Indian friendly relations. We believe that, following proper preparations, this question which has been carried over from the past can certainly be settled reasonably on the basis of the Five Principles of peaceful co-existence through friendly talks. To this end, the Chinese Government has now proceeded to take certain steps in making preparations.'

And the result is that what had been said earlier does not hold!

His reply on the McMahon Line, and the implications of China having accepted it in the case of its boundary with Burma also knocks the bottom out of what Panditji has been assuming in regard to the Sino-Indian border. The line was a result of imperialist aggression by Britain. It is illegal. China has never accepted it. Tibet too was dissatisfied with this unilaterally drawn line:

> An important question concerning the Sino-Indian boundary is the question of the so called McMahon Line. I discussed this with Your Excellency as well as with Prime Minister U Nu. I would now like to explain again the Chinese Government's attitude. As you are aware, the 'McMahon Line' was a product of the British policy of aggression against the Tibetan Region of China and aroused the great indignation of the Chinese people. Juridically, too, it cannot be considered legal. I have told you that it has never been recognized by the Chinese Central Government. Although related documents were signed by a representative of the local authorities of the Tibetan Region of China, the Tibetan local authorities were in fact dissatisfied with this

unilaterally drawn line. And I have also told you formally about their dissatisfaction.

But China is for balancing complex factors: the need for a 'more or less realistic attitude towards the McMahon Line' and the need to 'act with prudence', Chou says. Hence, China needs time to deal with this matter.

On the other hand, one cannot, of course, fail to take cognizance of the great and encouraging changes: India and Burma, which are concerned in this line, have attained independence successively and become states friendly with China. In view of the various complex factors mentioned above, the Chinese government, on the one hand finds it necessary to take a more or less realistic attitude towards the McMahon Line and, on the other hand, cannot but act with prudence and needs time to deal with this matter.

There is a vital change. Earlier, Chou En-lai has told Panditji that, in view of this Line having existed for so long, and in particular because of the friendly relations between China and India, China is prepared to accept this line in demarcating the Sino-Indian border. He now says, 'However, we believe that, on account of the friendly relations between China and India, a friendly settlement can eventually be found for this section of the boundary line.' The affirmation that, in view of the friendly relations that have come to prevail between China and India, China is prepared to accept the line, has vanished.

Next, Chou En-lai turns the question of those maps being old on its head. Precisely because the boundary has not been defined, it is natural that the maps in use in the two countries will differ, Chou states. As for the maps currently in use in China, 'the Chinese boundaries are drawn in the way consistently followed in Chinese maps for the past several decades, if not longer. We do not hold that every portion of this boundary line is drawn on sufficient grounds. But it would be inappropriate for us to make changes without having made surveys and without having consulted the countries concerned.'

And there is the practical difficulty in making changes. You say that you have to face difficult questions in regard to our maps, well, so have we in regard to the maps published in India! 'Furthermore, there would be difficulties in making such changes, because they would give rise to confusion among our people and bring censure on our government,' Chou tells Panditji. 'As a matter of fact, our people have also expressed surprise at the way the Sino-Indian boundary, particularly its western section is drawn on maps published in India. They have asked our Government to take up this matter with the Indian Government. Yet we have not done so, but have explained to them the actual situation of the Sino-Indian boundary. With the settlement of the boundary question—which, as our Government has repeatedly pointed out, requires surveys and mutual consultations—the problem of drawing the boundary on the maps will also be solved.'

As for recent incidents, like the one at Barahoti, Chou proposes that both sides keep to the areas that are under their control at the moment, and that disputes be resolved through consultation.[3]

Chou's reply must have caused great consternation. That trust had been misplaced, that the premise that not raising issues in a strong and forthright manner had been wrong—these had become undeniable. Information about happenings in Tibet also showed that the Chinese were unrelenting in their efforts to suppress and subjugate the Tibetans.

The foreign secretary puts up a draft letter to be sent to the Chinese government. Panditji suggests an additional sentence to the effect that the continued publication of those maps 'is a matter of great concern to us'. In his note to the foreign secretary, he adds, 'The idea struck me that in view of developments in Tibet, perhaps this was not the right time

---

[3] *SWJN*, XLVII.557–60.

to send this letter. But, on reconsideration, I think it is right for us to send it as soon as possible.'[4]

Treaties, revenue records

Two days later, on 22 March 1959, Panditji sends his reply to Chou En-lai. Yes, it is true that the border has not been delineated on the ground in all the sectors, Panditji says, 'but I am surprised to know that this frontier was not accepted at any time by the Government of China.' The traditional frontier follows the watershed on the crest of the Himalayan Range, he points out. Moreover, in most parts, it has the sanction of specific international agreements between the Government of India and the Central Government of China. Panditji lists these one by one. He also notes that old revenue records establish the areas as having been under Indian administration. As for the McMahon Line, Panditji points out that, apart from the advantage that this line 'runs along the crest of the High Himalayan Range which forms the natural dividing line between the Tibetan plateau in the north and the sub-montane region in the south,' 'In our previous discussions and particularly during your visit to India in January 1957, we were gratified to note that you were prepared to accept this line as representing the frontier between China and India in this region and I hope that we will reach an understanding on this basis.'

Panditji moves to the happenings at Barahoti to which Chou has referred. What he records is of interest—the pattern of what China has been doing since is exactly what it did then, and we too have been doing the same thing which the government was prepared to do then: that is, to desist from sending our personnel even to areas which we were convinced were well within India. We provided 'extensive documentary proofs that this area has been under Indian jurisdiction

[4] *SWJN*, XLVII.450.

and lies well within our frontiers,' Panditji points out. We proposed that neither side send their civil or military officials to the area. 'Unfortunately, your delegation did not agree to our suggestion.' But there has been a change since: 'I learn that a material change in the situation has since been effected by the dispatch of Chinese civil and military detachments, equipped with arms, to camp in the area, after our own civil party had withdrawn at the beginning of last winter. If the reports that we have received about an armed Chinese party camping and erecting permanent structures in Hoti during winter are correct, it would seem that unilateral action, not in accordance with custom, was being taken in assertion of your claim to the disputed area.'

Panditji is hurt by the counter-charge of Chou that Indian maps have been showing large parts of China as being in India. 'I need hardly add that independent India would be the last country to make any encroachments beyond its well-established frontiers,' he writes. 'It was in the confidence that the general question of our common frontier was settled to the satisfaction of both sides that I declared publicly and in Parliament on several occasions that there is no room for doubt about our frontiers as shown in the published maps. We thought that our position was clearly understood and accepted by your Government.'

Panditji accepts Chou's suggestion about maintaining the status quo, with two additions. He proposes that 'as unfortunately there is some difference of views between our two Governments in regard to the delineation of the frontier at some places, I agree that the position as it was before the recent disputes arose should be respected by both sides and that neither side should try to take unilateral action in exercise of what it conceives to be its right. Further, if any possession has been secured recently, the position should be rectified.'[5]

---

[5] *SWJN*, XLVII.451–54.

'Fanned out' vs. 'Massed at'

The situation in Tibet continues to deteriorate. The Chinese have moved a large number of troops into Tibet. The people of Tibet are being put down with great force. Panditji is now seeing a different side of Chinese character. His sister, Vijaya Lakshmi Pandit, at the time India's High Commissioner in London, has sent him an article by Kingsley Martin, the editor of *New Statesman*: the latter has lauded Panditji for his cautious policy in regard to the Chinese suppression of Tibet. Panditji is happy at what Kingsley Martin has written. He is as displeased with the article that Hugh Richardson—an ICS officer, he spent eight years in Tibet—has written in the *Observer.* Panditji sets out his approach to the developments, and contrasts it with the approach of persons conditioned by the cold war. He turns to the Chinese: 'The Chinese always and, more especially, now are given to arrogance and throwing their weight about. I have no doubt that they have treated the Tibetans very harshly, though I imagine that some of the reports are rather exaggerated. Anyhow, I just do not see what India could have done more than she has except, of course, for condemnation and denunciation.'[6]

Members of Parliament are agitated—both on account of what has been unleashed on the Tibetans, and because such a large number of troops in a region bordering India can present a threat to India. Questions are asked in Parliament and outside. Adjournment motions are tabled. Panditji downplays what is happening. As is his custom, he finds fault with a word here, a word there—in what has been said on the floor or what has been stated in a formal motion. An MP from Mysore has tabled an adjournment motion on the happenings in Tibet, and the fact that Chinese troops in large numbers have fanned out throughout that hapless region. Panditji takes exception to the use of the expression

---

[6] *SWJN*, XLVIII.457–59.

'massing of troops on the border'. (The member had actually spoken about Chinese having 'fanned out' their troops, and that, as a result, there being 'masses of troops' on the south and south-eastern border of China.)

'May I also refer to what for instance, hon. Member Shri Imam has talked about that is, the massing of troops,' Panditji tells the House. 'Now, I am completely unaware of this. In fact, I have not heard a rumour to that effect, leave out the facts. And he wants an adjournment motion because there is "massing of troops on the Indian border"!'

A member points out, 'He said about fanning out of Chinese troops.' The member himself says, 'That is the word I used in my adjournment motion.'

Panditji is not allayed. 'All kind of things are appearing in the Press,' Panditji says, 'which, again are based sometimes, presumably on reports not from within Tibet but from outside Tibet, whether it is Hong Kong or whether it is any other place. I do not say that any such rumour must necessarily be wrong. How can I say that? But, normally speaking, they are not correct. Anyhow, my information is that there is no massing of troops on the Indian border, so far as I know. How can I discuss it when I do not accept that fact?'[7]

That is the end of the question of the forces that China has thrust into Tibet.

During his extensive speech, Panditji also says, that, while the extent of hold of the Chinese over Tibet has varied in history, 'Our attitude, and historically, previously—I am not going into the past history of 500 years—the position of all previous Governments of India and elsewhere has been recognition of some kind of suzerainty or sovereignty of China over Tibet and Tibetan autonomy…' Notice that just a few years earlier, the Government of India headed by Panditji himself was talking in terms of the 'Government of

---

[7] *Lok Sabha Debates,* Second Series, Volume XXVIII, cols. 8461–68, 30 March 1959. Also *SWJN,* XLVII.471.

Tibet', it was treating it as a country on its own; and also that Panditji is now conflating the two words which he had stoutly maintained did *not* mean the same thing—'suzerainty' and 'sovereignty'.

The basic point is different: we cannot do anything in the face of China having marched its troops into Tibet. This comes through: 'The measure of the autonomy has varied,' Panditji tells the House, 'because the strength of China, the weakness of China, the strength of Tibet, the weakness of Tibet has varied in the course of the last hundreds of years. But, that is the position. Every Government in China has claimed that. Many Governments in Tibet have repudiated that. So, there it is. Anyhow, we could not become judges or interfere or intervene either in law, or in fact, or in the circumstances, we could do nothing. That is just past history.'

Panditji recalls that during his visit to India, Chou En-lai had placed great emphasis on the autonomy of Tibet and had said that, while Tibet is a region of China, it would be given 'full autonomy'. I had not raised the matter with him, Panditji says. Chou En-lai had brought it up himself. 'He told me then that Tibet had always been, according to him and according to the Chinese position, a part of the Chinese State; that is, they have always claimed it and they have had it, according to him; but yet, Tibet was not China,' Panditji recalls Chou telling him. 'Tibet is not China; Tibet is not a province of China. Tibet is an autonomous region which has been a part of the Chinese State—that was, as far as I remember, his words—therefore, we want to treat it as an autonomous region and give it full autonomy.'

'That is how he explained the Chinese Government's attitude to Tibet,' Panditji says. 'All I could say was that we had to recognize Chinese sovereignty over Tibet. But, I was glad to hear Mr. Chou En-lai laying such stress on Tibetan autonomy. I said if this was fully acted upon and was well known to Tibetans, possibly the difficulties would be much less, because, I remember, difficulties had arisen already, three years ago.'[8]

The bulldozer continues

The Chinese assault becomes more and more oppressive. Lhasa itself is crushed. Shells land in the compound of the Dalai Lama's residence. His closest advisors and he decide that he must leave immediately. After an arduous journey, he and his small group reach the Indian border. The Government of India receives him with due honour, and he is formally given asylum. Till final decisions can be taken about where he will set up his residence, he, his closest relatives and colleagues are taken to Mussoorie.

The developments create a sensation around the world. Public opinion is aroused in India also. The decision that Panditji has taken about giving the Dalai Lama is indeed a far-sighted one. It is based on principle. It has been taken in the full knowledge that China will be incensed by it. For all these reasons, the decision is a bold and principled one. And there can be no doubt that Panditji is the one to whom we owe this decision, and to whom, accordingly, we owe gratitude.

Parliament is in furore at what China has done.[9] Panditji

---

[8] *Lok Sabha Debates,* Second Series, Volume XXVIII, cols. 8461–68, 30 March 1959. Also *SWJN,* XLVII.473.

[9] Conventions are held outside also—denouncing China, and the suppression of the Tibetan people. Jayaprakash Narayan and his socialist colleagues are in the forefront of organizing these protests and conventions. 'The Tibetans have the same claim to the right of self determination as any other nation in the world,' the resolution they pass at one of their conventions affirms. 'Racially, linguistically and culturally different from Chinese, they are a nation according to all standards of nationality. Although China claimed and intermittently exercised suzerainty over Tibet since the eighteenth century, that suzerainty was not based on the willing consent, and they had virtually shaken it off in

is at pains to balance several considerations. He says our policies must rest on three objectives. First and foremost, we have to take care of India's interests and security. Second, we want to maintain friendly relations with China—that these relations remain friendly is vital for us, for China and for the world. Third, we have to bear in mind the close ties we have with Tibet—of culture, of history, of religion; and, of course, there are the reverence that people here feel for the Dalai Lama and the sympathy they have for the people of Tibet in these trying times.

The fact is that the brutal suppression that China has unleashed flies in the face of everything that Panditji has been saying about China and the Chinese—at least in public. It undercuts the basic premises on which he has been

---

the second decade of the twentieth century. The Sino-Tibetan agreement of 1951, which imposed Chinese rule over Tibet was the result of force and violence...' (Reproduced in *SWJN,* XLIX.562.) Unexceptionable and true. But by giving asylum to the Dalai Lama and by receiving Tibetan refugees in India, Panditji feels, we have already triggered anger in Peking. He feels that such criticism of China, and such conventions and resolutions make his task infinitely more difficult. He criticizes the conventions, resolutions and those organizing them, in particular J.P., and takes every opportunity to make sure that everyone sees that the Government has nothing to do with them. '...I think that whatever that convention appears to aim at or whatever it seems to represent, seem to be very wrong,' Panditji tells Parliament in regard to that particular convention. 'It is a wrong approach, an approach which will do no good to anybody at all, and may do a good deal of harm if really it was the approach of any responsible people in India. For, we must realize first of all one thing. What do we want? What are we aiming at? How can we get there? What can we do about it?...' The contrast with China—then and now—can hardly be greater: as we see even today—over the accidental bombing of the Chinese embassy in Belgrade, or the protests against Japan now and then—the Chinese Government orchestrates minatory demonstrations and protests, and not just sedate conventions, whenever these suit its purpose.

proceeding in regard to China—including on the border question; in particular, his premise that the Chinese will be amenable to reason and good faith, and that he has time to work out a solution with them.

In public, he does not want to upset them more than giving asylum to the Dalai Lama will in any case. And he is loath to acknowledge that the very premises of his policy have turned out to have been misconceived, that he has allowed himself to be misled and thereby brought the country close to a grave crisis. Hence, faced with a barrage in Parliament, he is by turn, factual, evasive, petulant, 'philosophical'—and, ever so often, as was his wont, he just wanders off. All too often also, his presumption also comes through—the presumption that he alone has the necessary learning, the lofty perspective which are required to assess the developments and their implications for India; a presumption that will become such a cruel memory soon.

Less than the whole truth

It isn't just the Chinese who are publishing maps that show large swathes of India as being in China. Now, Russia too has published similar maps. Questions come up in Parliament. Panditji says, 'I think they [the Soviet Government] had merely taken those maps or copied them from the Chinese maps without probably going into the matter, and when we addressed them they said they would enquire into this—look into this.'

But what about the Chinese? Where do matters stand regarding their assurances on the maps? 'So far as the Chinese maps are concerned, we are still in correspondence,' Panditji says. 'As I have previously informed the House, their answer has been that "these are old maps and we are not sure of the exact border and we shall look into it and that the status quo should continue."' He adds, 'That is not a very adequate answer, if I may say so, after so many years. We have pointed that out to them. I wrote to them again on the subject about a month or so ago, may be a little more or a little less. We have not had any further reply from them.'

Panditji doesn't reveal that Chou En-lai has in fact completely changed his stand vis-à-vis the maps: what he tells Parliament is not untrue, but it is not the whole truth. Chou En-lai had added that the maps were old in the sense that China had been consistently publishing the same maps. If they show what you say are parts of India to be in China, he had said, we have to face censure from persons in China who say that India is continuing to publish maps that show large chunks of China to be in India.

In a moment, Panditji's answers become even more opaque. A member from his own party, the Congress asks, 'May I know if there is any dispute about any border territory or any kind of territory between China and India and, if not, why is it that some parts of India which are obviously in India have been shown as parts of China?'

'It is rather difficult for me to answer that question,' Panditji replies. 'We have discussed one or two minor frontier disputes which comprise tiny tracts of territory, maybe a mile this way or mile that way, in the high mountains where nobody lives and those are pending. We have discussed them and for the present no settlement has been arrived at. No other question has been raised for discussion; except that one sees this map, no other question has been raised that way.'

These exchanges take place on 22 April 1959. Chou En-lai has sent his letter on 23 January—a letter in which he has opened the entire boundary to dispute.

The members are not at all satisfied. 'Apart from the maps, because after all, the question of the maps is academic, may I know whether there are certain portions of land between India and Tibet where they are encroaching on the basis of these maps—encroaching into our territory—particularly in Taklakot which is near the border of Almora?' asks a member of Panditji's own Party, the Congress. He represents the Nainital constituency in the Lok Sabha. 'At Taklakot they have come six miles this way, according to their map. It is not a question of map alone. They have actually encroached on our territory; six miles in one pass.'

Once again, Panditji minimizes what the Chinese have done. 'I should like to give a precise answer to such questions,' he says, and does the exact opposite. 'I would not like to venture to give an imprecise answer. Taklakot and another place—Hoti—have been places under argument and sometimes, according to our reports we have received, some Chinese have advanced a mile or two, maybe, in high mountains. It is true. We have been enquiring into it. The difficulty is that in the winter months most of these places are almost inaccessible and more inaccessible from our side than from the other side.'

The Speaker suggests that, instead of members taking up the entire Question Hour on this matter, it can be discussed in a 'half-an-hour discussion'. Panditji says he is not willing for that. So, a few more questions get asked.

A member asks, 'May I know whether Government's attention has been drawn to the news item published in several papers alleging that the Chinese have claimed some 30,000 sq. m. of our territory and they have also disputed the McMahon line?'

Panditji's answer is true to form: it is misleading. 'No, Sir,' he says, and puts the onus on the members. 'I would suggest to hon. Members not to pay much attention to news items emanating sometimes from Hong Kong and sometimes from other odd places. We have had no such claim directly or indirectly made on us.'

By now the Chinese have seized Aksai Chin. They have endorsed the maps that claim all of what is now Arunachal Pradesh and large parts of Assam as being parts of China. They have gone back on their willingness to accept the

McMahon Line. What more would they have to do to make a claim 'directly or indirectly'?

'The Prime Minister told us not to attach much importance to the news items appearing in the papers,' a member observes. 'May I know whether his attention has been drawn to a reference made by Mr. Chou En-lai in the Chinese National Assembly to the effect that boundaries between China and other countries are to be settled again peacefully? Does it mean and has it been enquired by our Ambassador that they do not accept the McMahon line as the border line between India and China?'

'I did see something, some kind of a report to that effect,' Panditji says—not mentioning that in his formal letter Chou En-lai has gone much farther. 'What exactly it means, I cannot interpret that. We are actually corresponding on this issue with the Chinese Government. I would like to wait for their answer before I interpret their meanings.'[10]

Instructing the Dalai Lama

The Dalai Lama—all of twenty-four years of age at the time—and his party have been taken to Mussoorie. The Birla House there has been requisitioned for their stay. Panditji travels to Mussoorie to meet the Dalai Lama.

The two meet for four hours on the 24 April 1959.

Panditji is alternately solicitous—and in the years to come, the Dalai Lama will always acknowledge the affection and concern with which Panditji treated him—and interrogatory. Panditji naturally has the Dalai Lama narrate the exact sequence of events that compelled him to decide to leave Tibet.

The Dalai Lama acknowledges how Tibet had fallen

---

[10] For the preceding questions and answers, *Lok Sabha Debates*, Second Series, Volume XXX, cols. 12715–21, 22 April 1959. Also *SWJN*, XLVIII.465–71.

behind, and how this had made it vulnerable to the Chinese invasion. He is looking for ways by which Tibet would get another chance—to become modern and to be able to stand on its own feet. He gently explores whether any help can come from outside—the UN, other countries, India. This is when Panditji becomes impatient with such hopes. He disillusions the Dalai Lama of such hopes—but in the process he also shows that India is helpless in the matter, that what it has already done in giving the Dalai Lama sanctuary is having consequences, that it can do no more.

The counsel to be realistic is actually a proclamation of helplessness.

The Dalai Lama is saying that the Tibetans themselves are now anxious that reforms be brought about, but that these reforms should be instituted 'by the Tibetan people themselves and not by foreigners and especially the Chinese, who were non-religious.' He says that Tibetans 'must gain complete independence, and attain real peace which can only be had by practice of religion.' The Tibetans are no longer as conservative as they used to be, he says, and want reforms to be carried out but in accordance with their own wishes. Tibetan students have been writing to him along these lines, he says, and they also express strong nationalist feelings.

'Interrupting D.L. [Dalai Lama], P.M. said emphatically,' the official record of the meeting states, 'Let us be relevant. I agreed with all this conception of a new world, etc. I myself would like to see a new India, but these are only wishes and one does not know whether I would actually live to see it. We have to see the situation as it is and understand realities. We understand about religion. If religion is really strong and dynamic it should be able to face up to a situation like this and if it is not able to do so, then there is something radically wrong with it.'

He tells the Dalai Lama, 'There are only two choices, either an armed struggled in which case the party with the bigger arms wins. The example of the students and their nationalist feeling is no doubt a good one and it goes to prove that you cannot convert a whole nation into anything unless they are themselves convinced that it would conform to their interests.'

But such feelings are not enough.

Panditji continues: 'If one has to fight for anything one should choose one's weapons carefully, weapons which are to one's own advantage and not to that of enemy. Violence is all right if one can be equal or superior to the enemy in arms. One must also know how to use violence in that case. I am not criticizing but only analysing the factors of the situation in Tibet. Spiritual efforts and physical force are two different things. In an actual physical conflict the physical force that can be brought to play and its result will have to be taken into account. Something to this effect I had spoken to the D.L. [Dalai Lama] at the time I met him during the Buddha Jayanti Celebrations. Speaking practically and not philosophically, Tibet became an economically and socially backward country. Such a country is physically weak and a poor country which cannot easily resist the force of a powerful country. To say "Now give us a chance to become a strong country" ignores the actual position. We cannot go on, on that basis. In all such cases, the effort of the people themselves is required to improve their position. Take India's own case. We had a background of relative backwardness ourselves and how hard the Indian people had struggled before they actually achieved independence.'

At the very next moment, having instructed the Dalai Lama that strength alone can determine the outcome, Panditji ignores this fact. Recall that Chou En-lai had told Panditji at length how China was going to ensure that Tibet had 'full autonomy', and that Panditji had counselled the Dalai Lama to accept Chou En-lai's assurance in good faith. Now Panditji scolds the Dalai Lama:

> P.M. then asked: Did D.L. at any time speak to Premier Chou-en-Lai and Gen. Tan[11] that autonomy given to Tibet was not working or it was not real?
> D.L.[:] Yes, I spoke to Chang-Kuo-hua.[12] In 1959 about the reforms in Kham being carried out against the wishes of the people there, but not about autonomy.
> P.M.[:] When did D.L. and Premier Chou En-lai last meet?
> D.L.[:] In Delhi.
> P.M.[:] Why did he not say this not once but a hundred times to Premier Chou En-lai that there was not real autonomy in Tibet? Now to say that it was not working is not very effective.

But, on Panditji's own analysis—realism, power—what difference would repeating this a hundred times have made when Tibet was weak?

The Dalai Lama was not the one who could be splitting hair. 'The main point is that when they (Tibetans) tried to resist some of the harmful policies, the Chinese opposed them and got angry with them,' he tells Panditji. 'Since then, they are suspicious and now they are called rebels. D.L. confessed that it was their mistake not to have mentioned to Premier Chou-en-Lai about autonomy. The Chinese, although outwardly make a show of welcoming criticism, were extremely angry when any criticism is levelled against them. There was, therefore, no chance to tell them about this.'

Panditji is clear—both about what the Tibetans cannot do, as well as about what India cannot do: 'The choice is between recourse to arms or standing up to the Chinese in frank talks in a direct manner. As regards help from India,

---

[11] General Tan Kuan-san, Acting Representative of the Chinese Government in Tibet and the Political Commissar of the Tibet Military Area Command.

[12] Chang-Kuo-hua had led Chinese forces into Tibet in 1951; commander of PLA in Tibet.

undoubtedly there is a good deal of sympathy for Tibet in this country, undoubtedly, we do not want the Tibetan religion to be suppressed or submerged by the Chinese or by Communism. But exactly what do they want us to do? We cannot go to war with China or Tibet and even that would not help Tibet. What else do they expect us to do?'

When Panditji does not want to or cannot do anything, he tends to frame the question in terms of 'either/or'. Either peace or World War.

The Dalai Lama says that 'Tibetans expect the achieving of independence in the long run.'

'Let us face facts,' Panditji tells him. 'One cannot bring heaven to the people in India even if I wish it. The whole world cannot bring freedom to Tibet unless the whole fabric of the Chinese State is destroyed. U.S.A., U.K. and others or anybody else cannot do this at present. D.L. should realize that in the present context Tibet's independence would mean the complete break-up of the Chinese State and it is not possible to envisage it as likely to happen. To defeat China is not easy. Only a world war, an atomic war can perhaps be the precursor of such possibility. Can one start a world war? Can India start a world war? Let us talk of the present and not of the future and be more realistic.'

'Help is required for the present juncture,' the Dalai Lama says. 'Since 20th March, the Chinese have been killing indiscriminately and burning large numbers of people. Can't this be stopped?'

'How can I stop it?' Panditji exclaims. 'How can I stop anything from happening inside Tibet?'

'There are killings by machine-gunning from the air. If there can be only a solution to this?' the Dalai Lama inquires.

Panditji turns logician: 'There is a definite contradiction between this talk of a fight and this fear of killing. Ultimately if Tibet's independence is to be achieved, it will be due to its own people's courage and ability to stand up to suffering, whatever it may be, and not due to any help anybody else in the whole wide world can give.'

'We do not have a speck of a desire to fight the Chinese violently for our independence,' the Dalai Lama protests. 'It was the Chinese who said that the Tibetans started the fight but this is completely untrue.'

'It does not matter who started the fight and there is no good complaining,' Panditji says. 'Only old women complain! Physically it is not possible to fight on behalf of Tibet. Even such a suggestion will harm them and their cause. Sympathy at present for Tibet cannot be converted into help by any country. D.L. should be under no illusion and, therefore, should fashion his policy with reference to actuality.' No other country can help at present, and India has gone to the limit: '…at the present moment if the D.L. reads newspapers he will find the anger of the Chinese against India. See for example the Panchen Lama's statement.[13] We have gone to the limit of our efforts. It is true not much has been done. Today we cannot even privately advise Chinese, because of this suspicion. The so-called help being given to you would close all the doors to such help.'

The conversation continues in the same vein. '…As a practical question, what can we do about it?' Panditji asks. 'We are anxious to help but our capacity to help is very limited and the moment we try to extend it, it would stop even that capacity. War was not possible. Cursing the Chinese was no alternative. It would only stop every possibility of a peaceful settlement. P.M. himself intended to keep very quiet except when necessary in speaking in Parliament. His own advice would be to let the present excitement go down so that talks would be possible. The Chinese say India wants to grab Tibet and with this suspicion they suspect everything we say.'

The tactic of hurling wild charges—that the Tibetan

---

[13] The Panchen Lama had asserted that India had coerced the Dalai Lama into making the statement that he had left Tibet of his own free will.

uprising is being organized from the 'command center' of Kalimpong; that India is conspiring with the Tibetans to break it away from China; even Chou En-lai has himself told the National People's Congress in Peking on 18 April 1959 that the Dalai Lama has been abducted to India! The Chinese Ambassador tells the Indian Foreign Secretary that the uprising in Tibet has been 'caused by India'!—has worked.

The Dalai Lama agrees that the best course would be for India to develop good relations with China so that a solution can be found.

'The mere fact of D.L. living in India has some consequence to India, to Tibet, to China and to the rest of the world,' Panditji reminds the Dalai Lama. 'In China it is immediately one of irritation and suspicion. D.L. being in India keeps alive the question of Tibet in the minds of the world. Tibet, as it were, cannot close up without news. It becomes a difficult thing to manage. The tendency of the Chinese authorities would be to crush Tibet as soon as possible. Nobody can help…'

Panditji advises the Dalai Lama to say as little to the press as possible. 'The only kind of statements, if at all necessary, could relate about peace and ending of fighting in Tibet. An indication that despite all her sufferings Tibet had no quarrel with the Chinese may be helpful. P.M. deprecated the taking up of an attitude like "we must have independence or nothing else". This would not help, nor would the cursing of China help. Stress on peace and stopping of fighting and killing will help in keeping the subject in the right place and level.'

Panditji then inquires about the report that there is a proposal to set up a Tibetan government-in-exile. The Dalai Lama gives some details.

'Certain consequences follow from this,' Panditji says. 'We as a country cannot recognize this Government under international law. The moment we do this, we will have to withdraw our C.G. [Counsel General] in Lhasa and lose all touch with Tibet.'

The Dalai Lama asks whether the Counsel General was not responsible to the old Tibetan Government and since it had been dissolved, did the position not change?

Panditji: 'It is an act of war against China, a step like that of withdrawing our C.G. and recognizing the new Government.'[14]

Again: 'all or nothing'.

Panditji returns to Delhi, and gives an account of his conversation, rather of his conclusions from the conversation with the Dalai Lama to the press and to Parliament.

'Deepest regret and surprise'

In Parliament, Panditji gives an account of the troubles in Tibet. He gives glimpses of his conversations with the Dalai Lama. Manifestly, the charges that the Chinese have been hurling are much in his mind. 'All I can say is that I have been greatly distressed at the tone of the comments and the charges made against India by responsible people in China,' he says. 'They have used the language of the cold war regardless of truth and propriety. This is peculiarly distressing in a great nation with thousands of years of culture behind it, noted for its restrained and polite behaviour. The charges made against India are so fantastic that I find it difficult to deal with them...' He recounts the events that have led to the situation in Tibet and to the Dalai Lama having to leave Lhasa. We gave up the extraterritorial rights that the British government had acquired in Tibet. All that we have wanted to do since then is to preserve the traditional contacts between India and Tibet, he protests repeatedly: '...our actions in this matter and whatever we have done subsequently in regard to Tibet are proof enough of our policy and that India had no political or ulterior ambitions in Tibet. Indeed, even from the narrowest practical point of view, any other policy would have

---

[14] SWJN, XLVIII.478–98.

been wrong and futile. Ever since then we have endeavoured not only to act up to the agreement we made, but to cultivate the friendship of the Chinese State and people.'

He continues: 'It is therefore, a matter of the deepest regret and surprise to us that charges should be made which are both unbecoming and entirely void of substance. We have conveyed this deep feeling of regret to the Chinese Government, more especially at the speeches delivered recently in the current session of the National People's Congress in Peking'—a reference that includes what Chou has told the body about the Dalai Lama having been abducted to India against his will.

He recalls what Chou had told him about respecting the autonomy of Tibet.[15]

A different view of Chinese character

In private he is expressing a different reading of Chinese character. In a telegram he sends to India's Ambassador in Peking, G. Parthasarathi, he writes:

> Recent developments in Tibet have raised difficult problems not only for India but for China also and of course for Tibet itself. I can appreciate to some extent Chinese attitude, constituted as Chinese are at present. We realize that Tibet is very backward. Nevertheless the regimented and virulent attacks on India in China and their insistence on patent falsehoods have surprised and distressed me. It seems to me that Chinese authorities have developed a habit of trying to bully and imagining that offensive language will produce results they desire. It produces exactly opposite results in any self-respecting country. It is difficult enough to restrain these strong reactions in India, but we shall do so. Our general policy will remain firm, though not unfriendly to China. We realize the importance of these friendly

---

[15] *Lok Sabha Debates,* Second Series, Volume XXX, cols. 13493–503, 27 April 1959. Also *SWJN,* XLVIII.503–10.

> relations, but friendship cannot be obtained by threats and coercive attitude. If Chinese friendship is necessary for India, so is Indian friendship for China. The time for any country to display arrogance in dealing with India is long past. We have still some remains of what we learnt from Gandhiji. We shall, therefore, continue to be polite and seek friendship and at the same time to hold firmly to the policy we consider correct.
>
> I do not know if you will have any chance of talking informally to people who count. If so, you might explain to them how opposition parties have full freedom to function here and in fact they frequently hold demonstrations against Government and criticize it in strong language. Obviously this is not understood in China where no opposition is allowed. Also that during twelve years of our Independence, no country big or small, has used such offensive language towards India as Chinese leaders and press recently. In spite of this grave provocation, we have remembered Gandhiji and will continue to keep our tempers.[16]

A week has not passed, and on 4 May 1959, the Rajya Sabha is debating the events in Tibet and the situation that has arisen as a consequence. Panditji reverts again and again to the charges that are being made by the Chinese leaders and their press. What has happened is a tragedy for Tibet, of course, he says, but it is also a 'deeper tragedy for many of us that something that we have laboured for, for all these years, which may be said to be enshrined, if you like, in the Panchsheel or in Bandung, has suffered very considerably in people's minds'. He says, 'I may say I shall hold on to it, but the fact is in people's minds there is that crack, there is that suffering, there is that uneasiness that something they valued might slip away. These words like all other words Bandung, Panchsheel; it does not matter what word you use—begin to lose their shine and to be hurled about without meaning, and in fact, just like even the word "peace" becomes almost like a

[16] *SWJN*, XLVIII.511–12.

thunderbolt or a minor war the way it is used, sometimes the manner of using it—it is the manner that counts...' Panditji drifts from facts to words, to the meaning attached to words, to means and ends.

He recounts the charges that are being levelled by the Chinese: 'These are very serious charges against a country's leaders being made irresponsibly in this way by the leaders of a people whom we have not only honoured and respected but whom we have considered particularly advanced in culture and politeness and the gentler art of civilisation. It has been a shock to me beyond measure because, quite apart from everything else, I have looked up to the Chinese and I look up to them still because of their great accomplishments, because of their great culture and all that, and it has been a shock to me that this kind of thing should be said and done in the excitement of the moment. I hope that excitement will pass...' They are now citing some memoranda we wrote when their armies marched into Tibet, Panditji tells the House—and 'very polite memoranda they were'. They are citing these and saying that we sent these after consulting the British government, 'that though we called ourselves independent we really acted as the stooges or tools of the British government'.[17]

As I mentioned, the Chinese tactic—it used to be at the time the Standard Operating Procedure of Marxists—of hurling extreme and wild charges, in extreme language, that tactic has worked: instead of focusing on what the Chinese have done and are doing in Tibet, Panditji is forever defending what he and his government have said in regard to the Chinese.

Changing perceptions of Chinese nature

In the years that follow his trip to China, Panditji sees many good things in what is happening in China. He doesn't

[17] *Rajya Sabha Debates*, Volume XXV, cols. 1671–84. *SWJN*, XLIX.545–55.

exactly fall for their drive for collectivization but he gets even more convinced than he has been that we should go in for cooperative farming—delegations are sent to China to study what they have done in agriculture. He writes about their approach to family planning—about how they have changed from Mao's original proposition that, there is no such thing as overpopulation to the new policy of limiting the growth of numbers... The conference in Bandung takes place—where he goes out of his way, and quite unnecessarily, to ensure for Chou En-lai a prominent role... By now, Panditji has begun to take the word of China's leaders, and accounts emanating from there at face value. 'There is a tendency also in China towards less rigidity of thought,' he writes to the chief ministers in his fortnightly letter of 12 June 1957, 'and a remark by Chairman Mao has become famous. This was "letting all flowers blossom and all schools of thought contend". This has resulted in some relaxation of the old cultural controls...'[18]

A year and a half later, a few journals abroad publish some accounts of rivalry between India and China. Panditji will have none of this. There have been reports in the foreign press, he tells the chief ministers in his letter of 31 December 1958, 'about the rivalry of India and China and some kind of apprehension growing in India because China is supposed to be going ahead fast in industrial production and in other matters'. 'Apparently people used to the cold war cannot think except in terms of rivalry,' he writes, not just dismissing what has been written but also smearing a colour on anyone who thinks in these terms. 'There is no rivalry between India and China. There may be a healthy spirit of emulation and of learning from each other which we certainly propose to do. Then there are stories about increasing tension between

---

[18] Jawaharlal Nehru, *Letters to Chief Ministers, 1947–1964*, G. Parthasarathi, General Editor. Henceforth, *Letters*. *Letters*, Volume 4, 1954–1957, p. 503.

India and the U.S.S.R. and China. I have failed to notice any marked tension. There are of course some things happening in the U.S.S.R or China, which we may not approve. Indeed, there are many things happening in India which we do not approve. It is well known that we follow certain basically different policies in India from those prevalent in China and the U.S.S.R. That does not mean that there should be tension or unhealthy rivalry. We continue to have friendly relations both with the Soviet Union and China and I hope you will not be misled by reports to the contrary.' His policy direction is firmly set: 'Even if something is said or done in China or the U.S.S.R., which is not to our liking, we shall continue to pursue our own policy of friendship and co-operation wherever this is possible.'[19]

But, he now has to explain the policy he has been pursuing vis-à-vis China, and Tibet in particular. The Khampas have mounted a fierce movement to resist the Chinese occupation, the suppression of the Tibetans, and especially the Chinese policy of settling a large number of Hans in Tibet. The Tibetans clearly see the danger: they will be reduced to a minority in their own land. Panditji devotes a large part of his letter of 25 March 1959 to justifying the policy he has followed. He goes over grounds that have become familiar to us by now: no Chinese government gave up its claim to Tibet, even though it could not exercise effective control over the region; we could do little when Chinese forces went into Tibet; the seventeen-point 1951 Agreement—how it recognized autonomy of Tibet under the sovereignty of China, how the Dalai Lama was a party to this agreement, 'it is true that even that Agreement was accepted by the Tibetans without joy and under the compulsion of circumstances. But it was accepted...'; the facts about who started the violence—the Khampas or the Chinese—are not clear...,[20] remarks which

[19] *Letters,* Volume 5, Letter of 31 December 1958, p. 192.

[20] *Letters,* Volume 5, Letter of 25 March 1959 in particular pp. 227–32.

we should pause to consider—as they help explain how Panditji was able to not see for so long what was patent.

A Mental Habit

As the principal object of this brief book is to set out the evolution of India's China-policy in Panditji's own words, and to show how those assumptions and habits continue to endanger us today, I have kept annotations to the minimum. But what Panditji did and said and wrote in regard to China does deserve to be analyzed almost at the psychological and linguistic level! For his stance, his formulations, his rationalizations are rooted in habits, in mental processes. Not just his assumptions and premises persist among policy-makers, those very habits and mental processes persist. In the 1950s, they went unquestioned because of the lofty position that Panditji occupied in our lives and discourse. Today, they go equally unquestioned—though for a different reason: discourse has got so dumbed-down that no assumption or premise is examined as it should be. An illustration will bring home the consequence.

Among the habits that persist, one is especially harmful as it rationalizes going-along at an almost subliminal level. This is the habit of slipping in a thought or sentence which excuses one from facing the facts. We see this in Pandit Nehru's writings and spoken word at every turn. We see it in India 'always' having recognized Chinese suzerainty over Tibet; in 'suzerainty' meaning the same thing as 'sovereignty'; in our rights and position in Tibet having really been the result of British Imperialism and, therefore, things that we *ought not* to be defending; in the roads China has built being just rudimentary in that they just entailed leveling the ground a bit and putting some markers; in Chinese concentration of forces in Tibet being natural, in reports about it being alarmist... A sentence or word is slipped in, and thereby an argument is insinuated.

The letter that Pandit Nehru wrote to the chief ministers on 25 March, 1959, and which we just encountered, provides a typical example. Recall the context. The Chinese have begun another full-scale programme to crush the Tibetans, one that is just at that time compelling the Dalai Lama to leave Tibet. They have completed the roads through Aksai Chin. They have commenced a series of incursions across our border. They have claimed large parts of India to be parts of Tibet, and, hence, of China. Panditji is explaining the policy he has pursued to the chief ministers. He slips in a clause and sentence:

> The 17-point Agreement, *to which the Dalai Lama was a party,* assured that autonomy. It is true that even that Agreement was accepted by the Tibetans without joy and under the compulsion of circumstances. *But it was accepted...*[21]

In the letter, Panditji is justifying his accepting China's sovereignty over Tibet in return for China agreeing to preserve Tibet's autonomy. The argument that Panditji is advancing is that, even by that Agreement, China is bound to respect the autonomy of Tibet. But the impression that the clause and sentence that I have italicized above are liable to insinuate into the reader's mind is that there was an Agreement which the Dalai Lama and the Tibetans accepted, and what is happening there, and the policy that Panditji is pursuing flows from that Agreement. That sort of an impression is particularly likely to take root as most of the Chief Ministers, and, I dare-say, almost all of us today, would not have read the 1951 Agreement!

But the text of the 'Agreement' itself speaks to the *exact opposite* conclusion—namely, that it was no 'Agreement' at all, that it was, as the Tibetans have pointed out times without number, a document that they were compelled to sign under duress.

---

[21] Jawaharlal Nehru, *Letters to Chief Ministers, 1947–1964,* G. Parthasarathi, General Editor, Volume 5, op. cit., p. 228.

Look at the Preamble to this so-called Agreement. Which Tibetan government, to say nothing of the Dalai Lama, would of its own free will describe the recent history of Sino-Tibetan relations in the following way?

> The Tibetan nationality is one of the nationalities with a long history within the boundaries of China and, like many other nationalities, it has done its glorious duty in the course of the creation and development of the great motherland. But over the last hundred years and more, imperialist forces penetrated into China, and in consequence, also penetrated into the Tibetan region and carried out all kinds of deceptions and provocations...
>
> The Local Government of Tibet did not oppose imperialist deception and provocations, but adopted an unpatriotic attitude towards the great motherland. Under such conditions, the Tibetan nationality and people were plunged into the depths of enslavement and suffering...

Which Government of Tibet, to say nothing of the Dalai Lama and his representatives, would describe of their own free will the Chinese invasion and the reaching of the 'Agreement' in the following terms?

> In order that the influences of aggressive imperialist forces in Tibet may be successfully eliminated, the unification of the territory and sovereignty of the People's Republic of China accomplished, and national defence safeguarded; in order that the Tibetan nationality and people may be freed and return to the big family of the People's Republic of China to enjoy the same rights of national equality as all other nationalities in the country and develop their political, economic, cultural, and educational work, the Central People's Government, when it ordered the People's Liberation Army to march into Tibet, notified the Local Government of Tibet to send delegates to the Central Authorities to hold talks for the conclusion of an agreement on measures for the peaceful liberation of

> Tibet. At the latter part of April, 1951, the delegates with full powers from the Local Government of Tibet arrived in Peking. The Central People's Government appointed representatives with full powers to conduct talks on a friendly basis with the delegates of the Local Government of Tibet. The result of the talks is that both parties have agreed to establish this agreement and ensure that it be carried into effect...

And yet, that is what the Preamble records! And Panditji would have us believe that this was an 'Agreement', an Agreement 'to which the Dalai Lama was a party', an Agreement which was 'accepted'—even if without joy in their hearts—by the Tibetans!

Which Tibetan Government, to say nothing of the Dalai Lama and his representatives, would of their own free will put their obligations as follows?

> The Tibetan people shall be united and drive out the imperialist aggressive forces from Tibet; that the Tibetan people shall return to the big family of the motherland—the People's Republic of China.
>
> The Local Government of Tibet shall actively assist the People's Liberation Army to enter Tibet and consolidate the national defenses.

But that is the text of Clauses 1 and 2 of the 'Agreement'!

Which Government of Tibet, to say nothing of the Dalai Lama and his representatives, reeling as they were in those months from the Chinese invasion, would of their own free will put their faith in the following procedure for selecting their rulers and administrators?

> In order to ensure the implementation of this agreement, the Central People's Government will set up a military and administrative committee and a military area headquarters in Tibet, and, apart from the personnel sent there by the Central People's Government, it will absorb as many local

> Tibetan personnel as possible to take part in the work. Local Tibetan personnel taking part in the military and administrative committee may include patriotic elements from the Local Government of Tibet, various district and various principal monasteries; the name list is to be prepared after consultation between the representatives designated by the Central People's Government and various quarters concerned, and is to be submitted to the Central People's Government for approval.

And yet, that is clause 15 of the 'Agreement'!

On top of all this, as Tsering Shakya was to record in his *Dragon in the Land of Snows,*[22] the Dalai Lama is supposed to have put his own seal on the Agreement by having written of his own free will to Mao and Co. in Peking later in the year a letter in which he assured them as follows:

> The Tibet Local Government as well as the ecclesiastic and secular people unanimously support this agreement, and under the leadership of Chairman Mao and the Central People's Government, will actively support the People's Liberation Army in Tibet to consolidate national defence, drive out imperialist influences from Tibet and safeguard the unification of the territory and the sovereignty of the Motherland.

The hand of the Chinese draftsman gives the game away. And yet, Panditji slips those words in—'The 17-Point Agreement, to which the Dalai Lama was a party... But it was accepted...'

There is another point. Recall that Panditji put great faith in Chou En-lai telling him that the Chinese Government was going to respect Tibet's autonomy and religion, that it would not interfere with either. Panditji wrote and spoke about this assurance on several occasions—at first as

[22] Tsering Shakya, *The Dragon in the Land of Snows,* Columbia, New York, p. 90.

evidence of what he had secured for Tibet and then, much later, when it was too late, as evidence of the Chinese having gone back on their assurances to him. But should the matter not have been evident to him in 1959 when he was writing this letter justifying his policies? After all, the so-called 1951 Agreement had contained many clauses to this effect:

> 3. In accordance with the policy towards nationalities laid down in the Common Programme of the Chinese People's Political Consultative Conference, the Tibetan people have the right of exercising national regional autonomy under the unified leadership of the Central People's Government.
> 4. The Central Authorities will not alter the existing political system in Tibet. The Central Authorities also will not alter the established status, functions and powers of the Dalai Lama. Officials of various ranks shall hold office as usual.
> 5. The established status, functions, and powers of the Panchen Lama shall be maintained.
> 6. By the established status, functions and powers of the Dalai Lama and of the Panchen Lama is meant the status, functions and powers of the 13th Dalai Lama and of the 9th Panchen Lama when they were in friendly and amicable relations with each other.
> 7. The policy of freedom of religious belief laid down in the Common Programme of the Chinese People's Political Consultative Conference will be protected. The Central Authorities will not effect any change in the income of the monasteries...
> 11. In matters related to various reforms in Tibet, there will be no compulsion on the part of the Central Authorities. The Local Government of Tibet should carry out reforms of its own accord, and when the people raise demands for reform, they must be settled through consultation with the leading personnel of Tibet.

Each and every one of these clauses had been violated. 'National regional autonomy' had been crushed under the heel of the PLA. 'The existing political system' had been obliterated.

'The status, functions and powers of the Dalai Lama', and of his officers, instead of being maintained, had been cast to the winds. 'Freedom of religious belief had gone the way of other freedoms in Mao's China. Far from the income of monasteries being preserved, the monasteries themselves had been erased and, those that had survived physically, had been brought to heel. As for clause 11, reforms or no reforms, there was compulsion all round. Yet, in the face of all this, Panditji thought fit to advise the young Dalai Lama to put faith in Chou En-lai's 'friendly approach' and assurances. Recall what Panditji himself acknowledged in the Lok Sabha on 27 April, 1959, that is just about the time he wrote the foregoing letter to the chief ministers:

> I told him [the Dalai Lama] of Premier Chou En-lai's friendly approach and of his assurance that he would respect the autonomy of Tibet. I suggested to him that he should accept these assurances in good faith and cooperate in maintaining that autonomy and bringing about certain reforms in Tibet...

Each rationalization paves the way for the next ruinous step. Once the Indian Government says that India has 'always accepted Chinese suzerainty over Tibet,' it is but a step to saying that it has always accepted Chinese 'sovereignty' over Tibet. Once it says that India has always accepted Chinese sovereignty over Tibet, it is but a step to signing the 1954 Agreement with China 'on trade and intercourse between Tibet Region of China and India'—an Agreement which refers to Tibet as the 'Tibet Region of China' not once but six times. Once it signs off on 'Tibet Region of China' six times, it is but a step to signing on to 'the Tibetan Autonomous Region of China' as was done in 2003, thereby accepting not just that Tibet is a region of China but that the 'Tibet' which is a region of China is what the Chinese Government says is 'Tibet'—that is, a Tibet with two of its three parts lopped off.

But to get back to the cascade of events...

10
Prelude

The Opposition members of Parliament are up in arms. The subject is debated four times during the Budget Session of 1959. How he has sacrificed Tibet. How he has wrongly trusted communist China... In the debate on 30 March 1959, Panditji is put on the defensive. But as is his wont, in defending his policy, a policy which he will soon be regretting, he goes even farther in repudiating the rights and position that India had in Tibet till the 1954 agreement. He says that these were nothing but the results and residues of British imperialism. The British decided to interfere in the affairs of Tibet. That is why they sent the Younghusband Expedition. 'They sat down there and imposed the British Government's will,' he says, '... and imposed our troops there in Tibet, in Yatung, Gyantse. All kinds of extra-territorial privileges were imposed on Tibet because Tibet was weak and there was the British Empire. With some variations, we inherited these special extra-territorial privileges when India became independent.'

Given the fact that we had ourselves waged a struggle against British imperialism, we could not, we would not, we just *should* not have sought to retain even fragments of that position, Panditji tells the House. 'Regardless of what happened in Tibet or China or anywhere, we could not, according to our own policy, maintain our forces in a foreign country, even if there had been no change in Tibet,' he says.

'That was a relic of British Imperialism which we did not wish to continue. We had to withdraw them back. It so happened that soon after this change in the Government in China—about that time, soon after—their armies marched into Tibet. What I am venturing to say is that the policy we adopted towards Tibet would have been adopted regardless of what China did, and we would have withdrawn our forces, etc. That was the main thing we did.' 'Apparently people seem to imagine that we surrendered some privileges in Tibet,' he continues. 'The privileges which we surrendered in Tibet were privileges which we do not seek to have in any other country in the world.'

He will soon have to recount a different bit of history. If China had been repudiating the acquisitions that resulted from its expansionism and imperialism, where would the modern state of China be?—he will be asking soon, and very justifiably, for the original Chinese Kingdom was a third of what it had become by 1949. But that is three years hence. For the time being, his reading of history is the way the Chinese rulers read it—Tibet has never been independent; no Chinese government has given up its right to Tibet; all Indian governments of the past have always recognized Chinese 'sovereignty' over Tibet; whatever rights and position we had were the result of British imperialism and expansionism.

But the Chinese have trampled on Tibet. Their armies are crushing the people. There has been a full-scale invasion. Our attitude historically has been to recognize Chinese suzerainty or sovereignty over Tibet with Tibetan autonomy... 'Anyhow,' Panditji says, 'we could not become judges or interfere or intervene either in law, or in fact, or in the circumstances, we could do nothing. That is just past history... All I could say was that we had to recognize Chinese sovereignty over Tibet.' 'We could not become judges?' He is sitting in judgement all the time—over events from Korea to Indo-China to Congo to Guatemala. But on Tibet, 'Anyhow, we could not become judges...' Yes, the Chinese are accusing us of instigating the trouble. We have repudiated that. In any case, I cannot speak more, as 'whatever I may say, whatever the Government may do, may have far-reaching consequences.'[1]

Soon after this debate, on 3 April 1959, Panditji informs the House that the Dalai Lama has crossed into India with a small party, having escaped from Lhasa after the Chinese began shelling the Potala Palace.

China, which had already been blaming India for the upheaval in Tibet, now escalates its denunciations to fever pitch. Panditji and his colleagues are dubbed the 'Indian expansionists', and are denounced for carrying forward the intrigues of the British imperialists. China declares that India is instigating the 'upper strata reactionaries' in Tibet who fear the loss of their feudal privileges. 'Indian enthusiasts have mistaken a handful of rebels for the entire Tibetan people,' the Chinese papers fume, and thus supported the rebellion. India wants to convert Tibet into a vassal state, they charge. India has abducted the Dalai Lama and is holding him under duress, they shout. With these denunciations flying about, and the Embassy of China in Delhi circulating handouts to the press containing them, the Lok Sabha is seized of the matter again on 27 April 1959.

Panditji makes a long statement explaining the restraint with which India has been reacting. He protests once again that there is absolutely no interference from India in Tibet. He expresses his great pain and his 'deepest regret and surprise' at the denunciations. He appeals to all within India to speak and act with the utmost restraint in spite of the strong emotions that the happenings in Tibet have evoked. 'It is not for me to make any similar appeal to the leaders, the press and the people of China,' Panditji observes. 'All I can say is that I have been greatly distressed at the tone of the comments and the charges made against India by responsible

---

[1] *Lok Sabha Debates*, 30 March 1959, cols. 8509–27.

people in China. They have used the language of cold war regardless of truth and propriety. This is peculiarly distressing in a great nation with thousands of years of culture behind it, noted for its restrained and polite behaviour. The charges made against India are so fantastic that I find it difficult to deal with them. There is the charge of our keeping the Dalai Lama under duress...'

'Another and even stranger allegation has been made about "Indian expansionists",' Panditji tells the House, 'who, it is alleged are inheritors of the British tradition of Imperialism and expansion...' In refutation, Panditji describes how, on the contrary, India has consciously given up all the privileges and influence it had in Tibet, how it has entered into an agreement with China recognizing Tibet as a region of China, and, even more so, how 'we have endeavoured not only to act up to the Agreement we made, but to cultivate the friendship of the Chinese State and people.' He recalls that he has already made it clear that the Chinese charge that the rebellion in Tibet is being organized from Kalimpong is 'wholly unjustified'. To imagine that such a large upheaval deep inside and across Tibet could be organized by a small group sitting in Kalimpong 'makes a large draft on imagination and slur over obvious facts'.

'The Khampa revolt started in an area of China proper adjoining Tibet, more than three years ago,' Panditji observes, and asks, 'Is Kalimpong supposed to be responsible for that?' Moreover, even within Tibet, to say that a handful of 'upper strata reactionaries' are causing the trouble 'appears to be an extraordinary simplification of a complicated situation', Panditji says. 'Even according to the accounts received through Chinese sources, the revolt in Tibet was of considerable magnitude and the basis of it must have been a strong feeling of nationalism which affects not only upper class people but others also...' 'The attempt to explain a situation by the use of rather worn-out words, phrases and slogans, is seldom helpful,' Panditji points out.

A substantial advance, you would have noticed, from the time, not so long ago, when he was scotching all proposals for keeping our options open in regard to Tibet on the ground that the order there had been feudal, and resentment against the Chinese was among classes that feared losing their position and privileges.

'We have no desire whatever to interfere in Tibet,' Panditji says, setting out the first of three limbs around which he says our policy is built; 'we have every desire to maintain the friendship between India and China, but, at the same time, we have every sympathy for the people of Tibet, and we are greatly distressed at their hapless plight.'

He speaks at length in this vein. The Chinese are right—the more vituperative they are, the more the liberal will strain to ensure that he does not come in their way. After all, sympathy carefully encaged within our hearts will not hurt them.

But there is one point in Panditji's speech that pains even after all these years. It gives us yet another glimpse of the enormous suffering his misjudgement inflicted on others. We have earlier been through the conversations of Chou En-lai and Panditji during his visit to Delhi in 1954. Chou En-lai had discussed the situation in Tibet with him 'at considerable length', Panditji recalls. Chou told him that 'while Tibet had long been a part of the Chinese State, they did not consider Tibet as a province of China;' that they recognized that 'it was absurd for anyone to imagine that China was going to force Communism on Tibet'—communism could not be forced on a backward country by force; that even reforms would be deferred for a considerable time. In a word, Tibet would maintain its autonomy. All this, Panditji recalls for the House.

We have also seen how the Dalai Lama had beseeched Panditji for help, and how Panditji had given him an instruction in realism instead of help. It turns out that Panditji had done more, and he now narrates it to the Lok Sabha. He tells the House:

> About that time, the Dalai Lama was also here and I had long talks with him then. *I told him of Premier Chou En-lai's friendly approach and of his assurance that he would respect the autonomy of Tibet. I suggested to him that he should accept these assurances in good faith and cooperate in maintaining that autonomy and bringing about certain reforms in Tibet.* The Dalai Lama agreed that his country, though, according to him, advanced spiritually, was very backward socially and economically and reforms were needed.[2]

How the judgement of a great man misleads not just him but others too, and brings about great suffering!

The reactions that Panditji's reasoning evokes

Two weeks later, on 8 May 1959, the Lok Sabha is seized by yet another discussion on the upheavals in Tibet. To follow such debates in full will take us too far away from our present concern, namely, the lessons that Panditji's thinking holds for the country. It will be enough to recall some of the salient points from just Acharya Kripalani's intervention, and that of a young member. Kripalani had crossed swords with Panditji over Tibet and China often. Many of his sharp criticisms had been vindicated by time. The speech he delivers now gives a flavour of the reactions that Panditji's reasoning was inviting.

China has been issuing one vituperative denunciation after another: India is the base of the 'bandits' who are destabilizing Tibet. Kalimpong is the 'command center' of the conspiracies. India is interfering in the internal affairs of China in brazen violation of the Five Principles. The denunciations are by themselves a complete answer to the friendship that Panditji has insisted on attributing to the Chinese rulers for years. Moreover, Acharya Kripalani observes, 'It is nothing unusual for countries to criticize each

---

[2] *Lok Sabha Debates,* 27 April 1959, cols. 13493–503.

other in their internal and external policy. Nobody takes this criticism to be interference in the internal affairs of the country. If it were so, the hard criticism that is being leveled by China itself against Yugoslavia would be considered interference in the internal affairs of the country. But in the Communist world there are two standards of judgement—one for themselves and the other for others with whom they think they are in opposition.'

Acharya Kripalani reminds the House that five years earlier, in 1954, when the Sino-Indian Agreement was signed, he had said on the floor of the House, 'Recently we have entered into a treaty with China. I feel that China, after it had gone Communist, committed an act of aggression against Tibet. The plea is that China had the ancient right of suzerainty. This right was out of date, old and antiquated. It was never exercised in fact. It had lapsed by the flux of time. Even if it had not lapsed, it is not right in these days of democracy by which our Communist friends swear, by which the Chinese swear, to talk of this ancient suzerainty and exercise it in a new form in a country which had and has nothing to do with China.'

'England went to war with Germany not because Germany had invaded England, but because it had invaded Poland and Belgium,' he reminds the House. Acharya Kripalani recalls that the same argument was being put forward in 1954, and he had pointed out at that time, 'It is also well-known that in the new map of China other border territories like Nepal, Sikkim, etc., figure. This gives us an idea of the aggressive designs of China. Let us see what the Chinese themselves did in the Korean War. As soon as the U.N. troops, or more correctly the American troops, reached the borders of China, it felt insecure and it immediately joined the Korean War.' 'I do not say that because China conquered Tibet, we should have gone to war with it,' he says. What he had been suggesting from the beginning, he recalled, was that we should not rush in to recognize the new regime. Let it show its colours first, he had counselled. Let us not go around the world pushing others to hurry up and recognize it. Let us not push its case for the seat in the UN to the exclusion of everything else. True, we could not go to war with it because of its aggression against Tibet, Acharya Kripalani had said, 'But this does not mean that we should recognize the claim of China on Tibet. We must know that it is an act of aggression against a foreign nation.'

He recalls that the previous year, in 1958, talking about Panchsheel, he had said, 'This great doctrine was born in sin, because it was enunciated to put the seal of our approval upon the destruction of an ancient nation which was associated with us spiritually and culturally.'

He turns to the hypothesis that Panditji has been advancing—we have seen it in the minutes of his remarks at the Commonwealth Prime Ministers' Conference—that, had China been a member of the UN, history would have been different, the Korean War may never have taken place as China would have been subject to the discipline of the UN—and punctures it: 'They think that as a member of the United Nations, China would be subject to some public opinion there. This is not a fact. There is South Africa; there is France; there is Russia and [there are] many other aggressive nations. Because they are members of the United Nations they have not ceased to be aggressive.' '*Panchsheel* implies a *mutuality* of respect for each other's integrity and sovereignty,' Kripalani points out, that is the essence of it—respect for *each other's* territorial integrity, non-interference in *each other's* internal affairs... 'How can there be respect for these things unless there is mutuality?' Is there mutuality in the way China is conducting itself vis-à-vis countries like ours?

They have charged that Kalimpong is the 'command center' of the troubles they are facing in Tibet. Their charge was investigated last year, Acharya Kripalani recalls. It was found to be totally unfounded. The report was sent to them.

'Yet our efforts to save it [China and its goodwill] will only result in this that they will not give us credit for good intentions. They will only give us credit for cowardice. It will never appear to a bully that you are doing things out of your goodness; it will only appear to him that you are frightened.'[3]

A young member advances telling points. We have been advocating the case for China in international councils even more fervently than China itself, hc says—*muddai sust aur gavah chust*... Under the agreement of 1951, Tibet is to have autonomy in its internal affairs. But China has violated the agreement. It has interfered in the internal affairs of Tibet. Lakhs of people from China are being settled in Tibet so that the Tibetans shall be reduced to a minority in their own land... Thousands have been taken from Tibet for inculcating a new religion in them... When we recognized the suzerainty of China over Tibet, we made a great mistake. That was an unfortunate day... China has violated the agreement that it signed with India... When people cannot protect and practise even their religion under communism, how can one say that communism and democracy are compatible?... Tibet is not the internal affair of China... The Government of India should think again about the policy it has been pursuing... If we can champion the cause of Algeria's independence, why can we not speak out for the independence of Tibet? On the same criteria, is Algeria not the internal affair of France?... Our party supports the independence of Tibet... Can Tibet conceivably attain autonomy within China? Communism and autonomy are antonyms... When we were championing the cause of China in the UN, we could as well have championed that of Tibet. Ukraine is a part of the Soviet Union but it has its own membership of the UN... With howsoever much restraint our prime minister may pursue our policy, if that

[3] *Lok Sabha Debates,* 8 May 1959, cols. 15878–85.

policy does not help solve the problem of Tibet, then we will have to acknowledge that there is need to inject some firmness into that policy, some activism... A large country has swallowed a small one... As far as India is concerned, China has a malevolent eye towards us... How come, the new Government of China has thrown Chiang Kai-shek out but kept his maps?... This is hidden aggression against India. In Uttar Pradesh, China is squatting over two places that it has wrested. Such incidents point to a gathering calamity... The Tibetan refugees now in India should be allowed to campaign for the freedom of their country just as our freedom fighters campaigned in foreign lands for India's freedom... This is a new imperialism. Its danger is that it comes wearing the disguise of revolution. It comes shouting the slogans of a new era. But this is imperialism, it is expansionism...[4]

Panditji speaks immediately after him. 'I may say in passing that we have laid no limitations on the Dalai Lama,' he says, 'except the limitations of good sense and propriety of which he himself is the judge.' And then he turns on the young member. 'But for the hon. Member to suggest that we should allow him to do something which he has not himself suggested, that is, making India the headquarters of some kind of a campaign and that we should allow the hon. Member and his party to join in this campaign,' Panditji pronounces, 'is something which seems to be so odd, so remarkable of utterance that I cannot imagine how even he could have made it if he had thought about it. I need not say much about it, because it has no relation to facts, no relation to what is happening in the world, or in India, or in Tibet, or in China or anywhere.'

He takes up the criticism that has been levelled at the Sino-Indian Agreement on Tibet. 'It was a correct Agreement and we shall stand by it and it is not correct even for him to say

[4] *Lok Sabha Debates,* 8 May 1959, cols. 15918–25.

that that Agreement has been broken,' Panditji pronounces, and advances a quibble as argument. 'It may be said that he thinks that certain implications of that Agreement have not been, according to him, or according to anybody else, carried out. That is a different matter. But there is no question of that Agreement having been broken. It lasts; it functions.'

By now he is in flight. As we have seen him put civil servants down, so we see him come down on members of Parliament—it is a characteristic way: like so many men placed high on pedestals, Panditji talks often of ancient virtues like humility, but he doesn't come through as all that humble. Dealing with arguments and facts that members have cited, Panditji says,

> I do not know how many hon. Members here know the history, the background of Tibet, of China, of Mongolia, of Bhutan and Sikkim and Nepal in the last few hundred years. I wonder how many have cared to look into them. I do not know whether the hon. Member who just spoke knows anything about it at all. I happen to know something about it and I have taken the trouble to read quite a number of books of history, Chinese chronicles, Indian reports, etc. Here is the history of six or seven hundred years, or more...

Panditji proceeds to expand on what Chengiz Khan did... what happened during the time of Kublai Khan... down to the Manchu dynasty. And then ends with, 'But, all these do not count. In considering the present day situation, we have to take things as they are and have been recently.'

That young member who has advanced a proposal that is 'so odd, so remarkable of utterance that I cannot imagine how even he could have made it...'; that young member about whom Panditji says 'I do not know whether the hon. Member who just spoke knows anything about it at all'—about those history books which Panditji has read in piles, that young member is Atal Behari Vajpayee...

Panditji berates those who have been using strong words:

'Peaceful solutions are not brought about by warlike speeches and warlike approaches...'

He mentions two factors—an apologia for China can be built on them. The first is change. Tibet has been stuck in the rut of the past. It has suddenly been catapulted 'into the open, events throwing it into the mad world of ours, cold wars and all kinds of things happening, dynamic policies and ferocious policies and authoritarian policies'. It would have been better if the change had been slower, and in fact that is what the Chinese rulers had planned: 'It was the policy, I believe, of the People's Government of China, who realized that a country like this cannot be treated in a sudden way, to go slowly about the so-called reforms or whatever it may be...' But uprooting is 'a terribly painful process' whenever it occurs... It would have been better if the changes had been brought through cooperation. But 'I cannot judge of what is happening in Tibet. I do not have facts, neither does anybody in this House, except broadly some odd fact here and there. But I am merely venturing to say that all these complicated systems—not so easy to disentangle; anyhow, whatever it may be—have brought undoubtedly a great deal of suffering to the people of Tibet. And I should have liked to avoid it. But what can I do?'

But had Chou En-lai not promised that Tibet would have autonomy, that its religion would be respected? Did the seventeen-point agreement not guarantee that autonomy? True, Panditji's argument runs, but maybe the problem is linguistic!

'There is another difficulty in my or our dealing with these matters, and that is, that the words we use have a different meaning for other people,' Panditji tells the House. 'For instance, we talk of the autonomy of Tibet. So do the Chinese. But, a doubt creeps into my mind as to whether the meaning I attach to it is the same as they attach to it. I do not think so. There are so many other words. I am not talking of any deliberate distortion. That apart, quite apart from any distortion, the ways of thinking have changed. They have changed anyhow and the cold war methods have made them change even more. It is frightfully difficult really to talk the same language, the same language of the mind, I mean. Difficulty arises because of that also, and tremendous misunderstandings arise. However, I cannot go into all these matters...' Could the Chinese have asked for a more convenient exculpation?

He devotes most of the remainder of his speech to counselling Indians to avoid angry words, to maintain dignity, maintain their rights, maintain their self-respect, 'and yet not allowing ourselves to drift into wrong attitudes, hostile attitudes...'

At the same time, he advances a different reading of the Chinese than he has been stressing hitherto: '...I believe I am not wrong in saying the Chinese rather look down upon the Tibetans from the Mongol times. The Chinese rather look down upon every country other than their own. They consider themselves as the celestial race, a great country, whether it was the Tang kingdom, or the Ming kingdom or ultimately the Manchus for a long period...'

He does turn in passing to the Chinese maps, and his tone is a bit, just a bit different. He expresses irritation—not so much at the maps as at their continuance:

> One thing which was referred to by two or three Members was the question of maps. Now, there is no doubt about it that this continuance of what are called old maps by China, which show certain, fairly large areas of Indian territory, as if they belong to the Chinese State, has been a factor creating continual irritation in the minds of people in this country. It is not some crisis that has arisen, but it has been difficult for our people, naturally, to understand why this kind of thing continues indefinitely, year after year. It is not, mind you, a question of some odd little pocket here and there which may be in dispute on which we can argue—there are two or three pockets about which we have had, and we are going to have

> discussions—but this business of issuing these maps which are not true to fact, which are factually untrue, and which can hardly be justified on the ground of history, of Marshal Chiang Kai-shek's regime or any previous regime.[5]

Chinese propaganda continues to condemn and denounce India, in particular Panditji. Indeed, it becomes sharper with each volley. Disquiet with the policy that our government is pursuing grows in proportion.

That even the little that has been done has occasioned such charges becomes an argument for not even thinking of doing anything more. An officer who used to be the Indian Consul-General in Lhasa has been deputed to liaison with the Dalai Lama. On 7 May 1959, the Dalai Lama writes to Panditji about what the Chinese are doing in Tibet. Panditji dictates a note for the officer and instructs him to give an oral answer to the Dalai Lama. 'I can very well understand his deep distress at happenings in Tibet,' Panditji tells the officer. 'But on reading his letter, it seems to me that he has not fully appreciated the situation.' To work for the terms the Dalai Lama has suggested would require that the Chinese have been completely defeated in war—'No Government, least of all the Chinese Government can accept such terms or conditions. Even if there was war, such terms would not be accepted by it because they involve a complete surrender of their position in Tibet. It is impossible for a strong and powerful nation to accept these terms even if these are put forward by all the great powers in the world.'

And it is even more difficult for India to do anything more in the matter: 'During the last few weeks, the Chinese Government have attacked India and its leaders with extreme virulence. This itself shows how much they have been upset by India's attitude, moderate as it was. India has, in fact, gone as far as it can. Any further step would mean a break with China. In any event, India cannot put forward any demands

---

[5] *Lok Sabha Debates,* 8 May 1959, cols. 15925–39.

on China. The most that can happen is for a situation to develop gradually which will induce the Chinese Government to moderate their attitude on Tibet. There is no other way ... It must be realized that nothing can happen soon in Tibet. A situation has been created which cannot be reversed quickly. We have to function carefully and await events.'[6]

A major part of Panditji's letter of 18 May 1959 to the chief ministers has perforce to be devoted to justifying his policy towards China and Tibet. The chief ministers are taken through the familiar sequence—India has always recognized Chinese suzerainty over Tibet; couldn't do anything when Chinese forces entered Tibet; therefore, emphasized autonomy; the 1954 agreement entered in good faith... The only new point that Panditji makes in the long explanations is to reject once again the proposal that is being made that, at the least, India should take up the matter in the United Nations, it should, at the least, support the move if some other country takes the initiative to have the UN consider the fresh Chinese onslaught. 'We do not understand also how it is feasible for the matter to be raised in the United Nations when the UN does not even recognize the People's Government of China, and more or less treats it as a hostile country,' Panditji exclaims. 'The UN cannot have it both ways, to ignore China and at the same time to condemn it.'[7]

The Chinese escalate—the verbal denunciations as well as the frequency and the extent of incursions on the ground. At a press conference in the first week of August, Panditji expresses his surprise and distress at 'the strange silence' that the Chinese government is maintaining in response to our protests about their maps that show thousands of square miles of Indian territory as parts of China.

Suniti Kumar Chatterji, a distinguished linguist and man of letters, and at the time the President of the India-China

---

[6] *SWJN,* XLIX.569–70.

[7] *Letters,* Volume 5, Letter of 18 May 1959, in particular pp. 236–41.

Friendship Association in West Bengal, requests Panditji for a message on the anniversary of the Panchsheel Declaration. Panditji's response shows what has become of those principles, and the deep injury that events have caused him. He replies to Chatterji,

> I do not quite know what kind of a message to send you, because we have seen repeatedly cases of the violation of these Five Principles by those very countries which spoke loudly in their favour.
>
> The Government of the People's Republic of China accuses us of having violated these Principles because we have given shelter to the Dalai Lama and other Tibetans and because the Indian press as well as some others have criticized Chinese policy in Tibet. We think that China has offended against the spirit of those Principles on several occasions.
>
> What then am I to say in a message? I do not wish to go on criticizing the Chinese Government. That does not help. At the same time, I can hardly shout in praise of something which is not being acted upon.[8]

Just incursions, no 'fixed occupation'

Parliament is up in arms. There are spirited exchanges in both Houses on three occasions during Question Hour, by way of Adjournment Motions, members struggle to extract information about what has been happening.

Panditji does his best to minimize the incursions, to play down their significance for the defence of the country. He deflects and dodges the pointed questions that the members ask. It is only because of the prestige he commands that he is able to get away with the responses he fields. But it is a capital he is expending.

---

[8] *SWJN*, XLIX.583.

On 8 May 1959, Panditji had answered a starred question about the Chinese incursion in Bara Hoti. Several members have tabled a question inquiring whether negotiations with the Chinese about that area and incursion have been concluded. The negotiations have not been resumed, the members are told. But what is the current position? Members demand to know. Is the area still in Chinese possession? No, a party of the UP police is sitting at the place at present, Panditji tells them. 'It should be borne in mind,' Panditji says, 'that this piece of flatland is about one and a half square miles, it is a small piece of flatland. During winter one cannot even go there.' During summers, 'shepherds come with goats, etc., for grazing. They come mainly from the Tibet side because on our side there are steep mountains…'

Is some arrangement being made so that even during the winter months our soldiers can remain there? a member inquires. It is true that last year, when our soldiers remained there during the cold of winter, a few Chinese soldiers also came over, Panditji replies. 'Now, for this I do not quite see why we should put our soldiers to so much trouble to sit through such cold, through the winter...' The negotiations have not been abandoned, Panditji explains. What has been agreed by both sides is that, till the matter is settled, both sides will treat the patch of land as neutral territory. Neither side will send personnel with arms. Such matters have to be settled by discussions, he tells members. I do not understand how they are to be settled by remaining perched on hilltops. It is a matter of maps—we have our maps, they have theirs. How can the matter be settled by sitting there, by roaming around in the area?[9]

Several members have filed another question: 'Occupation of Ladakhi territory by Chinese forces.' Is it a fact, they want to know, that a large part of Ladakhi territory has been recently occupied by Chinese forces? Panditji's written answer begins

---

[9] *Lok Sabba Debates,* 28 August 1959, cols. 4756–60.

by explaining, as usual, how remote and inaccessible the area is: 'There is a large area in Eastern and North-Eastern Ladakh which is practically uninhabited. It is mountainous, and even the valleys are at a high altitude generally exceeding 13,000 ft...' The government has set up some check-posts in this area...

He then mentions two separate sets of incursions by Chinese forces—one in October 1957 and another one in February 1958—and that the attention of the Chinese government had been immediately drawn to these. Then a third, much more serious incident had occurred. In July 1959 two patrol parties had been sent. One of these, while proceeding towards the place where the Chinese had intruded in 1957 and 1958, was apprehended by a stronger Chinese force. It turned out that the Chinese had established a camp at Spanggur 'well within Indian territory'. A protest was lodged. The Chinese said they had apprehended the Indians as they had crossed into territory which belongs to China. 'We expressed surprise at this claim, Panditji explains. No reply has been received to this communication as yet...'

'Of course, there have been some frontier troubles in two or three places widely separated,' he tells the Lok Sabha, and adds, 'and it would be hardly correct to say that our area is under occupation of the Chinese, that is, under any kind of a fixed occupation. But their patrols, so far as we know, have come within our territory two or three miles or thereabouts. That is our knowledge, so far as we know.' And when it turns out that the Chinese *have* occupied an area, and it is no longer possible to deny that—soon, the road they have built cutting off a wide swathe of Aksai Chin will become the focus of public censure—it will be said that it is now too late to get the area back from under their 'fixed occupation'.

Panditji explains how and why the Indian patrol was sent, how it was captured by the Chinese, and how it has been released after a month in captivity. Panditji is pressed. But haven't the Chinese built a road cutting through Ladakhi territory? N.G. Goray asks. 'Yes, that is in Northern Ladakh,' Panditji acknowledges, 'not exactly near this place but anyhow in the Ladakhi territory.'

'About a year or two ago,' Panditji now tells the House, 'the Chinese had built a road from Gartok towards Yarkand, that is, Chinese Turkestan; and the report was that this road passed through a corner of our north-eastern Ladakhi territory.'

A year or two ago, and the House has not been told? And what has the government done to recover the area? 'The House will appreciate,' Panditji says, 'that these areas are *extraordinarily remote, almost inaccessible, and even if they can be approached, it takes weeks and weeks of march to get there*.' Moreover, the border in that remote area is not clearly demarcated on the ground. 'So far as we are concerned,' Panditji tells the House, 'our maps are clear that this is within the territory of the Union of India. It may be that some of the parts are not clearly demarcated. But, obviously, if there is any dispute over any particular area, that is a matter to be discussed.' The question we should bear in mind when we read such responses is, 'How would China have reacted to an inch, to say nothing of 9,000 square miles of territory it regards as its own being hacked off by some other country?' The answer will tell us how territory is guarded; more than that, it will acquaint us with the inference China will draw when the way Panditji is responding is how we respond to usurpation. Why will not they be emboldened to do more of the same?

N.G. Goray asks Panditji, 'Does it mean that in parts of our country which are inaccessible, any nation can come and build roads and camps? We just send our parties, they apprehend the parties and, because of our good relations, they release them. Is that all? The road remains there, the occupation remains there and we do not do anything about it.'

Panditji's response is typical of this phase: 'I do not know if the hon. Member expects me to reply to that.' He proceeds to differentiate types of intrusion and types of borders: regions where it is demarcated—any incursion in such an area is aggression and we have to have it vacated; those in regard to which there are rival claims; areas where the maps are clear but the border has not been demarcated on the ground, etc. In regard to the area where our patrol party was abducted, he says, 'we have been carrying on correspondence, and suggesting that it should be considered by the two Governments.'

Atal Behari Vajpayee asks what has been done to enforce security measures in this area. Instead of using the question to spell out the measures, Panditji takes recourse to a put-down: 'There are thousands of miles of border. The hon. Member should be a little more specific in his question. If he is referring to this particular corner, the Aksai Chin area, that is an area about some parts of which, if I may say so, it is not quite clear what the position is. In other places, we are quite clear and certain. The border is 2,500 miles long...'

Sushila Nayar asks whether the troubles are occurring in areas that the Chinese are claiming in their maps to be theirs, and, if so, what are the implications of that for the future?

The Speaker intervenes: 'Any further encroachments within the limits of the map?' he asks Panditji.

Panditji yields another bit of ominous information, almost as an aside: 'This particular question that I answered related to one area. *There are other areas too where we have had, and we are, in fact, having, some trouble now.*' It is, of course, for the benefit of the members that he is keeping matters distinct: 'I do not want to mix it up with this. Then there will be confusion in one's mind. This is a frontier of over 2,000 miles.'

Atal Behari Vajpayee: 'What is the use of repeating that it is a long frontier? Are we not in a position to defend it?'

Panditji: 'I was only venturing to say that by putting two or three places together, there would be confusion in the Members' minds...'

But what about the maps that the Chinese government continues to circulate? Do they not show large parts of Ladakh to be part of China? Panditji's answer is typical:

> The Chinese Government's maps are on such a small scale and in such broad splashes that some parts of Ladakh appear to be included in them. But they are not accurate enough. What we are discussing, and the question which I have answered, relates to about two or three miles. Two or three miles are not visible in these maps. But it is a fact that part of Ladakh is broadly covered by the wide sweep of their maps.[10]

Is the reason that the maps are on a small scale? Or is it that these small-scale maps are continuing to be circulated and relied upon for a reason?

China sends troops, we send representations

Immediately after the Question Hour, the Lok Sabha takes up Adjournment Motions that several members have filed about the situation along the north-eastern border. It is during the exchanges that Panditji has to inform Parliament about what will turn out to be one of the most serious precursors to the full-scale invasion in 1962. He informs the Lok Sabha that Chinese forces have been marshalled across the borders in strength. He says that they have made deep incursions at three places in the north-east. A serious lunge has been made into the village of Longju.

'In the course of the last two or three years, there have been cases—not very frequent—of some kind of petty intrusion on our border areas by some platoon or other of the Chinese troops,' Panditji says. 'This was nothing

[10] *Lok Sabha Debates*, 28 August 1959, cols. 4793–800.

extraordinary, because there is no demarcation at all and parties may some times cross over. We drew the attention of the Chinese Government in 1957/58 to this and they withdrew. There the matter ended.' Now two incidents have occurred. In one, around 200 Chinese soldiers crossed our border in the Kameng Division, surrounded our patrol which consisted of ten or twelve personnel, and pushed it back. The Chinese withdrew. Our party re-established its position. 'All this was over a question of about two miles,' Panditji says. On 25 August a large Chinese force came three or four miles into our territory, surrounded and apprehended our picket of a dozen or so. Seven or eight of them escaped, and reoccupied the check-post. The Chinese surrounded them. Fire kept being exchanged for a long time. Overwhelmed, our soldiers had to abandon the check-post at Longju village.

The entire NEFA has been placed under the army, Panditji tells the House. 'I need not say that, while I do not wish to take an alarmist view of the situation—in themselves these are minor incidents—it is a little difficult to understand what lies behind these minor incidents. In any event, we have to be vigilant and protect our borders as best we can.'

Panditji goes on to describe the policy he has followed in regard to China and Tibet and the border. He is at pains, as is his custom, to urge the balanced view, tilted in favour of finding a peaceful solution, which in this case boils down to sending representations. Minor border incidents, like minor disagreements about the precise alignment of the border should be settled through negotiations. On the other hand, 'the broad approach of the Chinese maps which have brush-coloured hundreds of miles of Indian territory' is 'totally and manifestly unacceptable and we have made it clear'. '...It is not a normal, peaceful way of approaching the question for their forces to come, envelop our check-posts and capture them after firing. This matter becomes much more serious than some incidental or accidental border affray.' Members have asked me what lies behind this, Panditji remarks. His answer is important:

> I cannot say. It is not fair for me to guess—it will be guesswork, of course—but I cannot imagine that all this is a precursor to anything more serious. It seems to me to be foolish for anybody, including the Chinese Government, to function in that way, and I do not give them the credit or rather the discredit for folly. Therefore, I do not think they will do it. But so far as we are concerned, we should naturally be prepared for any eventuality and without fuss or shouting keep vigilant.[11]

A gross error, that: to assume that because a course of action seems foolish to me, the adversary will not adopt it. Remember, this is exactly the ground on which Panditji had first ruled out the Chinese invasion of Tibet, and later its plunge into the Korean War.

On 31 August 1959, the Rajya Sabha is seized of the matter. What about the intrusions? What about the road in Aksai Chin? What about the soldiers who were captured?

According to an official announcement of the Chinese government, Panditji informs members, the road was completed in September 1957—remember, that the discussion is taking place in August 1959. 'Representations were made to the Chinese Government in a Note presented to the Chinese Ambassador in New Delhi on October 18 1958,' Panditji says, 'drawing their attention to the construction of the road through Indian territory and the arrest of fifteen members of the Indian reconnaissance party within the Indian border.'

In their reply, the Chinese said the Indian party had been released, and that the road was in Chinese territory. 'A Note expressing our surprise at the Chinese contention was presented to the Chinese authorities on November 8, 1958,'

---

[11] *Lok Sabha Debates,* 28 August 1959, cols. 4860–71.

Panditji says. 'Reminders have been given subsequently. No further answers have been received.' He proceeds to dilate upon the remoteness and high altitudes of Ladakh...

Why was Parliament not taken into confidence earlier in regard to this matter? A member, D.P. Singh, asks.

'There was not much to take into confidence about, Sir,' Panditji says in reply. 'Without our knowledge they (the Chinese) have made a road in that extreme corner and we have been dealing with it through correspondence. No particular occasion arose to bring the matter before the House, because we thought that we might make progress by correspondence and when the time was ripe for it we would inform Parliament.'

Hardly the answer that would satisfy anyone. D.P. Singh persists: 'What are we to do when the Chinese Government does not even answer our protest sent as far back as August or so?'

The chairman corrects him: the House is debating the matter in August 1959, the protest was sent on 8 November 1958, he interjects. That makes D.P. Singh's question even more pertinent.

Panditji says, 'After that we sent them reminders to which they did not send an answer. That is true.'

'In spite of reminders?' asks another member.

Panditji: 'In spite of reminders. We can only send further reminders.'

But doesn't the road stay? Does the area not remain in their occupation? 'The road was built,' Panditji concedes, and immediately underplays what has been done. 'Roads in these areas, Sir, are of a peculiar type. In these very high areas the ground is so hard, harder than normal cement, and the only thing you have to do to build a road is to even the ground a little and remove stones and shrubs...'

In response to a further question from D.P. Singh, Panditji has to acknowledge that a Chinese detachment has been observed in another place 'a considerable distance away from this area'. 'This matter arose this month, and we are carrying on correspondence about that territory.'

Another member, Jaswant Singh, inquires, 'The Prime Minister stated a little while ago that this portion of Ladakh is absolutely desolate and unfertile and that not even a blade of grass grows there. Even then, China is attaching importance to the area and is building a road there. I would like to know, when China is attaching so much of importance to this desolate bit of land, why, when the territory is ours or is under dispute even, do we not attach any importance to it?'

Panditji: 'I talked only about the Yehcheng area, not about the whole of Ladakh, although the whole Ladakh, broadly speaking, is 11,000 to 17,000 and 20,000 feet high. Presumably the Chinese attach importance to this area because of the fact that the route connects part of Chinese Turkestan with Gartok-Yehcheng. This is an important connection.' Apart from everything else, is the fact that the place is an important connection between two parts of China not the precise reason why the area should be of vital, strategic significance to us?

The effort of Panditji to minimize the significance of what the Chinese have done, the road they have built, the area they have hacked off, is bad enough But he adds something that amounts to casualness: '*I cannot even now say when it was built. But reports about it, as I said, reached us from a small Chinese map two years ago.*'

Panditji does not just underplay what the Chinese have done. Thrice during these exchanges, he makes out as if their coming in is just an incident of the way things are, that their claims to the areas in question are at par with, that they are just like our claims in the region. He says this to minimize Chinese incursions and to explain away the government's failure to safeguard the territory. But the sentences he uses have significance far beyond the immediate incursions.

'The hon. Member started by saying that this is admittedly

Indian territory,' Panditji says while responding to the pointed questions of D.P. Singh, 'but the Chinese would not agree to it. That is a contradiction in terms. As a matter of fact, it is Indian territory and we claim it so because we think that the weight of evidence is in our favour—maps, etc. But the Chinese produce their own maps, equally old, which are in their favour.' As both claims are at par, why fight over the areas? That is the clear implication.

Not just that. Panditji returns to the 'not a blade of grass grows there' thesis. 'And the territory is sterile. It has been described as a barren, uninhabited region without the vestige of grass and 17,000 ft. high.'

Thus, there is not just one, there are two reasons not to get excited about the road and incursions.

Another bit of information slips out, and Panditji takes the same position. D.P. Singh asks whether the Chinese have occupied areas in addition to the area cut off by this road. Panditji evades: 'Not about that particular area, Sir, but I think there is another question, I am not quite sure...'

Seeing Panditji trail off, Dr Radhakrishnan, who is presiding, inquires, 'There is another question?'

Panditji: 'That is different. There is no question about it. There was a report this month, in August, not about this area, but an area near Ladakh, a considerable distance away from this area, on the eastern area of Ladakh border of Tibet, where a Chinese detachment was seen by a reconnaissance party, a small Indian patrol in that area; and ultimately I think 7, 8 or 10 persons—I do not remember the number—were apprehended by the Chinese and later released.'

Information having come out, Panditji swiftly seeks to play down its significance, and thereby for the second time puts China's claim to the areas at par with that of India:

> The same claim arises here, they say it is their territory and we say it is ours. And the matter arose, as I said, this month and we are carrying on correspondence about that territory. These

> places are not demarcated on the land. We go by our maps which the Chinese do not recognize and they go presumably by their maps, whatever they have. And this was four or five miles according to our maps, may be seven or eight miles, I am not sure where the Chinese patrol came. And we are told they have established a small check-post a little within our side of the international border there, just on the eastern Ladakh border of Tibet. This is near a place called Chusun [sic] near which we have one of our check-posts.

The discussion moves to the north-east. Panditji describes the Chinese foray into Longju five days earlier. We lodged a protest immediately, he says. The situation on the ground is not completely clear: 'It is not clear whether the Chinese patrols have occupied Longju or are merely moving round about it,' Panditji says. Two of our border guards escaped, and have given an account of what happened. 'I do not quite know where the remaining six are...'

Members want to know what steps are being taken to prevent incursions of this kind. Panditji says that one cannot prevent an incursion over a 2,000-mile frontier. 'What we can do is to take steps to repulse it if one takes place.' We have to follow a 'double policy': strengthen our defences, and, at the same time, when such incidents occur, sort them out through conferences.

A member, Jaswant Singh, asks whether there is any doubt about the ownership of this particular area in which this incursion has taken place. Panditji again puts China's claim at par with our rights to the area:

> Yes, the Chinese not only doubt it but claim ownership of that particular strip. I do not know how far it is correct but they claim that particular strip and they said to our men that that strip belongs to them. Whether they are justified in doing so or not is another matter.[12]

[12] *Rajya Sabha Debates*, 31 August 1959, cols. 2281–92.

Panditji uses these expressions to minimize what the Chinese have begun doing. He does so to imply that these things are happening simply because of the terrain and the fact that the border is not demarcated on the ground. He does so to explain away the government's dereliction.

Yet two things will be obvious. First, even in his own assessment, the claims are *not* at par, things are not as vague as he makes them out to be in public. The tone of what he writes about these incidents to the chief ministers, as we shall see, is very different. Second, the words have significance far beyond the immediate incidents: for getting over the embarrassments of the moment, Panditji has used expressions that undermine our case along the entire border.

At last, on 8 September 1959, Chou En-lai replies to the letters and protests that the Indian government has been sending. He does not just reject them. He lays claim to over 40,000 square miles of territory as being that of China. Panditji in turn rejects the claim. He proposes that the two sides meet to settle differences, and that, in the meantime, the status quo be maintained.

Two days have not passed, and the Rajya Sabha is again debating the Chinese incursions. Even senior members who have been associated with Panditji for long, like Dr Kunzru, say that the events and what has by now become evident about China's intentions have thrown our foreign policy in the melting pot; that they have shown that the assurances which the government has been giving about adequate steps having been taken to safeguard our borders were incorrect.

Panditji begins by referring to the correspondence of both sides that has been published in the White Paper, and the new letter that has been received from Chou En-lai. As he does in his letter to the chief ministers, Panditji lays at least a part of the problem on language! 'I often wonder if we, that is the Government of India and the Government of China, speak quite the same language, and if, using the same words or similar words, we mean the same thing,' he tells the House. 'Secondly, and I know this from experience, it is a terrific problem to translate Chinese into any other language...'

As for foreign policy having been thrown into the melting pot, Panditji won't have any of it. He refers to Dr Kunzru and declares, 'So far as I am concerned and so far as our Government is concerned, our foreign policy is as firm as a rock and it will remain so. The present Government will hold to non-alignment because it is a matter of principle, not of opportunism or the convenience of the day. That surely does not mean that we should not be vigilant or that we should not protect India's interests or India's border. That would be a foolish inference to draw from it...' Again, that 'all-or-nothing' way of posing the question.

'Right from the first few months of independence, I repeatedly stated in Parliament that the McMahon Line, by which I simply mean the defined frontier, was our frontier,' Panditji recalls. 'When I say something in Parliament, it is meant for the outside world and it was meant, if I may say so, for the Government of China. We said this to the Chinese Government in communication too, orally and otherwise. Their answer was vague.' But the question is different: even without events having taken the course they have, it is evident that it is never enough to just proclaim one's position, certainly not vis-à-vis a country like China; the question is: have we done enough to stand by the position we have proclaimed?

For the first time Panditji uses a self-deprecating expression: 'Seven or eight years ago I saw no reason to discuss the question of the frontier with the Chinese Government, because, foolishly if you like, I thought that there was nothing to discuss.'

It isn't just that there was such a colossal misjudgement about whether the matter should have been taken up earlier in discussions. The sentences that follow disclose the criminal extent to which the very areas that the Chinese maps were alerting us were their targets, were neglected. Panditji tells the House,

> When we discovered in 1958, more than a year ago, that a road had been built across Yehcheng in the north-east corner of Ladakh, we were worried. We did not know where it was. Hon. Members asked why we did not know before. It is a relevant question, but the fact is that it is an uninhabitable area, 17,000 feet high. It had not been under any kind of administration. Nobody has been present there. It is a territory where not even a blade of grass grows. It adjoins Sinkiang...

He proceeds to recall the fate of the patrol that was sent, and how they were captured by the Chinese. For the second time, he uses words that show how events are leaving him no alternative but to look at the consequences of his insistences of the past few years. 'We sent a small party, practically of explorers, numbering eight to ten, to find out the facts... The men belonging to that group were released later. Now, it was possibly an error or a mistake on my part not to have brought the facts before the House. Our difficulty then was that we were corresponding with the Chinese Government and we were waiting for that little party to come here and tell us as to what happened to them. It took two or three months for them to come. We thought at that time that it might be easier for us to deal with the Chinese Government without too much publicity for this incident. We might have been wrong, but it was not a crisis...'

Panditji swings—in one breath he is arguing the imperative of peace, and minimizing the area in question:

> But nothing can be a more amazing folly than for two great countries like India and China to get into a major conflict and war for the possession of a few mountain peaks, however beautiful the mountain peaks might be, or some area which is more or less uninhabited.

In the next, he is stressing the gravity that lurks behind the surface happenings:

> But it is not a question of a mile or two. It is something more precious than a hundred or a thousand miles. People's passions have been brought to a high level not because of a patch of territory but because they feel that we have not received a fair treatment in this matter and have been treated rather casually by the Chinese Government and an attempt is made, if I may use the word, to bully us.

'A few mountain peaks', 'some area which is more or less uninhabited', 'a patch of territory'—is that all that the claim to 40,000 square miles amounts to?

Panditji recalls his talks with Chou En-lai. '...Premier Chou added that he did not think that it was a valid line, and that the British had gone on extending it; nevertheless, they were recognizing it because of long usage and because we were friendly countries.' 'When I heard it I wanted to be quite sure that I had not misunderstood him,' Panditji says. 'Therefore, I went back to the subject three times and made him repeat it. And because the matter was of some importance to me, I put it down in writing when I came away.'

'It is a matter of sorrow to me that this is now ignored, if not practically denied, and another line is adopted,' Panditji continues. He still wants to believe that he was not wrong in trusting the word of Chou En-lai: 'It may be that things have happened in China compelling a change in policy,' he says, only to contradict that hypothesis in the sentences that follow: 'This change-over is not sudden. Those who read the White Paper will see that the answer about the McMahon Line was not quite so strong and positive as in Premier Chou's letter of yesterday. Gradually, step by step, the policy of China in regard to this matter has become more rigid. Why, I cannot say.'

How is one to continue to trust the word of the Chinese rulers? That is the question. And if one cannot trust their word, what is the alternative? That is the one question Panditji does not want to face. He says, 'This is a matter of concern to us, not only because of its consequences but because such developments produce a lack of confidence in each other's words and assurances. That is a more important thing, as some hon. Members said, than a few yards of territory'—members, at least not the ones who have been warning him that the assumptions on which he has based his entire policy are baseless, and worse, have *not* said 'a few yards of territory'.

The very maps which Panditji was explaining away—recall his remarks to the press about how these were old maps—he now cites as compounding the uncertainties: 'Take these maps where large areas of India are marked as if they were China. They say that the maps are not precise and accurate, and can be changed if necessary, except that they do not recognize the McMahon Line. Nobody knows exactly what they may have in mind as to where the Line is. This is an extraordinary position for a great State to take up. Even if we subscribed to that, it would mean leaving the matter vague, with the possibility of trouble always there. So far as we are concerned, administratively we have been there. We function and we have functioned for years there. To be told that this [our being there] is aggression is an extraordinary thing.'

'Take the Sino-Indian Treaty about Tibet five years ago,' he says, pointing to another circumstantial factor. 'The whole context of those discussions was that we were dealing with all the remaining problems as between Tibet and India in that treaty with China. And to have it at the back of your mind that you are going to change the whole frontier between Tibet and India and later bring it up does not seem to be quite straight or fair play.' Two assumptions in that, two assumptions with no basis at all—and, as we have seen, both enforced by Panditji. First there is the assumption that the agreement had dealt with 'all the remaining problems' including the border. Then there is the second assumption that the Chinese had committed themselves to be straight and play fair. Surely, Panditji, with all those books and chronicles that he had read on Chinese history, and the stratagems by which the Chinese communists had wrested power ever so recently, surely these accounts and events gave no warrant for this assumption.

The point he makes next is both telling, and a bit embarrassing: isn't it the very point that Sardar Patel had urged in the letter with which we began this account? But it is a telling answer to the Chinese canard about India continuing the policies of British imperialism. Panditji says,

> Now, a very favourite word with the Chinese authorities is 'imperialism'. It seems to me that sometimes this word is used to cover every sin and everything, as if that was an explanation of every argument. The Chinese State today is a great, colossal State. Was this Chinese State born as such from the head of Brahma? How did it grow so big and great? Surely, in past ages by the ability of its people and the conquest of its warriors; in other words, by Chinese imperialism. I am not talking of the present, more enlightened days of China, but of the old days. The Chinese State grew in that way, and came into Tibet.

Quite a different tone than he has insisted upon in the past. And then his realization, his lament:

> In the final analysis, the Chinese have valued India's friendship only to a very small extent.

Exactly the value that the Sardar had said they would place on our friendship.

Panditji's conclusion is as much a conclusion as a confession:

> Of course, it is fantastic to talk about war, etc. Nevertheless, the matter is serious enough. It is serious because I just do

> not know how the Chinese mind works. I have been surprised at the recent developments. I have great admiration for the Chinese mind, logical and reasonable and relatively calm. But sometimes I wonder if all these old qualities have not perhaps been partly overwhelmed.[13]

That last sentence—which betrays the intellectual's reluctance to give up the conclusions he has broadcast about character and the innate desire of the Chinese for friendship, conclusions he has deduced from his copious reading of history—may be overlooked for the time being. The Chinese will, and soon enough, rid him of those conclusions also.

Another two days, and it seems that the enormity of what Chou En-lai's letter implies as well as the very strong reaction in the country have both gone home. The words Panditji uses in his reply to the debate in the Lok Sabha on 12 September 1959 are much more explicit. Where he had been the advocate of the Chinese position the world over, he is now at pains to distance himself from it.

He says he has also been reading reports of Chou En-lai's speech at the Congress that is taking place in Peking at the time, as well as the other speeches, all of which have naturally been along the same lines, the line namely, 'expressing their great surprise to find Mr. Nehru defending British Imperialism... Prime Minister Nehru and the Indian Government treat the aggressive plot of British Imperialism against China in the last century as an accomplished fact. Does this accord with the Five Principles advocated by Mr. Nehru?'

'Now, what is happening in China today?,' Panditji asks. 'I do not wish to use strong words, but it is the pride and arrogance of might that is showing in their language, in their behaviour towards us and in many things that they have done.'

---

[13] *Rajya Sabha Debates*, 10 September 1959, cols. 3848–916.

There has been sharp criticism to the proposal that Panditji has mentioned to the Chinese, namely that disagreements about the border can be referred for mediation or arbitration. 'When I talked about mediation and conciliation—and I even used the word arbitration—I meant that minor alignments could always be talked about in a peaceful way,' Panditji explains. 'But the claim laid down in the Chinese maps, for the first time, is something bigger. This claim is taking definite shape in this last letter of Premier Chou En-lai and the speeches delivered at their Congress. At first, whenever the maps were referred to, they said they were old maps and they would revise them. It was a totally inadequate answer, but it was some kind of an answer—postponement of an answer, if you like. But what is now held out is something definite.'

'We do not know exactly where their line is,' Panditji tells the House, as the Chinese have never specified it, 'but they hold by it. Even a petty spot, even a yard of territory, is important if coercively and aggressively taken from us. It is not the yard of territory that counts but the coercion. It makes no difference to China or India whether a few yards of territory in the mountains are on this side or on that side. But it makes a great deal of difference if that is done in an insulting, aggressive, offensive, violent manner, by us or by them.'

He returns to the Chinese attempt to give their claims some verisimilitude by invoking history—in their very special, selective way. 'It is fantastic and absurd for them to base their demand on what happened in past centuries,' Panditji exclaims. 'If this argument is applied, I wonder how much of the great Chinese State would survive this argument. This extraordinary argument takes us back to past ages of history, upsetting everything. It really is the argument of a strong and aggressive power.'

Panditji is now characterizing the Chinese attitude and claims in words that the facts demand. But he is still not prepared to see the distance that the Chinese have already travelled to enforce their claims. Tibetan refugees, and others have been bringing reports that Chinese troops have spread out across Tibet and right up to our border in very large numbers. Panditji dismisses these reports:

> The impression seems to have grown that there are masses and masses of Chinese armies perched on the frontier, or pouring into the frontier. That is not a correct impression. Such a thing is not easy to do, and, if it is done, it will be met.

He ends on a note of conditional contrition:

> If I have erred in the past by delaying the placing of papers before the House, I shall not err again. This very reply from Premier Chou has come six months after my letter of March. But the situation is such that we have to keep the country and especially Parliament in full touch with the developments. This apparent change in the attitude of the Chinese Government has come out quite clearly with a demand which it is absolutely and wholly impossible for us to look at...[14]

[14] *Lok Sabha Debates*, 12 September 1959, cols. 8108–129.

11

'These are not excuses, but merely facts'

By now, Panditji's assurances are not enough for Parliament. There is great disquiet. They demand that the entire gamut of policies we have been sticking on to in regard to Tibet and China be reviewed. Panditji places a White Paper in Parliament. It contains the complete set of letters that have been exchanged between us and the Chinese since 1954.

He devotes a large part of his letter of 1 October 1959 to the chief ministers again to the events that have erupted along the frontier with Tibet and China, and to the policies that he has been pursuing. He writes of the White Paper that has been issued. He says it is likely that another one will be issued soon. The tension that has arisen is of great concern, he says. 'That does not mean that we should get alarmed in the present or fear any serious consequences,' he writes. Yet he is compelled to add, 'But the basic fact remains that India and China have fallen out and, even though relative peace may continue at the frontier, it is some kind of an armed peace, and the future appears to be one of continuing tension. It is this future that troubles me because it will involve both a mental and physical strain on our country, and it will somewhat come in the way of our basic policies.'

'Those policies, I believe, have been correct and I see no reason whatever why we should vary them,' he tells the chief ministers. One feature of his reasoning is important. Whenever anyone raises a question about the policies, he reduces the policies to just three general expressions, and makes out that the critic is demanding that these be jettisoned: the attempt to find peaceful solutions to problems, and thus avoid war; non-alignment; and peaceful coexistence. And then traduces the person. Panditji now has a new reason for not changing the policies: 'At any time, any change in policy would have been wrong; at the present time, when the world appears to be moving towards a new adjustment aiming at peaceful settlements and possibly far reaching disarmament, such a change in policy would be even more unfortunate and uncalled for. Therefore, I am convinced that we should hold to that policy.'

Sensing the reaction such reasoning is liable to evoke, Panditji writes, 'To some people, this may appear rather odd and not in conformity with the realities of the situation. That argument would mean that the policies we have pursued were temporary and opportunist and liable to change with changing situations.' He makes a distinction: 'Undoubtedly, no policy should be rigid and inflexible; it has to be varied from time to time to fit in with objective realities. But if these policies were based on some firm principle, as I believe they were, then there should be no question of our discarding that principle for what appears to be some momentary and opportunist gain.'

Surely, that is to make a caricature of the proposals that are being made for change of policy. Yet, this is almost a reflex with Panditji by now: anyone advocating some nimbleness in alliance systems, for instance, is at once denounced as one who wants to push India into one of the power blocs. The end of such reasoning will, of course, be that we do, in fact, become completely dependent on the Soviet Bloc.

And then there is the predictable conflation—those who are proposing changes are deep down propelled by fear. 'No principle and no policy can be pursued through weakness or fear. I have no fear of China, great and powerful as that country is. China will undoubtedly grow in physical might. Even so, there is no need for us to be afraid and indeed fear is never a good companion. But we shall have to be vigilant all the time and balance firmness with a continuation of our policy...'

The troubles and the face that China, in particular Chou En-lai, has shown do lead Panditji to read the great tides of history in a somewhat different way than he has been putting out till just four months earlier. He now sees a problem, a problem that is basic, that is grave, and that is liable to continue to plague us for long. 'Behind all this frontier trouble, there appears to me to be a basic problem of a strong and united Chinese State, expansive and pushing out in various directions and full of pride in its growing strength,' he writes. His reading of history now leads to a different conclusion: 'In Chinese history, this kind of thing has happened on several occasions. Communism as such is only an added element; the real reasons should be found to lie deeper in history and in national characteristics.' These two large states—India and China—have come face-to-face now. The Chinese population is increasing rapidly. The Chinese are homogeneous. All this will spell danger. We can face it, indeed some good may come of it... 'I have no doubt, however, that in the face of danger there will be much greater cohesion in India than we have at present. Perhaps, that may be one of the good effects of this new and unfortunate development.'

The familiar discourse follows: 'In any event, we have to be firm and vigilant and, at the same time, calm and restrained, and we must realize that real strength does not come from strong language, or even by the addition to our armed forces, but from the general development of our country, from industrialization in a big way and from unity. We come back, therefore, to the basic problem of India's growth and development through our Five Year Plans and the like...'

We have to be alert also to the strategic and, indeed, deep cultural consequences of what the Chinese are demanding.

'Minor controversies about the frontier might not be of importance,' Panditji points out. 'What we have to face, however, is something much deeper and more serious. This is a demand for considerable areas, more especially in the NEFA. All this means the Chinese want to come down on this side of the Himalayan barrier. This has two vitally important aspects: one that if a foreign Power comes down on this side of the Himalayas, our basic security is greatly endangered; the other that a sentiment which has been the life-blood of India through past ages, is shattered. That sentiment appertains to the Himalayas. As I said in Parliament, we are not going to make a gift of the Himalayas to anybody whatever the consequences.'[1]

A fortnight later, he again has to give reasons to the chief ministers for staying with the policies. The alternative is to plunge us into hatred and war, he says. To change will rob us of the reputation we have acquired across the world... In his letter to them of 16 October 1959, Panditji tells the chief ministers,

> It is not an easy matter to follow a policy which is firm and dignified and, at the same time, friendly. And yet that is the only reasonable and mature policy to adopt.

By implication, those advocating a review of our policies are pushing the country into unreasonableness, into immaturity, into undignified conduct. Worse,

> The other leads to a plunge into the bitter ocean of hatred and cold war. For the last dozen years or more, we have kept our heads up and avoided being submerged by waves of this cold war, except sometimes to a little extent in regard to Pakistan. Because of this, we have built up some kind of a reputation the world over and we are respected even by those who do not agree with us.

---

[1] *Letters,* Volume 5, Letter of 1 October 1959, in particular pp. 285–88.

'Why did I get an unusually warm reception from the peoples of Afghanistan and Iran recently?' he asks. 'It was because of this reputation built up gradually year after year. And yet it is easy to fall off from this height in a gust of anger or emotion.' Unfortunately, there are hotheads all round: 'But some people imagine that strength and courage are exhibited by strong and intemperate language and by brave gestures...' And not just that. They have definite objectives: 'In the international field, there appears to be an attempt to push us out of our policy of non-alignment and non-commitment; in the domestic field, an organized attempt by certain conservative and reactionary groups to oppose some of our basic policies. This is an unfortunate development...'

But what about the UN? Why are we standing in the way of the UN even discussing the issue? Ireland and Malaya have tabled a proposal that the item be put on the UN General Assembly's agenda. On 13 October, 1959, we abstain from voting on it. Panditji says that it was decided long ago that we should not encourage a reference to the issue in the United Nations; that he had told the Dalai Lama about this; that most of the other nations have also been of the view that it would not be desirable to bring the matter up in the UN. 'However, the exigencies of the cold war led some later to support this proposal,' he says—could it not be that these countries realized at long last that they had been wrong to fall in line with India's Micawberish attitude? But 'the exigencies of the cold war' it is. And so, our representatives there decided to abstain...

Not only are those who have introduced the matter for discussion in the UN propelled by an ulterior motive—'the exigencies of the cold war'—those who have opposed our abstention from the debate are also propelled by a collateral, hidden agenda: 'Some excitement has recently been caused, mostly in newspapers, by the debate on Tibet in the United Nations... In the event, it was decided by them [our representatives on the spot] not to participate which I think was quite correct. This has, however, led to much criticism in the press. If one examines that criticism, it will be seen that it is based not on this particular development but is rather against our basic policy of non-alignment...'

In any event, 'to talk grandiloquently in such matters without any regard for consequences is hardly the proper approach. It is the approach of passion and unreason and, if pursued, this would lead us to the pit of cold war.'

Correspondingly, it should have been obvious to this keen student of history, to go on repeating grandiloquent vacuities, to clutch on to fixed postures when circumstances are changing will lead us to the pit of defeat.

The main task is to strengthen our position on the border, and on that '*we have taken adequate measures for this protection.* No one can guarantee the absolute protection of a border 2500 miles in length. *But for all practical purposes, it is adequately protected, and any attempt at aggression will be difficult to maintain. I have no apprehension on that score, and I do not think there is going to be a major conflict there.*'[2]

By now, the assault on Longju in NEFA has been followed by another serious incident in Ladakh. The previous year, there had been no Chinese troops or structures near our border in north-east Ladakh. This year, patrol parties notice structures as well as troops. A party that has gone on patrol, does not return. A second party is sent. It comes upon entrenched Chinese soldiers. The latter attack them with mortars and the rest. Some of our men are killed, others are disabled. Several are captured by the far more numerous Chinese.

Though a fortnight hasn't elapsed since his last letter, Panditji writes to the chief ministers again on 26 October 1959. He describes this new escalation. He tells the chief ministers that in August it was decided to make the army responsible for the protection of the entire border.

---

[2] *Letters,* Volume 5, Letter of 16 October 1959, in particular, pp. 294–97.

He describes Ladakh: 'It is treeless and even without grass. It is on the other side of the main Himalayan range and hardly has any rain or snow. The outlook is thus dreary in the extreme with bare rocks, though this has a very definite beauty of its own...'

Panditji describes the place where the clashes have occurred: 'The place where the conflict with the Chinese troops took place is a three weeks' hard journey by mountain tracks from Leh. We have an airfield at Chushul which can be used when conditions are favorable, but Chushul itself is about sixty miles or more from the place of this recent incident. On the other side, that is, the Chinese side, the terrain is somewhat better because we have crossed the principal mountains and the plateau of Tibet and the highlands of the Chinese Turkestan lie there. Even that is by no means easy going, but it is far easier and more accessible from the other side.'

He repeats what he has been saying about the reasons on account of which the Chinese have had an easier time building up their infrastructure: 'We hear of Chinese roads being built in Tibet and near and across our border. These roads are of the simplest type. All that is done there is to level them to some extent and to place some kind of roads marks. The ground is so hard because of the cold that it is almost like stone or cement. It requires little treatment. These roads are, of course, hard going, but they can be used by trucks or lorries.' Surely, the inference can only be that, precisely because the terrain is easier for them, we should have been striving harder.

He acknowledges that there is a heavy concentration of Chinese troops in the region. But he ascribes it to a special circumstance—the rebellion that has taken place in Tibet—as if the fact that the concentration has been caused by a special factor makes it temporary, and therefore of less consequence for us. 'Before the recent Tibet rebellion which began in the spring of this year, the number of Chinese troops in Tibet was not very large and most of them were concentrated in Central and Eastern Tibet. Probably Western Tibet had a small number also. After the rebellion the Chinese poured large numbers of troops into Tibet and they spread them out all over in order to crush the rebellion. In this way their forces gradually reached our frontiers both south and west of Tibet. Apart from crushing the rebellion, the object was to cut off refugees from escaping and to prevent any contacts with elements across the border which, the Chinese thought, might be aiding the rebels. Thus the Chinese troops came into direct touch with our frontier at NEFA. Fortunately we had established a number of check-posts there and it was not possible for the Chinese troops to advance any further without a conflict...'

That is why, apart from Longju, there has been no major conflict on the NEFA border, he says. In the Ladakh region, the area is uninhabited. The border is undefined on the ground. We have been establishing check-posts, but these have as yet been few... 'It has been a difficult and adventurous task to set up these check-posts during the past few years. In effect it meant high skill and great endurance for our men in addition to various types of dangers having to be faced.'

The last few months have certainly begun to make Panditji see that the Chinese are pursuing a definite policy: 'The policy of the Chinese Government appears to have been to creep forward with their forces and to occupy any of these empty areas where there was no opposition.' After suppressing the Tibet rebellion, they had their forces move into Ladakh, Panditji says. 'Presumably, they wanted to get possession of as big a part of this empty and more or less uninhabited area as they could without a conflict and to establish themselves firmly there. It was not difficult for them to do so as the terrain was more suitable for them and some of their principal military centers in Western Tibet were not far off.'

He immediately sees the problem an explanation of

this sort raises. 'It may be asked why we did not go there first. The question is a relevant one,' he acknowledges. But spreading so far away from our bases in central Ladakh, and then keeping the forces supplied would not have been easy. But he sees that his answer cannot settle the doubts that events have raised. So, he leaves the matter open: 'Whether it would have been desirable for us to lock up and isolate a good part of our Army in these distant areas is a matter on which opinions may differ,' he concludes.

'Anyhow, we have to face the position as it is,' Panditji observes. 'We have, in fact, to face a powerful country bent on spreading out to what they consider their old frontiers, and possibly beyond.' He is now reminded of another characteristic of China and its history: 'The Chinese have always, in their past history, had the notion that any territory which they had once occupied in the past necessarily belonged to them subsequently. If they were weak, then they could not enforce their claim, but they did not give it up. If they were strong then they tried to enforce that claim and seize territory with the firm conviction that they were in the right and they were only taking back what belonged to them. Most countries, I suppose, have a rather one-sided view of their rights and responsibilities. The Chinese certainly have that one-sided view in ample measure. That past view has now been perhaps confirmed by the present communist government there and a sense of growing strength has given them an additional measure of arrogance.' Shades of what the Sardar had warned him about almost a decade earlier would be the case—a decade that would have been enough time to prepare. But at that time, Panditji read only other features into Chinese history, he drew contrary inferences alone from the rise of communism in China. And don't forget to notice the frequency with which he uses the word 'communist' these days, the very adjective for which he reprimanded an officer—using such words, he had declared not long ago, 'prevents intelligent thought'.

'The Chinese would not willingly come into conflict with India,' he writes explaining the different tendencies in Chinese policy. 'But at the same time they are not likely to change their basic policies merely to please India or anyone else. Their thinking, in spite of or because of their Communism, has reverted to the old imperial days of China when they considered themselves the "Middle Kingdom", the centre of culture and enlightenment and the other nations on their fringes were to be treated in a superior and patronizing way, provided they recognized the broad fact of China's superiority.' That is why, he says now, while the present situation is difficult enough, 'what is of far greater concern to me is the future that is gradually unrolling itself. I view this not with any fear but certainly with great concern.'

Panditji says this, but, in fact, he still is not prepared in his mind to face that situation. After all, facing a situation cannot mean just acknowledging it verbally. It means that the leader initiate the steps that the situation demands, howsoever contrary to his preferences they may be, and that he bear, and he inspire his people to bear the costs that the steps demand. Instead, Panditji is Hamletian: 'But I do not like the idea of continuing tension and potential conflict between India and China. This is not because I am enamoured of China, but because I am enamoured of India and of peace. The burden of constant friction on a long border with a powerful country will be great and even worse than that burden will be the spirit of hostility that this arouses and which leads us to think in wrong directions.' Who will respond to an uncertain trumpet?

'It is a fact, however, that our attempts at friendship with the Chinese Government have failed and there is unfortunately some actual and a great deal of potential conflict in the air,' Panditji acknowledges. His inference is that we must hold on all the more tenaciously to the policies he has pursued. These policies he always lists as 'non-alignment and peaceful coexistence'. But, surely, there were steps that could be taken within these parameters. As he always poses the question as an 'all-or-nothing' affair—'the choice is either non-alignment or joining a Power Bloc'; 'the choice is either peace or war, and thence, probably, world war'—he has little difficulty in rejecting all talk of alternatives. 'For us, in a moment of excitement or weakness, to join the ranks of the cold war protagonists and to seek military alliances would indeed be a tragic failure not only of our policy but of all that India has stood for.' In any case, no country will sacrifice its interests just to help us when we are in trouble. On the other hand, if a war between China and India did break out and we were the military allies of some bloc, 'Probably what would happen is that that war would develop into a world war and the vast destruction and even annihilation which that entails. That is a poor kind of help that we would get.' As the poet has said,

Kisi aane vaale tufaan ka rona ro kar
Nakhudaa ne mujhe saahil par dubonaa chaahaa...

And there are trends towards peace in the world, aren't there? The Soviets and the Americans are inching closer. True, the Chinese government 'is not terribly keen on the success of these trends.' But there is a rift between the Soviet Union and China... and, in any case, when even the major powers are working towards peace in the world, 'for us to take any action which upsets this work will be bad for us and for the world...'[3] Hence, we persevere with our policies. Public criticism mounts. The situation that has erupted is exactly the one that critics have been warning *will* erupt. They have been saying that his policies—the trust he has been placing in China's rulers, his reliance on pieces of paper like the Panchsheel—are making that denouement inevitable. Panditji has been scolding them into sullen silence. And now all their forebodings have come true.

---

[3] *Letters,* Volume 5, Letter of 26 October 1959, in particular pp. 304–13.

'These are not excuses, but merely facts'

On 4 November, 1959, Panditji commences his letter to the chief ministers by drawing attention to those trends towards peace, disarmament, cooperation which he has listed in his last letter. The Chinese government remains an exception, he says, and, it is true that 'the bellicose attitude of China affects India in particular.' That is doubly unfortunate: 'Just when our broad policy is meeting with success in many parts of the world, it is a strange twist of destiny that we ourselves should have to face a situation which tends to push us in a contrary direction. In effect, whether we like it or not a cold war atmosphere is beginning to take shape as between India and China...'

The 1954 agreement with China in which we gave up our position and presence in Tibet for nothing has particularly been the subject of criticism. Panditji is incensed. That agreement, he tells the chief ministers, 'was not only a proper one, but logical and inevitable in the circumstances. It was a recognition of basic facts and it would have been absurd for us to ignore them. In any event, that would not have prevented the present crisis; it might well have accelerated it.'

As far as military preparations are concerned, he says, 'It is possible that we might have done something more but not much more, unless we concentrated on our border and on the increase of our defence forces to the detriment of our advance in the social and economic fields...' That would have forced us to cut back on industrialization and Five Year Plans—which are the real foundations of a country's strength in the long run. 'For us to place large forces on our thousands of miles of frontier would have meant a tremendous drain on us without any real advantage, and in fact at the cost of basic advance. At the end of the period, we would have been essentially weaker than ever.'

But at the least should we not have done more in regard

to roads and related infrastructure on the border? 'It is possible that we could have concentrated more on these roads,' Panditji concedes. 'I wish we had done so. But it must not be forgotten that what we had done was fairly considerable.'

'These are not excuses, but merely facts,' Panditji says. The Chinese have had an easier terrain to deal with. Their forces have been closer to their bases. To suppress the Tibetan rebellion they had already concentrated forces in Tibet—recall how he has come down not long ago on Apa Pant for his report about China concentrating forces in Tibet. 'It may be said that we should not have been so complacent when all this was taking place,' Panditji says. 'I do not think we were complacent at any time. But it is true that we did not expect a crisis to arise in this way and with such rapidity.'

Some persons, including 'a gallant ex-Commander-in-Chief of our Army' have begun saying that we should send our Army in large numbers to the border, and drive the Chinese out.[4] 'These proposals are singularly inane,' Panditji pronounces. The current military advisers are against such an approach, he says. 'In such maters military advice must normally prevail and we are accepting it and taking all the steps and precautions that they have recommended as being necessary and feasible. Those steps do not include rushing our armies all over and getting them in disadvantageous positions. That would only imperil them without our gaining any advantage. Wars are not fought in this adventurous way; nor are preparations for a possible conflict so made.'

Has anyone, least of all General Cariappa, suggested that we send our troops 'rushing all over'? As usual, Panditji

[4] The person in question is General, later Field Marshal K.M. Cariappa. Earlier he has had to disregard both the hesitations of Panditji as well as the devious aims of his superior British officer to save Kashmir from the marauders.

exaggerates a proposal he does not approve to the point of caricature and shoots it down.

'Even if any big army is situated at the frontier, it cannot wholly prevent incursions,' Panditji tells the chief ministers: does that hold for a better equipped, better trained, better acclimatized 'smaller than big' army also? Panditji does not wait to consider. He proceeds to reassure: 'But about one thing I should like to assure you, as I have been assured by our officers. This is that any attempt at a major invasion across frontiers, if this ever takes place, will be met by us adequately and with success. We are strong enough for that and we shall naturally increase our strength. If and when such an invasion takes place, the balance of advantage progressively tilts in our favour.'

'Progressively' means what? In time or space? Is it that the more time that elapses between now and that invasion, the better for us because the preparations that we are now making are at a faster pace than the ones China is making? Or that the farther the Chinese come into our territory, the easier it will be for us to handle them?

As for the future, Panditji sticks to formulating the alternatives in the same terms—non-alignment or joining a military bloc—and coming to the same conclusion: we adhere to non-alignment. He has a new reason for doing so: 'As I have said above, this policy has been remarkably successful. In a sense, though only partly, it might be said that it has isolated China.'[5]

Panditji writes to Chou En-lai on 7 November 1959: to minimize chances of further conflict along the Ladakh border, Indian forces should withdraw to the west of the line shown as the border by China; Chinese forces should withdraw to the east of the international border as indicated in successive notes of the Indian government...

---

[5] *Letters,* Volume 5, Letter of 4 November 1959, in particular pp. 323–30.

Seven weeks later, when Panditji writes to the chief ministers on 15 December 1959, he has to mention a telling fact: Chou En-lai has not sent any reply even after this period of over a month. Two days later, Chou sends a letter. He peremptorily rejects Panditji's proposals.

The Chinese have returned the soldiers they had captured in Ladakh. The soldiers testify to the cruel ways in which they were treated. Panditji remarks how 'grim and distressing' their accounts are. He still does not want to face the situation that the Chinese are forcing on the country. He writes,

> One may be driven into war, but no country likes the prospect, much less do we in India like it. Any such war will be disastrous both from our point of view as well as probably the Chinese. It may well be the beginning of a much wider conflict. All this would mean the end of the hopes that we have been nourishing about our own progress as well as world peace.

True, no country likes to face war. But what if the other country is determined to put it down through a war?

'An entirely new situation has arisen,' Panditji writes, not only for us but also for other countries of Asia. The long border with China was a 'dead frontier'. 'Now it has become a live and vital frontier and in the best of circumstances, it will remain a frontier of dangerous potentialities.'

'This is no new development and we have been conscious of this possibility at least for the last seven or eight years,' Panditji says. We were alert to this possibility for *seven or eight years,* and yet we have not prepared ourselves adequately?

No, we did begin setting up check-posts: 'Indeed, it was because of this that we started taking steps some years ago to put up check-posts and improve communications. It is true that we did not expect the rapid development that has taken place on the Tibetan side and we may be criticized for lack of foresight. But any excessive concentration by us on frontier development and defences would have meant, to that extent a slowing down of basic development programmes in the whole of the country. Even from the point of view of defence, the Five Year Plans were of vital importance. I do not see how we could have sacrificed them and thus sacrificed also any increase in our basic strength for defence for the sake of temporary arrangements.'

Is it correct to brush away the steps that should have been taken along the border as mere 'temporary arrangements'? Moreover, while it is absolutely true that eventually the country's strength depends on development programmes, can the immediate problem be neglected on that count? Panditji will himself be compelled to shift the balance soon.

He does, of course, make a valid and important point: it is not just governments that have to do the job; the people also have to be prepared for sacrifices, and, even as the government is being asked to do this, that and the other, the people and political groups are continuing with business-as-usual. 'The China crisis has led to a great deal of excitement, enthusiasm and emotion in our people,' he writes. 'In spite of this enthusiasm and emotion, I have a feeling that most people do not quite realize the gravity and the needs of the situation. We still continue our quarrels and our lack of discipline. We talk about offering our lives for the defence of the country, but are not anxious to do a little hard work for it.'[6] In Parliament, groups are shouting about shortage of grains, of sugar. You want to fight, he berates them, and with full justification, and yet are not prepared to cut down a bit even on the amount of sugar that you will take... Another lesson that we have not learnt, our leaders have certainly not learnt till today. It isn't that we don't want freedom, I remember reading Gandhiji remark once. It is just that we are not prepared to sacrifice anything to get it, and would be

---

[6] *Letters,* Volume 5, Letter of 15 December 1959, in particular pp. 335–39.

happier still if we could make some money while getting it. But to get back to Panditji's letters.

Relations continue to deteriorate. Chou En-lai and Panditji meet in Delhi in April 1960. They decide that officials of both sides should jointly examine documents each has for substantiating its claims.

Panditji remains busy with a host of issues at home and abroad. At his initiative, India has been active in promoting the Disarmament Conference in Geneva. The conference does not make the progress that was expected. President Nasser and Panditji point to the consequences that would follow were the Conference to fail. The Chinese government, Panditji reports to the chief ministers, 'have not only expressed their pleasure at the break-up, but have tried to run down India. Their attempt has been to break up the friendly relations that exist between India and the Soviet Union as this comes in the way of their own policies...'[7]

[7] *Letters*, Volume 5, Letter of 8 June 1960, in particular pp. 370–71.

12

The avalanche

In June and again in October, Chinese troops intrude—into NEFA and then into Sikkim. Panditji is compelled to address the situation that is unfolding. It is impossible not to see what the Chinese are driving towards—go on pushing India till it agrees to settle the issue at hand on their terms. Alas, Panditji still is hesitant to mobilize the country with the unambiguous call. He is still pointing to the costs that would befall as a result of exacerbation. In his letter of 23 October 1960, he gives a detailed account of troubles and tensions in different parts of the world, and then explains, 'I am writing all this to you so that you may have a full realization of the world today. There is danger in this cold war between the communist countries and the Western nations, there is danger in the basic attitude and the circumstances surrounding the People's Republic of China, there is danger in some accident or untoward happening letting loose war upon the world, there is danger in the situation in Germany and Berlin, there is danger in Indo-China and even in little Cuba. And then there is Africa, with its dynamism bursting out, often uncontrolled...'[1] Why should people gird up their loins if doing so is only going to push the world even faster over the brink?

Every passing month is full of problems, achievements,

[1] *Letters,* Volume 5, Letter of 23 October 1960, in particular pp. 413–16.

prospects, disappointments... Kashmir, Goa, debates in the UN...

China's language becomes increasingly bellicose with every passing month. As the editor of Panditji's letters to the chief ministers notes, in May 1962, China warns India that it 'will not stand idly by' in regard to Longju. Two weeks later, it accuses India of following a policy of 'out-and-out Great Power chauvinism'. Within another three weeks it is accusing India of 'increasingly frequent violations' of its air space. The government turns back these 'baseless allegations' and affirms that it is China which has wrongfully occupied Indian territory.[2]

In the letter of 10 July 1962, Panditji reiterates that, even as we prepare to meet aggression, we shall adhere to our policy of exploring every chance for a peaceful settlement of disputes—with China as much as with Pakistan. He notes that, seeing that 'we are strengthening our position and weakening theirs,' of late the Chinese government has become more aggressive in the statements that it is sending us. 'I do not know what this signifies and we have to be wide awake and careful.' 'But I would repeat that, apart from any high morality, it is the strictest good sense for us not to fall into the trap of cold war in regard to Pakistan and China,' Panditji tells the chief ministers. 'Even if [their] governments are, we must not think that the people are our enemies.' Gratuitous counsel, I would think, when 'the people' have no say in what the governments will decide.[3]

On 22 August 1962, the Rajya Sabha again discusses Chinese moves on the border and their increasingly vituperative statements. Panditji's reply covers facts which are by now familiar. He recalls how the Ladakh region had been under the maharaja of Kashmir; how it had been a peaceful region. There had been no occasion to extend the machinery

[2] *Letters*, Volume 5, note to Letter of 10 July 1962, at p. 508.

[3] *Letters*, Volume 5, Letter of 10 July 1962, in particular pp. 508–11.

for day-to-day administration up to the border. He describes the rights and privileges that even the maharaja's rule had in the heart of Tibet: 'In fact, there were four or five villages in the heart of Tibet, far from the Ladakh border, which were the *zamindari* of Kashmir,' Panditji recalls, 'and every second or third year the Kashmir Government sent a little mission to these villages to collect the revenue, Rs. 100 or Rs. 200, in order to assert its *zamindari* right. The process was peaceful. No question arose of having any protective apparatus on that border in the Maharaja's time.'

Panditji tells the House that he had himself brought the fact of the build-up of Chinese forces to the attention of Chou En-lai, and that too on the basis of what he had himself seen when he had visited Chushul. He describes the two occasions on which he has visited that remote region, and the airfield we have there:

> About six or seven years ago I went to that airfield. Therefore, I told Mr. Chou En-lai that I could speak from my own evidence, apart from others' evidence; that I went to the airfield and his people were not anywhere near the place; that I went a second time and I saw his people on a hill-top nearby, and they had come since. He had no particular answer.

'The main thing is that quite apart from any claims based on history, the Chinese were not there and they are there now.'[4]

As the editor of the *Letters* notes, on 27 August 1962, the Chinese government declared, 'the Indian Government's attempt to realize its ambitious territorial claims by force and to coerce China into submission is bound to fail.' If India persists in such activities, the statement said, 'the Chinese side will have to resort to self-defence, and the Indian side must bear responsibility for all the consequences arising

---

[4] *Rajya Sabha Debates*, 22 August 1962, cols. 2876–82, cols. 2981–3002.

therefrom.' On 28 August it went one better: it declared that India was accusing China of occupying its territory only to cover up its own aggressive activities! 'This clumsy tactics has long been seen through and will not work at all.'[5]

Who could miss the pattern behind the increasingly false and fabricated allegations? It was patent that the Chinese government was building a case for an assault. Panditji is properly awakened to China's intent by these statements, as well as by the reports he is getting of their massing their troops across the border. He tries to look for some sign of hope, of some toehold for resolving the matter through discussions... 'But the situation continues to be serious and the notes we get from the Chinese Government become progressively more strident and abusive,' he records. 'What this indicates it is difficult to say. But it seems to me obvious that we have to be on the alert and guard our country. At the same time, we have to be prepared for a long term of tension and possibly petty conflicts. That is presuming that there is no major conflict.'[6]

Within three days of this letter being sent, Chinese troops cross the Thagla Pass in the north-east, seize a few square miles, and sit. 'This was a new development, and we had immediately to take steps to meet the situation that had arisen,' Panditji observes in his letter of 12 October 1962. The vast chasm in the preparations that they have made and the half steps that we have taken stares Panditji in the face. He writes, 'As elsewhere, the Chinese have an advantage of lines of communication. They have roads almost right up to the international frontier in Tibet, while our people have to go through difficult mountain terrain for long distances.' But whose fault is that? The question, after all, is not about

---

[5] *Letters,* Volume 5, Editor's note to Letter of 3 September 1962, at p. 523.

[6] *Letters,* Volume 5, Editor's note to Letter of 3 September 1962, at p. 523.

this single patch. Panditji himself is saying *'As elsewhere,* the Chinese have an advantage...'

'This incident and other facts brought to light that the Chinese had been strengthening their forces very considerably in this area,' Panditji says. That being the case, the inference can only be that either no information about this build-up has reached our government at all or that it has been studiously ignored.

Panditji sees the ominous future: 'This situation in the North East Frontier is definitely a dangerous one, and it may lead to major conflicts.' Till last September, the Chinese were not present across the McMahon Line, Panditji records. Their crossing the pass and occupying this patch of territory, therefore, is nothing but fresh aggression.[7]

'A powerful and unscrupulous opponent'

Panditji's next letter, the one he dictates on 21 October 1962 is a relatively brief one. And for good reason. On 16 October the Chinese launch a major attack at Dhola in NEFA. On 20 October they launch a massive assault across several fronts in the north-east as well as along the western frontier.

As is their custom, along with their assault, the Chinese have announced that the Indian forces are the ones that have launched an 'all-out attack' on Chinese positions, and the brave Chinese troops have beaten them back! The places that they have captured, they say they have 'recovered'. With these setbacks in everyone's mind, with the policy he has held on to in a shambles, Panditji can now only express bewilderment and regret: '...It is amazing to what lengths the Chinese are going in disseminating utterly false accounts... It has become a habit for the Chinese to blame others for what they propose to do... It is apparently their habit to

[7] *Letters,* Volume 5, Letter of 12 October 1962, in particular pp. 530–32.

consider every place that they have occupied by aggression as their territory...'[8]

The next day, 22 October 1962, Panditji addresses the country over All India Radio. He describes the assault. He describes the efforts that he has made to ensure that the matter is resolved through negotiations. 'But all our efforts have been in vain in so far as our own frontier is concerned, where a powerful and unscrupulous opponent, not caring for peace or peaceful methods, has continuously threatened us and even carried the threats into action. The time has, therefore, come for us to realize fully this menace which threatens the freedom of our country...'

'A powerful and unscrupulous opponent... this menace which threatens the freedom of our country'—the Chinese have compelled him to state the facts in plain words.

'I do not propose to give you the long history of continuous aggression by the Chinese during the last five years and how they have tried to justify it by speeches, arguments and the repeated assertion of untruths and a campaign of calumny and vituperation against our country,' he tells the people. 'Perhaps, there are not many instances in history where one country, that is India, has gone out of her way to be friendly and co-operative with the Chinese Government and people and to plead their cause in the councils of the world, and then for the Chinese Government to return evil for good and even go to the extent of committing aggression and invade our sacred land. No self-respecting country, and certainly not India with her love of freedom, can submit to this, whatever the consequences may be...'[9]

On 4 November 1962, with the invasion proceeding apace, Panditji is addressing the meeting of the National Development Council—this is always a dilemma for leaders.

---

[8] *Letters*, Volume 5, Letter of 21 October 1962, in particular pp. 534–39.

[9] *Jawaharlal Nehru's Speeches, September 1957–April 1963,* Volume 4, op. cit., pp. 226–30.

Engagements have been scheduled earlier. A thunderbolt descends. The argument always is against cancellation of those engagements, even though, in the new context, they appear foolish: we must give confidence to the people; if we start cancelling programmes, they will think we have panicked. In the event, the one thing from which Panditji can take heart is the way people have responded. 'The Chinese invasion, in its quantity and quality, came almost like a thunderbolt,' he tells the assembled ministers and chief ministers, 'and reactions in India have also come like a thunderbolt. The response of the people all over the country, of all classes, of all areas, has been truly magnificent and wonderful. Most of the problems and conflicts that filled our newspapers have become things of the past. That itself shows the stuff that our people are made of. It is one thing to get entangled in small matters, but another to rise above those matters, when a big crisis comes. While much has happened in the past to depress us, what has now happened has heartened me and, I am sure, heartened all of you.'[10]

Of course, the people rose as one. And, of course, it would have been worse if they had not. But even such a magnificent reaction can be of little immediate help on the frontier.

'An experience worth having'?

Four days later, on 8 November 1962, Panditji introduces a resolution in Parliament. It sets out the efforts that India has made for friendship with China; the efforts it has made to ensure that such disagreements as exist over the border are resolved through negotiations; and it binds the country and Parliament to a firm pledge:

---

[10] *Jawaharlal Nehru's Speeches, September 1957–April 1963,* Volume 4, op. cit., p. 153.

> With hope and faith, this House affirms the firm resolve of the Indian people to drive out the aggressor from the sacred soil of India, however long and hard the struggle may be.

Panditji's speech while introducing the resolution is a mixture: of indignation at having been betrayed; of explanations of why more was not done to safeguard the border; and flashes of his well-known temper at critics, who after all have been proven right.

'For five years we have been the victims of Chinese aggression across our frontiers in the north,' Panditji says. At first the aggression was 'furtive'. Today, 'we are facing a regular and massive invasion of our territory by very large forces.'

'...curiously the very champions of anti-Imperialism, that is, the Peoples' Government of China, are now following the course of aggression and imperialist expansion,' Panditji says. This 'massive invasion' has 'shocked us'. 'This menace to our freedom and integrity...' 'We are shocked at this cruel and crude invasion...' Panditji retraces the recent incidents... Thagla ridge, Dhola... On 13 September, they sent us 'a threatening reply...'

'Their alleged frontier is a very mobile one,' Panditji now says—in contrast to the efforts at fairness in 1959 when he put their claims at par with India's. 'It is wherever they have laid the frontier and in this matter too they have stated many contradictory things...' Panditji spells out what actually is the standard Chinese negotiating tactic: 'Repeatedly, in the course of talks... we were given to understand something not absolutely, not clearly; as has now been discovered, always their phrases had a double meaning attached to them which could be interpreted any way, to assure us something and later to deny that they assured us...'

Panditji recalls the long conversations he himself had with Chou En-lai about the McMahon Line. 'We had a long talk and immediately after the talk I put down in a note I prepared the contents of our talk so that I might not forget,' Panditji tells the House. 'Much later I sent an extract of my note of that talk to the Chinese Government and they denied the truth of it!'

'I was very much surprised and hurt because I was quite certain,' Panditji says. 'When we were talking it was not once I asked; I asked the same question two or three times and definitely the answer was given to me...' Panditji recounts what Chou En-lai had told him about the McMahon Line—how, though it was not fair to the Chinese position, the Chinese government had decided to accept it because it is a settled matter and because of the friendly relations that now exist between China and India...

The Chinese assertions in regard to the recent events in NEFA are of the same piece, Panditji tells the House. 'They keep saying India attacked them and their frontier guards... are merely defending themselves. I must confess that this complete perversion of facts and the attempt to make falsehood appear to be truth, and the truth to be falsehood has amazed me because nothing can be more utterly baseless than what they have been saying...'

'To say that we are committing all this aggression on Chinese territory is a kind of double talk which is very difficult for a man of my simple mind to understand,' Panditji exclaims in remorse as much as in self-justification.

The new situation is a dangerous one not only for India but for the rest of the world also... 'an expansionist, imperialist minded country deliberately invading into a new country... naked aggression...'

Panditji narrates the way the Chinese built up their forces on the other side of the border during the preceding months: '...Now for them it was a relatively easy matter because they have vast forces in Tibet'—recall how he has earlier cast doubt on reports about the magnitude of the build-up. 'I do not know how much they have. They used to have 11 divisions, and I am told they now have 13 or 14 divisions in

Tibet. Just imagine the very vast armies they are having in Tibet alone.'

The member from Karnal, Swami Rameshwaranand, interjects: 'At least now you would have got to realize the Chinese mind-set.'

Panditji: 'I think, if the hon. Member feels keenly about it, we will send him to the frontier! Perhaps the speeches may convince the Chinese...'

Panditji recalls the advantage of terrain that the Chinese have had; how their forces have been long acclimatized to the high altitude; how 'the whole of Tibet has been covered in the last few years by roads, and the roads there, in that extremely severe climate, mean simply leveling the ground, removing boulders, etc...' Panditji talks about the massive numbers that the Chinese have deployed against our forces, of the way our soldiers have been outnumbered 'six, seven and eight times.'

Members interrupt him. H.V. Kamath, the veteran parliamentarian, intervenes, and remarks caustically, 'We do not want to interrupt; you may go on replying in your own way.'

'I say most of the talk is based on ignorance of facts,' Panditji shoots back. Some of it is true—for instance, it is true that we were not prepared for two or three divisions of Chinese forces descending on the forces we had there...

'I want to know what were *you* doing,' Swami Rameshwaranand butts in.

Interruptions. General commotion.

'I only want to know what he was doing,' Rameshwaranand insists. 'When they were invading us, what was he doing?'

Panditji: 'Swamiji, I am afraid has not acquired...'

A member intervenes, in Hindi: 'The trouble is that Swamiji does not understand the language. You explain to him.'

'That is exactly what I was saying,' Panditji resumes, this time in Hindi, 'that Swamiji does not understand anything.'

Panditji turns to the criticism that has been levelled, namely that our forces were not well armed. Interruptions follow interruptions.

'It is really extraordinary that many persons here who know nothing about arms talk about arms,' Panditji says in exasperation. Interruptions...

Panditji mollifies a bit: 'I do not wish to go into details. I merely wanted to indicate that the criticisms that are made, partly justified, are largely not justified.' He explains the approach to acquiring weapons that has guided the government—how we must build capacity for producing them at home rather than buying them abroad. Moreover, if we had tried to get them from abroad, 'we will have to spend enormous sums of money. Our whole planning, etc. will have gone... It is not a question of a few crores, but thousands of crores and it would have smashed our economy...' He explains what has been done to commence scientific research in this area...

'Anyhow,' he says, 'if there were mistakes committed or delays committed, it is not for me to go into that now. It is not a good thing for us to apportion blame and say that such and such officer or such and such Minister, etc. is to blame. We are all to blame in a sense.'

The members will have none of this. He is interrupted...[11]

The debate goes on in the subsequent days. A hundred and sixty five members speak.

Panditji responds on 14 November. It is a joyless birthday for him. Panditji speaks at great length—explanations follow explanations, all shattered by the traumatic events of the preceding weeks.

He introduced a long resolution, he says, and listening to the speeches, it is evident, he says, that the Resolution is welcome to the House and will be accepted... 'I have almost felt,' he says, 'that it would have been suitable to add

---

[11] *Lok Sabha Debates*, 8 November 1962, cols. 106–26.

a small paragraph to the Resolution thanking the Chinese government for taking this action against us which has suddenly lifted the veil from the face of India...'

He describes the way the people have reacted, and, in putting up a front as brave as possible, he goes overboard. Panditji says, 'This has been an experience worth having for all of us and it has been our high privilege to share in that emotion and experience...'

'Worth having?' The response cannot be separated from the stinging defeat that has ignited it, and what is going to live in the collective memory of the country is not the response but the defeat.

'We may... have failed here and there,' Panditji says. 'We might not have been quite prepared to meet this invasion. Our mentality may be built towards peace.' And that has been the basic reason. In making some of the criticisms that they have made about our unpreparedness, Panditji says, 'Members have done injustice, not to any Minister or others but to our Armed Forces as a whole in making various charges...' The basic point has been that 'our whole mentality has been governed by an approach of peace. That does not mean that we did not think of war or of defending our country. That, of course, we always had in mind. But there is such a thing as being conditioned in a certain way and, I am afraid, even now we are conditioned somewhat in that way.'

Assume for a minute that this is true: the lesson clearly is that if a country is to avoid traumas like the defeat of 1962, its people and leaders better purge their minds of such conditioning.

Panditji takes off on a word. A member, Frank Anthony, has said during his speech that India needs to brutalize itself, that Nehru must be brutalized. 'I hope that our nation, much less my humble self, will never be brutalized because that is a strange idea that one can only be strong by being brutal...' A disquisition follows on our civilizational values, on how Gandhiji was the essence of humility and peace and yet strong...

Then on the distinction between the Chinese government and the Chinese people...

At last Panditji turns to preparedness. How this is not just a matter of arms and armed forces. The wars of today are total wars—they involve everyone, they require the mobilization and application of the energy and mind of the entire nation...

In his anxiety, he seems to shift to others the charge that could as well be laid at his door. Panditji says, 'Before the 20th of October, it was not realized by the people at large what dangers possibly might confront us. They thought of frontier incidents. Hon. Members in this House criticized us for not taking steps in Ladakh to drive out the Chinese, not realizing that it was not such an easy matter. Perhaps they now realize it a little more that these things are not such easy matters, that they require not only strength but strength properly utilized, properly directed, and enormous preparation and consideration of military factors...'

Hardly warranted. Panditji is the one who has consistently underestimated the dangers that were liable to confront us.

One reason for the setbacks has been geographical: the strictly military assessment was that we should seek to defend ourselves further back inside our territory rather than at the border itself... How it was difficult even for the army men to go by this assessment...

The massive numbers that the Chinese deployed. They 'had slightly better arms...' Entirely wrong to say that our men were ill-clad and poorly armed. They had four army blankets per soldier, but these had to be left behind as they occupied too much space when the forces were being sent up. Hence, they had to be airdropped. The difficulties in doing so in that terrain. Many of the packets fell at a distance from the troops and were lost... The forces were well booted and well clothed... Except for the small numbers that had to be sent in summer clothing at the last moment when we realized how huge the concentration of Chinese forces was...

They had good arms... Even in England the changeover to semi-automatic weapons has just taken place... And then the difficulty of deciding between weapons systems, and buying and producing them... The passages have a resonance today also. 'For about four years now, we have been considering and discussing this matter,' Panditji says. 'Various difficulties arose. Points of view were different.

> The easiest way is always to order something—ready-made article. But the easy way is not always the good way. Apart from the continuing difficulty we have to face, that is, lack of foreign exchange, etc., it is not the way to build the strength of a nation. If we get something today, we have to get ammunition for that all the time and are completely in the hands of some other country. And specially if we have to deal with private suppliers in other countries, the House knows that the arms racket is the worst racket of all; because you need something, they make you pay through the nose...

That the words sound so current shows how our decision making has remained in a rut. 'These arguments, specially in peace-time take a long period to determine. Of course, if we had this crisis before this, we would have functioned better. But it took about two or three years to determine what type to have'—he is talking about the type of rifle to have. 'Ultimately, we started the first processes of manufacture and we have just arrived at a stage when within about three weeks or four weeks—in fact, some prototypes have been prepared...'

What was true of rifles then is true of so many weapons systems today.

Do not judge these matters from the circumstances of today, Panditji says. Once a crisis is upon a country, we have to buy from wherever we can get the arms, and things can be decided swiftly. But in peacetime, in the normal course... By contrast the Chinese have been fighting all the time. From the very beginning they have concentrated on building their military strength...

So, this outlook of producing the weapons ourselves 'covered our whole approach to this question'. And for acquiring the capacity to produce weapons, we have to have industrialization... And for that we must make a success of the Five Year Plans... And for that education...

The misplaced criticism against our diplomacy. Other countries are not going to go only by what we tell them... UAR and Ghana have now given proposals that are close to ours... The embarrassment into which the Soviet Union has been put having to choose 'between a country with which they are friendly and a country which is their ally'...[12]

A long speech, a very long speech—of a great and much loved man struck down by events, now having to offer explanations about boots and blankets...

Indian forces are thrown back in sector after sector. Panditji is distraught: 'My heart goes out to the people of Assam,' he sighs—a sentence that the Assamese cite to this day as proof that Delhi does not care for them, that even Panditji was prepared to abandon them to the invaders. On 21 November, having mauled the ill-prepared, ill-equipped Indian forces, the Chinese declare a ceasefire, and announce that they will withdraw 20 kilometres. Our army has never suffered such defeat. The nation is shocked and humiliated.

At last, the realization: '*The word of the Chinese Government cannot be relied upon.*'

Two weeks later, on 10 December 1962, Panditji is addressing the Lok Sabha. 'Any person who studies the painful history of the last few years, more particularly of the recent months,' he says, 'will come to the conclusion that Chinese interpretation of various lines changes with circumstances

---

[12] *Lok Sabba Debates*, 14 November 1962, cols. 1644–71.

and that they accept the line which is more advantageous to them. Sometimes they accept part of a line and not the rest of it which is disadvantageous to them...'

At last he is explicit about the approach of the Chinese, the very ones in whose word, in spite of warnings after warnings, in spite of evidence upon evidence, he has continued to place trust. Panditji tells the House,

> There has been an amazing cynicism and duplicity on the Chinese side. They come to a place where they have never been at any time in history. And they preach against Imperialism and act themselves in the old imperialist and expansionist way. Altogether their policy seems to be one of unabashed chauvinism. It is curious that acting in 'self-defence' they have occupied another 20,000 square miles of Indian territory. The whole thing is manifestly and outrageously improper and wrong, and involves utter misuse of words. It is a little difficult to deal with persons who indulge in double talk. I regret to say that I have been forced to the conclusion that the word of the Chinese Government cannot be relied upon... The imperialist and expansionist challenge of China is not only a challenge to us but to the world, as it is a flagrant violation of international law and practice...[13]

With the defeat haunting the country, Panditji has to lift the morale of a shattered people. In his letter of 22 December 1962 to the chief ministers, Panditji tries to put a brave construction on the humiliating defeat. 'This sudden and callous invasion of India by the Chinese, returning evil for good, would benefit our country,' he writes in words that ring hollow. 'More and more I have felt so, and therefore I have no feeling of depression; rather I have been feeling a sense of joy and satisfaction that we have to face this crisis as a united people and with good heart. I feel confident that we shall

[13] *Lok Sabha Debates,* 10 December 1962, cols. 5083–94, cols. 5195–22.

emerge out of it stronger in every way and chastened by what we have experienced and will experience.'

'The well-known 303 rifle'

He is driven to fight off the charges that are on everyone's lips. 'As for arms, our Army had the well-known 303 rifle which is still used by most countries and is a good rifle,' he writes in a pathetic passage. 'Even in Great Britain, till the present year, the changeover to automatic rifles had not been completed...' He attributes the defeats primarily to the advantage of terrain that the Chinese forces have had, and to the fact that Chinese forces were well acclimatized while our forces had to be rushed 'rather hurriedly' from the plains to great heights. 'It may be said that we ought to have thought of this and placed our forces at that high altitude long before,' he acknowledges, only to offer explanations that no one believes any longer. 'Even that was not very feasible because that would have meant supplying them with everything a large Army wanted by Air dropping. The only course was to build up good roads right up to the frontier. This was undertaken two years or more ago and many roads have been built. But the process was not completed. The terrain is difficult and road building requires high engineering skill. It takes time...' That only means that we should have started the work earlier, that we should have poured more men and material into it.

The whole country is incensed at the role that the defence minister, his close comrade Krishna Menon has played, and at that of the officers Menon has catapulted up in command. Panditji enters a defence on their behalf: 'The faults, such as occurred, were of the local Commanders of Brigades and the like who had to decide on the spur of the moment what they should do when they were being overwhelmed by large numbers of the enemy. The Chief of the Army Staff and the Army Commander who have resigned could hardly be said to be directly responsible. They were competent and brave men and it is very unfair to them to accuse them for something that was due to a large number of circumstances, many of them outside their control.'[14]

A postscript is in order about 'the well-known 303 rifle' and boots: the Indian Army was outgunned by the LTTE in 1987; and it did not have the requisite clothes and boots in Kargil in 1999.

[14] *Letters,* Volume 5, Letter of 22 December 1962, pp. 540–58.

13

A roundabout thesis

That guilt, remorse, defeat are weighing upon him is evident: this letter, the one he sends in the third week of December 1962, is one of the longest he will dictate. Apart from defending senior officers and the like, Panditji puts forward an explanation for why the Chinese decided to invade India. He says that the analysis flows from what the vice-president of Yugoslavia, who is on a visit to India, and a prominent Arab leader have told him. It truly is a roundabout thesis.

First, there is intense hunger for peace the world over, Panditji writes. And everyone sees that the way to this peace is peaceful coexistence. The Soviet Union under Khrushchev has also come to this conclusion. China is stoutly opposed to this approach—it believes in both, in the inevitability of war, and in the thesis that the war, including nuclear war, will accelerate the cause of worldwide revolution. As countries have begun to strive to avert nuclear war, China has seen that the war and violence through which it aims to bring about revolutionary changes are getting less likely. Hence, 'a sense of frustration has filled her.'

Therefore, China wants to ensure complete polarization of countries. For this purpose, it wants other communist countries to not follow the Khrushchev line of peaceful coexistence, it wants them to stick to the path of revolution through polarization. Simultaneously, it wants the non-aligned countries to choose—either to join the Western camp or the communist bloc. That will ensure the failure of the Khrushchev line... In a typical passage, Panditji writes, 'China wanted to show that Soviet policy was wrong. If this could be demonstrated then the Communist countries and those that followed them would veer round to the Chinese point of view and hegemony of that block would be created. At the same time, the Asian and African countries would have to choose one way or the other. Many of them would be frightened of China. In this state of affairs, China would get much more help from the Soviet and allied countries and her industrialization would proceed more rapidly. If war comes, well and good. If it does not come, the strength of the Communist and allied block would grow and there would be interdependence of Soviet Union and China.'

India is the chief obstacle to this vision being realized: it is in the forefront of advocating peaceful coexistence and non-alignment. The Soviet Union too has come to look upon it favourably. 'If India could be humiliated and defeated and perhaps even driven into the other camp of the Western Powers, that would be the end of non-alignment for other countries also, and Russia's policy would have been broken down. The cold war would be at its fiercest and Russia would be compelled then to help China to a much greater degree and to withdraw help from the nations that did not side with it completely in the cold war.' Hence, India must be humiliated.

There is a second set of factors also. China is having a series of internal problems. It is frustrated at its slow rate of industrialization. To accelerate this pace, it needs Soviet assistance. But this assistance will come forth only if the world is polarized, and tensions are intensified. Then, the Soviet Union will have to stop aiding these in-between countries, and direct its aid to China, and China's industrialization will proceed apace.

'I think there is a great deal of truth in what the Yugoslav Vice-President and the Arab leader said to me,' Panditji observes. 'This analysis of the situation is partly supported by the assessment made by the United Sates though, of course, there are some differences in approach,' Panditji proceeds. 'Even according to the latter, the attack on India, partly at least is a vicarious assault on Khrushchev's position. China was of course irritated at India not falling in line with her wishes in many ways. They were angry at our attitude towards Tibet, to our giving asylum to the Dalai Lama and others, to our strong attitude in regard to our frontier and generally to our opposing many of the contentions advanced by China... China's dispute with the Soviet Union was largely due to the Soviet Union's different concept of India.'

Hence, the assault on India...

Panditji sets out this roundabout thesis at great length.[1]

The pithy alternative

Chou En-lai, in whom Panditji has placed so much trust just a few years earlier, is to offer a more pithy explanation. In his conversation with Kissinger, he does link Khrushchev and Nehru—but in the sense that both failed. As for Panditji, Chou's explanation is that he had become too 'cocky' and China decided to put down his cockiness. Going over the assault eleven years later, Chou tells Kissinger, '...And it was exactly at that time that Khrushchev was about to collapse. And Nehru was getting very cocky. He wanted to put us on the spot, and we tried to keep down his cockiness. Khrushchev supported him. So, actually in history, both sides failed...'[2] In 1979, as he sits with the American president, Jimmy Carter, and informs him about

---

[1] *Letters,* Volume 5, Letter of 22 December 1962, pp. 540–58.

[2] Department of State, US Government, *Memorandum of Conversation,* 13 November 1973, at http://www.gwu.edu/~nsarchiv/nsa/publications/DOC_readers/Kissinger/docs/01-02.htm

the invasion they have decided to launch at Vietnam, Deng Xiaoping is equally pithy: they will launch a strike 'limited in scope and duration' at Vietnam to 'give them an appropriate limited lesson' as they had administered to India in 1962, Deng tells Carter...[3]

A contributing factor certainly must have been the contempt that Mao, Chou En-lai and others felt for India and Indians. This comes through again and again in conversation after conversation of the Chinese leaders.

- Chou and Kissinger agree on how India is the one that is causing the troubles in East Pakistan; on what China and US should together do to halt India in the tracks; they agree about not just what is 'the Indian tradition'—deceit, blaming others—but just as much about the Indian character—marked by ingratitude.[4] The contempt and coordination show through even more dramatically in the conversations that Kissinger later has with the permanent representative of China at the UN, Huang Hua, during which he asks Huang Hua to assure Chou En-lai that, should China take military action against India to divert it from pursuing its assault on Pakistan, the US will hold the Soviet Union at bay.[5]
- Nixon, Pompidou and Kissinger are exchanging views about the state of the world. Nixon summarizes the Chinese assessments: '...the attitude of the Chinese towards their neighbours can be summed up in this way. The Russians they hate and fear now. The Japanese

---

[3] For a full account of the meeting, Zbigniew Brzezinski, *Power and Principle, Memoirs of the National Security Adviser, 1977–1981,* Nicholson, London, 1983, pp. 409–11.

[4] Memoranda of Conversation on 10 July, 1971, at http://www.gwu.edu/nsarchiv/NSAEBB/NSABB 70/#11.

[5] William Burr (ed.), *The Kissinger Transcripts, The top-secret talks with Beijing and Moscow,* The New York Press, New York, 1998, pp. 48–57.

they fear later but do not hate. For the Indians they feel contempt but they are there and backed by the U.S.S.R.'[6]

- Indian philosophy, Mao tells Kissinger, is 'just a bunch of empty words'.[7]
- 'India did not win independence,' Mao tells Kissinger, 'If it does not attach itself to Britain, it attaches itself to the Soviet Union. And more than one half of their economy depends on you...'[8]
- In his important study, Garver reproduces a poem of Mao in which India is represented as a helpless cow with a bear—the Soviet Union—astride it. Garver cites the 'Maoist exposition' of the poem which explains the reference to India as follows: 'Chairman Mao's use of the cow as a metaphor for India could not be more appropriate. It is no better than a cow... it is only food or for people to ride and for pulling carts; it has no particular talents. The cow would starve to death if its master did not give it grass to eat... Even though this cow may have great ambitions, they are futile.'[9]

And so on. In a word, the 1962 invasion can as well be explained by simpler hypotheses than Panditji's roundabout thesis:

- The Chinese have subjugated Tibet.
- They have seen that the Indian leaders have offered no obstacle; indeed, that they have striven hard to not just reconcile their people to it, they have made the invasion

[6] Ibid., p. 42.

[7] Ibid., p. 195.

[8] Ibid., pp. 195–96.

[9] John W. Garver, *Protracted Contest, Sino-Indian rivalry in the Twentieth Century,* University of Washington Press, Seattle, 2001, pp. 112–13.

out to have been natural, inevitable, in a sense justified—recall those passages about the Tibetan order having been feudal, and how India could not be a defender of feudalism.

- The Chinese have consolidated their position in Tibet and along the border.
- They have built roads across Indian territory in Ladakh; the Indian leaders have suppressed the information from their people and Parliament; when the information has burst out, they have strained to minimize its significance—'not a blade of grass grows there...'.
- They have set up some matchbox check-posts, they have begun building some roads; but these are half-measures: the check-posts have no military backing, the roads have just about begun.
- Yet, the leaders are 'cocky' and go about lecturing everyone.
- Why not seize the opportunity, and put India in its place?
- That will force it to reconcile itself to settling the border on Chinese terms.
- The defeat it will suffer, as well as the fact that it has had to accept the Chinese diktat on the fixation of the border will be a salutary signal to countries in the region about who is who.

As for the construction that the attack on India, 'partly at least, is a vicarious assault on Khrushchev's position,' that may be an incidental advantage that the Chinese saw in assaulting India—for Mao had just as much contempt for Khrushchev and his line as he did for Panditji and India. It is, however, also reported by now that, having launched his most venturesome move—that of placing nuclear missiles in Cuba—Khrushchev was eager to ensure that Mao would not lunge at him from the rear. Accordingly, he is reported to have offered to support China in the event it attacked India.[10] But we have got ahead of the story.

'A continuing menace'

Having set out the possible motives that propelled China to attack India, Panditji reverts to what is to be done. We must continue to persevere in non-alignment. The real strength of a country does not lie in arms it may receive from others but from its ability to produce them itself. Hence, Five Year Plans. And the general morale of the country... Hence...

The Colombo countries put forward proposals. India accepts them on the condition that China accepts them in totality. China at first accepts them 'in principle' and then discards them. In his letter of 2 February 1963, Panditji points out that it would be naive to think that the conflict is just about territory. He says that it arises from China's objective of dominance; that the conflict is going to last a long time, and that, therefore, we must strengthen ourselves comprehensively. He notes the increasing tensions between Russia and China, and remarks, 'Fortunately for us China is becoming increasingly isolated in the world...'

He repeats many of the desirables—agricultural and industrial growth, building up our own war manufactures, and everything else that goes to strengthen a nation... But he also sees now that we cannot focus only on the long run: 'At the same time, we have to think continually of the military effort which may be required from us at any time. We cannot wait till our long-term efforts bear fruit. Therefore we have also to speed up our military machine, both in regard to production in India and by obtaining such help from friendly countries as we can and as soon as we can. All this involves a great burden on our economy but there is no help for it and

---

[10] Jung Chang and Jon Halliday, *Mao, The untold story*, Jonathan Cape, London, pp. 486–87.

we have to shoulder that burden as any country has to do when it is faced with a crisis...'[11]

China goes on rejecting proposal after proposal. Panditji has abandoned the faith he reposed in it and its leaders. He says at last,

> We have lost faith in the *bona fides* of the Chinese Government. They have a strange way of twisting everything and even getting round what they have said previously. We have thus to face a continuing menace and we cannot afford to take any risks about that based on the assurances of the Chinese. We shall have inevitably to shoulder this burden for a considerable time. This is the price we have to pay for our freedom.[12]

He now writes in terms of 'the Chinese menace...'[13]

'The Chinese Government is surpassing its own high record in vituperation,' Panditji says. He is addressing the press on 15 June 1963. He is dealing with the latest concoction of the Chinese—that the Indian government is torturing the Chinese who are staying in India, that it is preventing Chinese from going back to China, and, simultaneously, that India is forcing Chinese to leave India for China! Panditji states what is actually happening—that the Chinese who have been residing in India are completely free to go or stay. 'The Chinese propaganda—the daily spate of falsehoods, vituperations—is extraordinary in the light of these facts,' he says.

Panditji points out that of late he has become the special target of the daily slander. 'Apart from India and the Indian Government, they are particularly displeased, if I may use a mild word, with me,' he tells the press. 'The Chinese have written long theses about Nehru's philosophy or whatever it

---

[11] *Letters,* Volume 5, Letter of 2 February 1963, in particular pp. 563–74.

[12] *Letters,* Volume 5, Letter of 14 April 1963, in particular pp. 583–87.

[13] *Letters,* Volume 5, Letter of 21 May 1963, for instance p. 592.

is, and carry on their propaganda which is very efficient and very widespread. In a way, it amazes me because of its lack of any semblance of truth. I suppose they think that India is an obstacle in their way and therefore they want to remove that obstacle or make it less of an obstacle.'

A pressman asks, 'In their way of what? Domination of Asia?'

Panditji hasn't got over his habit of first putting down a person before saying more or less the same thing. 'Do not talk of domination of the world or domination of Asia,' he answers. 'These are big terms. It is not an easy thing to dominate Asia, much less to dominate the world. I meant their attempt to increase their influence over other countries. Whatever their ultimate aim might be, these things, if pursued, would inevitably bring about a major conflict.'

By now he has a very different view of Chinese character and nature than the one he formed after his visit in 1954: 'The Chinese are a military-minded nation, always laying stress on military preparedness,' he says. 'The result is that they do not have to make such a fuss about the defence preparedness as we have to make. We function with a different outlook and on a different plane. Right from the beginning of the present regime there, the Chinese have concentrated on the military apparatus being stronger. It is really a continuation of their past civil wars. They are normally strong and they only make dispositions of troops here and there. Therefore, it is difficult to say that they are specially making military preparations for an attack. They are normally of that frame of mind and disposition.'[14]

That they are 'military-minded'; that they 'are normally strong' and 'only make dispositions of troops here and there'—are these reasons that make it 'difficult to say that

---

[14] *Jawaharlal Nehru's Speeches, Volume 5, March 1963–May 1964*, Publications Division, Delhi, 1968, pp. 161–66.

they are specially making military preparations for an attack'? Or are they reasons to be extra alert? How do the hammers that Panditji used to squash officers like S. Sinha, B.K. Kapur, Apa Pant, to say nothing of the lofty air by which he ignored and brushed aside what the Sardar, Rajaji, Acharya Kripalani, Shyama Prasad Mookherjee, Vajpayee, the socialist leaders like N.G. Goray and scores of others were saying; how do those hammers and that disdain look now? Indced, the Chinese have taught Panditji to speak the language of the very ones he has been shooing down as 'naive', as ones who have not read the books and chronicles that he has. 'The whole of Tibet is a major military concentration,' he says. When Apa Pant had tried to suggest that, Panditji had come down on him—what are his sources? he had demanded. 'Because they have built plenty of roads there, they can take their troops into Tibet, to any border, with considerable ease and fairly quickly. They need not keep their troops perched on the exact border...' Exactly: shouldn't that have been obvious before 20 October 1962? *Shouldn't that be obvious to the Government today?*

On 16 August 1963, Panditji makes another detailed statement in the Lok Sabha. He informs the House that Chou En-lai has sent no response to the proposals that India had sent four months earlier; that, in the meantime, it has continued to build posts all along the border; that it has inducted fresh troops into Tibet, as well as along our border; that it has built fresh roads and airfields, and storage dumps near our border...[15]

A fortnight later, on 2 September 1963, he makes a similar statement in the Rajya Sabha. In spite of the note we sent containing constructive proposals, in spite of the reminder in my letter..., no answer has come to the proposals we sent in April, even though they keep sending notes on other matters and even though they put out false propaganda every day...

---

[15] *Lok Sabha Debates,* 16 August 1963, cols. 678–96.

Panditji now repeats the thesis that we have encountered above in his letter of 22 December 1962 to the chief ministers: namely, that the attack on India is tied up with Sino-Soviet tensions, that it is part of the Chinese stratagem to defeat the Soviet line within the communist world. 'China does not want India to be non-aligned,' he tells the House. 'Our being non-aligned, and our talking about peaceful coexistence, according to them, goes against their policy completely. They believe in a country being with them or against them. They believe in no middle course, and that is one of the reasons why they have fallen out with the Soviet Union. They think that by creating conditions when we cease to be non-aligned they could produce an effect on Russia and would show that their policy is wrong. According to their thinking, there cannot be any peaceful coexistence or any real non-alignment with countries which are not with them. The Chinese policy dislikes the presence of any great country next to them, particularly a country which adheres to a different structure of government and economic policy...'[16]

But Panditji is just going through the motions now. Nobody cares for these theses. The plain fact is that the Chinese have had their eyes on our territory from the beginning; that they have strengthened their positions for an invasion in plain sight; that Panditji and his tight band of officers and associates have resolutely shut their eyes to what the Chinese have been doing; and the country is paying the price... The theses are no more than excuses...

Panditji's spirit is broken.

He must have seen how colossal a misjudgement he has inflicted on the country that he has loved and served.

He never recovers.

Haan, khabardar ke ik laghzish-e-paa se kabhi
Saari taarikh ki raftaar badal jaati hai

---

[16] *Rajya Sabha Debates,* 2 September 1963, cols. 2351–62.

14

The chasm

Sounds incredible. In just 1980, around the time Deng's reforms were taking off in China, on one measure—the Purchasing Power Parity valuation of country GDPs—India's GDP was *greater* than that of China: our GDP registered at US$ 286 billion, that of China at US$ 248 billion. When I inquire about the current figures, Chetan Ahya and Upasana Chachra of Morgan Stanley Research tell me that in 2012, on the same measure, China's GDP clocked at US$ 12.4 trillion, ours at US$ 4.7 trillion—their GDP is by now more than two-and-a-half times ours. Correspondingly, China's per capita income in 1980 was around US$ 251; ours around US$ 419. In 2012, theirs was US$ 9162, and ours US$ 3,830.

The Chinese produce almost *nine and a half times* crude steel and cement that we produce. They generate 4.9 *trillion* kwh of electricity. We generate 912 billion, in a good year. They spent close to US$ 616 billion on infrastructure in 2011. We spent US$ 155 billion. On roads, they spent US$ 209 billion. We spent less than US$15 billion—with a 'dynamic' minister having replaced an even more 'dynamic' minister.

The magnitudes in agriculture are little different. Their yield of wheat per hectare is fifty per cent higher than ours. Their per hectare yield of rice is almost *three times* ours. That of cotton is more than *two and a half times* ours.

The relative figures on social indicators are just as skewed.

In India, of 1,000 live births, 47 infants die; in China, 12. In India, by the time they reach 5 years of age, 61 out of every 1,000 children have died; in China, 14. One indicator of malnutrition is weight at birth. In China, around 3 per cent of infants have abnormally low weight at birth; in India, 28 per cent. While enrolment rates in pre-primary schooling are comparable, in China only 0.75 per cent of children drop out at the primary stage; in India, 29 per cent.

All this translates into well-being of the people.

It translates into legitimacy of the regime, and the system of governance.

And it translates into strength. As recently as 1990, their exports of goods and services were around US$ 57 billion; ours around US$ 20 billion. By 2012, their exports had shot up to US$ 2,239 billion; ours were US$ 440 million: one-fifth of theirs. Our foreign exchange reserves in 2012 were around US$ 296 billion. Theirs: US$ 3.3 *trillion.* They are the largest holders of US Government paper—they finance the deficits of the US government; they are the ones without whom the US government could scarcely have put through its stimulus programmes in the wake of the 2008–09 financial and economic meltdown. And every US Treasury Secretary knows this: you have just to look at the self-effacing and courteous demeanour of successive US Treasury Secretaries as they troop to Beijing. After a summit meeting of the EU, in October 2011, the same President Sarkozy who had put it out that France may abstain from participating in the Beijing Olympics, telephoned the Chinese President Hu Jintao to seek a massive bailout loan for the EU. Similarly, that in the contention for influence in Central Asia, China can deploy resources of an order that Russia just cannot do today, has compelled the latter, anxious as it is to check US advances in these five states, to accept being a sort of junior partner to China in the region. With every seventh worker of Taiwan working in Mainland China; with such a large proportion of Taiwanese firms having shifted their production facilities to the Mainland, will China have to deploy military means to integrate Taiwan into China? Nor should we forget our own case: look at our silence on what the Chinese are doing in Tibet—from the oppression of its people, to the erasure of the culture and religion of the country, to the militarization of the plateau? Similarly, what is the argument that is being put forth for inviting Chinese companies to invest in and build our infrastructure? 'They are the ones who have the money,' we are told.

What holds for countries holds a fortiori for mere companies. We saw earlier how swiftly Carrefour, Peugot-Citreon, Christian Dior made amends; how they bent backwards with explanations, apologies, cancellations at the mere prospect that they may lose access to the Chinese market. Sanjeev Sanyal gives an example of special relevance to us—the way our borders are portrayed in maps on Google websites. Maps meant for non-Chinese viewers show both Jammu and Kashmir and Arunachal as 'disputed territories'. 'It is especially telling in the case of Arunachal Pradesh,' Sanyal points out, 'because it has been under Indian control for a long time and virtually all countries have accepted it as part of India. Even China appeared to have let go of the issue till it raked it up in recent years.' But that is not all: 'What is worse, however, is that the *Chinese* version of Google Maps clearly shows both Arunachal and Aksai Chin as part of China [there is no dispute here].'[1]

Is 'economic development' just economic development?

'We estimate that since 2003, China has provided loan commitments upwards of US$ 75 billion to Latin American countries,' begins a recent paper on China's lending programme. 'China's loan commitments of US$ 37 billion

---

[1] Sanjeev Sanyal, 'China's Rise and Its Implications for India', Working Paper, Indian Council for International Affairs, 2010.

in 2010 were more than those of the World Bank, Inter-American Development Bank, and the United States Export-Import Bank combined for that year...'[2] When rulers of other finance-hungry countries hear such accounts, are they not going to be straining to catch China's eye? And remember, as in the case of Ecuador and Venezuela, China goes out of its way to provide loans to countries that are finding it difficult to get loans from international financial institutions and financial markets, and which are, therefore, liable to be especially grateful. When rulers in Africa or Latin America read that China is contemplating a fund of *half a trillion dollars* to shore up countries that the Chinese leaders choose to help along, are they going to heed its gestures—howsoever elliptical—in regard to the reorganization of the UN Security Council or our elaborate arguments?

It is because of the resources that it can deploy that China can at its own expense undertake to build naval ports in Myanmar, in Bangladesh, in Sri Lanka, in Pakistan. It is because of them that China can undertake to develop oil fields in Iran at a cost of US$ 100 billion over the next twenty-five years—with oil to be marketed entirely to China. It is because of them that it acquires exploration rights over a vast proportion of Kazakhstan, and it builds a 2,230-kilometre pipeline costing 7.3 billion dollars to transport 20 million tonnes of oil a year from Atyrau in that country to Xinjiang and further into China; a pipeline to transport Siberian oil from Taishet in Russia to Daqing in northern China at a cost of 12.3 billion dollars; a pipeline to transport 40 billion cubic meters of Central Asian gas every year from Turkmenistan to Xinjiang and beyond into China at a cost of 7.5 billion

---

[2] Kevin P Gallagher, Amos Irwin, Katherine Koleski, *The New Banks in Town: Chinese Finance in Latin America*, Inter-American Dialogue, March 2012. The Report goes on to suggest that Chinese loans may not go on doubling every year as they did between 2008 and 2010, that they may plateau *because of a lack of demand.*

dollars, a total length of over 1,880 kilometres; a pipeline to transport 12 million cubic meters of Myanmarese natural gas a year from Sittwe in the Bay of Bengal to Kunming in eastern China, and further on to Guichou and Guangxi, a total length of over 2,800 kilometres; and another 770-kilometre pipeline to ferry Middle East oil across Myanmar into China so as to skirt the choke-point of the Malacca Straits that it fears the US and its allies may feel tempted to throttle in case of hostilities—the two pipelines costing 2.7 billion dollars.

When I request Abhijit Raha of BNP Paribas if he could help me tabulate the oil and gas assets that China has acquired in other countries during the last decade, his colleagues, Gautam Mehta and Manishi Raychaudhuri, the head of research at BNP Paribas, send a list that is as unnerving as can be. It turns out that since 2009 alone, Chinese companies have spent US$ 92 billion on energy acquisitions and joint ventures—in 2012 alone, they spent US$ 35 billion on these.

The magnitudes involved are fraught with foreboding. The acquisitions span the world—Angola, Brazil, Sudan, the Gulf of Mexico, Canada, several states of the US itself: China has bought minority stakes and entered into joint ventures worth over 15 billion dollars in Colorado, Louisiana, Michigan, Ohio, Texas, Wyoming. In some instances, our companies—like ONGC Videsh—had attempted to get some of the same assets. They were repeatedly outbid: in Ecuador, China's Sinopec and CNPC beat ONGC and won access to 143 million tons of proven oil reserves; in Angola, we had almost got the deal to takeover Shell's operations for offshore exploration—China swooped it away by extending a seventeen-year, US$ 2 billion soft loan to the country. Nor is it held back by merely financial considerations: 'The $ 15.1 billion that CNOOC paid for Nexen, for example,' analysts at BNP Paribas tell me, 'represented a 60 per cent premium over Nexen's share price.'

'O, but China is our biggest trading partner,' we are told. 'Our trade has already crossed 75 billion dollars. In the next four-five years, it is likely to cross a hundred billion dollars.' First, there is the huge imbalance—our exports to China in FY 2012 were US$ 18 billion; our imports from China were US$ 57.5 billion. Of course, that is in good part due to the fact that we have not developed our industries as well as we could have. But a good part of the trade deficit in our case has its roots in some of the same factors that cause deficits in other countries' trade with China: namely, undervaluation of the Yuan, and non-tariff barriers in the Chinese market. Second, who can overlook the *pattern* of trade between the two countries? It is the exact same pattern that colonies had with the imperial powers: almost two-thirds of our exports to China consist of ores, cotton, salt, animal or vegetable oils and fats, etc.—products that embody little value addition. From the Chinese side, such products constitute but 5 to 7 per cent of their exports to India. We sell them ore; we buy processed goods from them. Isn't this the exact pattern of trade against which leaders from Dadabhai Naoroji onwards fought so hard? When we chant only the overall figure—'75 billion dollars going to 100 billion dollars'—aren't we brushing these two facts under the carpet, rather under that heap of ore?

In a word, it is self-deluding to look upon Chinese economic growth as merely *economic* growth. Economic strength gives China the wherewithal to acquire influence across countries. It gives it the wherewithal to bottle up scarce natural resources—and oil and gas are just an illustration of the resources that China is pre-empting. It gives China the capacity to shut the mouth of European and other governments when they so much as squeak a word of protest or censure—about its trading practices; about the proper valuation of the Yuan; to say nothing of what it is doing to the people and culture of Tibet or to the Uighurs.

Because of the resources it can deploy, and because of the

focus with which it pursues the objective it sets for itself, the modernization of Chinese forces is proceeding at a pace faster than the intelligence agencies of any country had earlier thought likely. Moreover, much of what is seen as 'economic development' has direct bearing on military strength. Indeed, what is done to build military prowess counts as economic development—plants to manufacture cruise and ballistic missiles; space vehicles including devices to disable enemy satellites; equipment and personnel for electronic warfare. China has made major strides in each of these, and all them count as 'economic development'. The train to Lhasa that traverses 16,000 feet can ferry not just tourists. It can ferry military personnel and materials also. The all-weather roads that have been built across Tibet right up to our borders; the underground naval base in Hainan Island off the coast of southwest China from which nuclear submarines operate; the high-speed rail-link that will connect China to Thailand, Malaysia, Singapore, Laos, Cambodia, and thereby knit them closer to China in every way—all these also register in the data on 'economic development'.

Of even greater significance for us than the chasm that has already formed is the fact that China is speeding far ahead of us on the factors that will determine how India and China will stack up in the coming years. A single example will do.

The future

Around 2006, Dr R.A. Mashelkar made a presentation to the prime minister and his associates about what India needed to do to keep pace in the new knowledge-world. Reading that presentation later led me to two studies and the indices of intellectual output they sketched—*Science and Engineering Indicators,* 2006;[3] and R.N. Kostoff, D. Johnson, C.A. Bowles

---

[3] *Science and Engineering Indicators,* Volumes I and II, National Science Board, Arlington, VA, 2006.

and S. Dodbele, *Assessment of India's Research Literature.*[4] These showed an alarming slippage by us—of effort, of attainments, of standards, and, consequently, in outcomes.

Consider one index: the number of papers that are being published by China and India in high-calibre journals—the journals that are accessed by *Science Citation Index* and *Social Science Citation Index*. The Kostoff study indicated that in 1980, papers from China were *one-fifteenth* of the papers produced from India. In 1995, they became about equal. By 2005, papers originating from China had become almost *three times* those from India. Between these dates, papers from India increased two and a half times; from China, ten times. Kostoff and his associates had pointed out that even by then, that is seven to eight years ago, the scientific output of South Korea had come to exceed that of India, and that of Taiwan and Brazil was catching up fast. Dr Mashelkar's colleagues Chitralekha Yadav and Aravind Chinchure send me recent figures from the Elsevier catchment: they show the gap to have widened. In 2010, they point out, China published over four times the papers that India did: India published 233,027 papers; China, 969,315.

Nor was this accidental. The US National Science Board's *Science and Engineering Indicators* showed the focused effort behind China's leap. In 1991, China was spending around US$ 12 billion on R&D. By 2003, this figure had gone up to US$ 85 billion. Our total R&D expenditure was around US$ 5 billion. Over this period, China's expenditure on R&D in academic institutions alone increased tenfold. 'China's R&D expenditures are rapidly approaching those of Japan, the second largest R&D performing nation,' the study noted. 'OECD data show China's investment at 17% of

---

[4] R.N. Kostoff, D. Johnson, C.A. Bowles and S. Dodbele, *Assessment of India's Research Literature*, Office of Naval Research and Northrop Grumman, Arlington, VA, 2006.

Japan's in 1991 but at 74% of Japan's in 2003.' The National Science Board's analysts observed, 'such a rapid advance on the leading R&D performing countries and regions would still be unprecedented in recent history'. By 2011, China's R&D spending overtook Japan's to become second only to that of the US—over *ten times* that of India. (China devoted US$174 billion to R&D; India, US$16.5 billion.) On current projections, China's R&D expenditure may well exceed that of the US in just about ten years—what with cuts in the latter's outlays because of economic difficulties of the last five years.

Nor was it just the case that papers by Chinese researchers were becoming such an important proportion of high-impact publications, their work was being translated into products. Focusing on five high-technology industries, *Science and Engineering Indicators* showed that by 2007 China had surpassed Japan as a producer of high-technology goods. And many of those high-technology industries were ones that add sinews to military prowess.

Mashelkar had pointed out to the prime minister and his colleagues that China had set itself the target of having one hundred world-class universities. Towards this end, China was giving each of its ten leading universities US$ 125 million—around Rs. 550 crore each—to upgrade their labs and other facilities. The two foremost universities—Beijing and Tsinghua—were *not* being given US$ 125 million. They were being given US$ 225 million each—around Rs. 1,200 crore each! In the second phase, China had decided to allocate similar grants to thirty more universities. We remained on course: of undermining the few islands of excellence that had survived—the IIMs and IITs.

Two recent reports from Thomson Reuters—one done for the Department of Science and Technology, and the other about research in Brazil, Russia, India, China and South Korea—contain data that further document that the gap has been widening.[5] The number of research personnel, counted as full-time equivalents, in 2000 was 695,000 in China, and 116,000 in India. By 2008, the comparable figures had diverged to 1,592,000 and 170,000. (In South Korea, a small country with a population one-twentieth of ours, the number of researchers, counted as full-time equivalents, is around 244,000.) Even in the mid-1990s, India was spending a larger proportion of its GDP on research than China: 0.64 per cent as against 0.57 per cent. By 2010, Gross Expenditure on Research and Development was 1.75 per cent of GDP of China; it was close to 0.78 per cent in India. (South Korea's figure was 3.74 per cent of GDP.)

Naturally, these differences registered in output. In the most recent five-year period, 2007–11, China accounted for 11 per cent of global research publications; India for 3.4 per cent; South Korea—remember, its population is one-twentieth of ours—for 3.1 per cent. In chemistry, every fifth paper was by the Chinese, only every sixteenth by Indians. In materials sciences, every fourth paper was by the Chinese, every sixteenth by Indians. In physics, every fifth or sixth paper was by the Chinese—our comparable figure was every twenty-fifth paper. In engineering, the comparable figures were every sixth paper and every twenty-fifth paper. It is only in three-four disciplines—for instance, agricultural sciences—that we were anywhere near or higher than China. Even in computer sciences, their share was almost two and a half times ours.

Nor can we comfort ourselves on the ground of quality of research. One measure, an admittedly rough surrogate for quality, that is frequently used is the Citation Impact

---

[5] Jonathan Adams, David Pendlebury and Bob Stembridge, *Building Bricks: Exploring the global research and innovation impact of Brazil, Russia, India, China and South Korea*, Thomson Reuters, February 2013. I am grateful to Thomson Reuters and the authors of the report for data underlying the charts given in the report.

of research publications—that is, the number of times that a paper is cited in subsequent publications. Obviously, this number varies between disciplines; it varies over time—a paper published this year will take some time in getting noticed by others. Normalizing for these two, and taking the world average as 1, the Citation Impact in 2011 for China registered at 0.78; for India at 0.69. (For South Korea at 0.8.) The same order of difference registered on another proxy indicator for quality of research. Taking the world average as 1, the proportion of highly cited papers as a per cent of the national output of research publications in 2011 turns up as 0.72 for China and 0.52 for India, with the figure for South Korea at 0.74.

The quantity and quality of research and development are being put to work more effectively in China, the data show. In 2011, China leaped ahead even of the United States in regard to both the number of patent filings and the number of patents granted to residents. That year, 526,412 filings were made in China for patents; in the US, 503,582. That year, Chinese residents secured 112,347 patents; those of the United States, 108,626—only Japan exceeded China with Japanese residents obtaining 197,594 patents.

The comparable figures for India are truly disheartening. In 2010, the last year for which the figure was available for India, filings for patents in China numbered 391,177; in India, 39,400—about *one-tenth.* By the next year, the Chinese figure, as we have just noticed, had gone up by a third, to 526,412.[6]

---

[6] As mentioned above, the figures given in the text are from Thomson Reuters, *Building Bricks, op. cit.* For a detailed sector-wise review of India's research effort and its effectiveness, and how it holds up vis-à-vis that of other countries, see Thomson Reuters, *A Bibliometric Study of India's Research Output and Collaboration, Phase 1,* Department of Science and Technology, Government of India, December 2011. The report shows that, while R&D work in India is improving, we are still far below world averages. And not just in quantity. 'Amongst the emerging research economies, the trend [in regard

Again, policies pursued with clarity and determination along a host of dimensions, and sustained over decades account for the lead that China has secured even on this one element—policies from which, and from the implementation of which we should learn. A single fact that bears on the general lessons that we need to internalize will illustrate the contrast—between how we do not move on a matter, and the single-mindedness with which China has moved. Martin Jacques reports:

> The Chinese government has been intensifying its efforts to persuade overseas Chinese to return home: 81 per cent of the members of the Chinese Academy of Sciences and 54 per cent of the Chinese Academy of Engineering are now returned overseas scholars. Overall, it is estimated that around 20 per cent of Chinese professionals working overseas have now returned, thus repeating a similar pattern that occurred with earlier Korean migration…[7]

Suppose for a moment that a government in India were to try and get distinguished Indian scholars working in American or European Universities to return, and to induct them into our universities. Representations, demonstrations, perhaps strikes, questions certainly about parity of scales, PILs, questions as

---

to the Citation Impact of research output] witnessed in the earlier period is still apparent, in that India is second lowest to Russia,' the report notes. Citation Impact of emerging economies is improving, the report records—but clearly the average hides substantial variations: with the world average taken as 1, Singapore's Citation Impact improved from 0.86 in 1994–98 to 1.23 in 2006–10; South Africa also crossed the world average threshold by the latter period, the Report states. We came out at 0.69: Thomson Reuters, *A Bibliometric Study of India's Research Output and Collaboration, Phase 1, op. cit.*, p. 39. That the Citation Impact of research work done in tiny Singapore should be so much higher than that of ours, that South Africa should have exceeded the world average while our figure registers at 69 per cent of the world average—distressing, to say the least.

[7] Martin Jacques, *When China Rules the World*, Penguin, London, 2012, p. 217.

to why facilities—like labs and the rest—are being created for these scholars 'just because they have been working abroad'... Indeed, I can recall from my own conversations what C.K. Prahlad, the sagacious and distinguished management guru, told me of the efforts that he had made over the years to get successive Indian prime ministers and ministers to avail of the services of academics and technical experts of Indian origin who had distinguished themselves in the US; how the academics and experts had pledged to do their best for the country, for next to no cost; how nothing had come of the promises that successive Indian officials had made to him; and how disheartened the attempts had left him...

China's problems

Sure, China has problems—exacerbating inequality between individuals, between households, between coastal regions and the inner provinces; corruption; nepotism; the cost that is being inflicted on the country's environment; the sharp deterioration of health and educational infrastructure in the rural areas; a climbing dependency ratio. And, because of opaqueness, there are uncertainties. Has China become a 'credit junkie'? Is non-bank lending going out of hand? Can the Local Government Funding Vehicles be reined in without causing several dominoes to tumble? Do the new 'financial instruments' not bear a disturbing resemblance to the ones that eventually pulled down Western financial institutions, and markets? To what extent has the pyramid of credit come to rest on mutual guarantees—companies providing 'guarantees' to each other so that all of them may go on borrowing, prudence being scorned in a rising market? One of the principal drivers of Chinese growth has been the real estate boom—but is it a bubble? Will the new leadership be able to reorient the economy from its dependence on exports and investment, or are the institutional—and personal—interests in this pattern of growth—the garnerings from 'trophy projects', for instance—so entrenched that the government will, in the end, continue to dispense the same medicine—'a combination of accelerated investment project approvals for local governments, a booming shadow banking system providing much of the financing, and unprecedented net injection of liquidity into the money market by the People's Bank of China and a revival of hot money flows...'? And so on. The debates are as sharp as they are inconclusive.[8]

So, there are problems. There are uncertainties. More than anything else, there is the factor to which we shall turn in a moment: the reaction that has set in—to the unprecedentedly swift rise of what is seen by more and more to be the new predatory power and, since 2008–09, to China's maladroit diplomacy.

All true, but

- The gap between China and India has already become so vast that unless catastrophes erupt, the problems that confront China today are not going to slow it down to such an extent that the gap between it and us will automatically get reduced;
- The fact that China has problems is not going to solve our problems; it is not going to boost our ability to get things done;

---

[8] For diametrically opposite assessments of recent developments in China's credit system, see Edward Chancellor and Mike Monnelly, *Feeding the Dragon: Why China's credit system looks vulnerable*, GMO [Granthan Mayo van Otterloo] White Paper, January 2013, and Jonathan Anderson, *How to Think About China, IV*, Emerging Advisors Group, 1 February 2013. On the need for structural reform, a representative paper, Chen Xingdong, Ken Peng and Jacqueline Rong, *Challenges, Reform and Potential*, BNP Paribas China Conference, 31 October-1 November 2012, Kunming. On the recent and prospective slowdown, the high cost of the 'traditional medicine' which was dispensed in 2011–12 and 'the unpleasant menu of policy choices' that faces the new leadership in mid-2013, Richard Iley, *China: Running Out of Road*, BNP Paribas, 27 May 2013.

- All that China's problems might do is to hold out a possibility—that should these problems really cause China to stumble, we would have a little more time than we have because of the way things are proceeding at present.

Nor should we underestimate the ability of a rival to take care of his problems: after all, one of the most impressive things about the Chinese leadership in the last thirty years has been the way it has reinvented the nature of the Chinese State.[9]

And then there is the question of questions. Assume for a moment that China runs into real problems—that its economy slows down, that Xinjiang and Tibet mount substantial insurrections, that civil society erupts. How will the Chinese rulers react? Would an external foray not be a tempting way to unify the majority—as the 1962 lunge at India helped divert people's gaze from the disastrous effects of the Great Leap?

---

[9] Analyses of BNP Paribas that I cited earlier provide a ready example from what we have discussed above—China's massive acquisitions of oil and gas assets. In 2005, China's state-owned company, CNOOC made a high-profile US$ 18.5 billion bid to buy up the US oil company, Unocal. The US Congress blocked the bid. The Chinese learnt the lesson, and reverted to the Deng-ian profile, so to say: 'Seek minority stakes, play a passive role, and keep Chinese personnel at arm's length from advanced US technology.' With these as their operating rules, they have, as we saw above, acquired stakes worth US$ 17 billion in US and Canadian oil and gas companies. Similar adjustments have been made in regard, for example, to dairy acquisitions in Australia. Chinese moves to buy up Australian dairy companies ignited a backlash—especially among the country's farmers. The Australian prime minister declared that she would 'set up a register of foreign landholdings'. The leader of the Opposition declared that 'if he got elected, he would consider lowering the threshold at which foreign investments in agriculture become eligible for scrutiny'. The Chinese have accordingly switched to off-take agreements, to joint-ventures, to leaving Australians to run the operations. C.f., http://blogs.wsj.com/dealjournalaustralia/2013/01/25/australia-backlash-makes-chinese-dairy-investors-wary/

Learn from the Chinese themselves! Recall the counsel of Sun Tzu we encountered earlier:[10] instead of placing our hopes in the possibility that China will be overwhelmed by problems, reflect on whether we are preparing ourselves for a situation when it would have surmounted them. Instead of drawing comfort from the fact that China too has problems, we should reflect on the strength that it has already acquired, and reflect on what this strength implies for us.

A good example for us to follow is Gandhiji's reaction to that scurrilous book, Katherine Mayo's *Mother India.* Gandhiji nailed her exaggerations, concoctions, falsehoods—and he did so by writing a critique of her book. But his advice was, 'No foreigner should read it; every Indian should.' For it was liable to mislead the foreigner, he said. As for Indians, it would prove useful—we would see through the eyes of a critical foreigner the wrongs we perpetrate, and which we are apt to ignore as they are so familiar.

The same thing goes for China's growth, and the strength which it has acquired through it. Leave it to China whether or not it should think about the problems that confront it. We should reflect on what that strength entails for us, and emulate the reasons of China's successes:

- Focus
- The deployment of all instruments for attaining the chosen objective
- Sustained pursuit of goals—for decades
- Execution
- Scale

Just as getting the best and brightest Chinese back to work in China doesn't just enable the country to have more papers published in international journals, or get more patents, getting them to work in and for China directly feeds into technological advances that, in turn, boosts

[10] See p. 131.

military might, so also China's economic growth does not just mean 'economic growth', it directly translates into military strength.

Military might

Report after report documents how China has been making determined, extremely well-coordinated and successful efforts to acquire advanced weapons' technology by all means: its own R&D joint ventures with foreign companies; 'persuading' foreign companies that have shifted their manufacturing and R&D operations to China to part with high technology; industrial espionage; outright theft. In doing so, it has, with great skill, harvested contributions from witting and unwitting foreign firms and individuals.[11]

Along with the growth and transformation of China's military strength has gone the transformation of China's military doctrine. Long ago, when 'People's War' dominated Chinese thinking, the main publicly expressed apprehension of the Chinese was that a superpower would invade the

---

[11] The Cox Committee's Report contained a detailed description of several systems that the Chinese secured, and of the clever means by which they did so: *U.S. National Security and Military/Commercial Concerns with the People's Republic of China,* US House of Representatives, Select Committee on National Security and Military/Commercial Concerns with the People's Republic of China, Washington DC, US Government Printing Office, 1999. The recent report of the US Defence Secretary to the US Congress contains a few more illustrative instances: Office of the Secretary of Defense, *Annual Report to Congress: Military and Security Developments involving the People's Republic of China,* Washington, DC, 2013, pp. 12–13. And the recent, informative study, William C. Hannas, James Mulvenon and Anna B. Puglisi, *Chinese Industrial Espionage: Technology acquisition and military modernization,* Asian Studies Series, Routledge, 2013, contains many more: this detailed study shows how China uses a network of overseas organizations and individuals to secure technologies developed by other countries; and how it uses patriotic sentiments in overseas Chinese to spur them along.

Mainland. They maintained that such an invasion was inevitable; at many junctures, that it was imminent. Accordingly, the idea was to draw the adversary deep inland, and then, through techniques that had been honed during the War for Liberation, to exhaust and defeat him. It could be argued that the doctrine was essentially defensive, and that, therefore, it provided a degree of security for countries that were not out to do China in. That, of course, would have been too sanguine a reading. After all, at that stage China also saw exporting revolutions to other countries to be its history-ordained mission. And presumably, the doctrine did not preclude invasions of countries such as India and Vietnam to 'teach them a lesson'.

In any event, under Deng, the assessment changed. Outright invasion, like a new World War itself, came to be seen as unlikely. Accordingly, efforts were to be directed at thwarting the enemy at the borders. This redirection got further impetus after the Kosovo war and, in particular, the Gulf War. Both engagements made a deep impression on Chinese strategic thinkers and military planners, what with high-precision and deep penetration bombing sorties being displayed on television. Chinese efforts now came to be directed at winning 'local wars under high-technology conditions'. Full-scale 'Revolution in Military Affairs' became the order of the day.

Books, monographs, papers were put out by strategic theorists, by service personnel and others that urged China to prepare for 'unrestricted war', for 'no-contact warfare'. They argued that sending troops across borders, wholesale bombing of an the adversary's cities, etc. were outmoded modes of warfare—both in the sense that, given modern conditions, for instance the speed at which others could intervene to help the targeted country or international organizations could rush in with calls to cease fire; and in the sense that such measures could not ensure more than a limited victory. Accordingly, the strategists urged that

China acquire capabilities to bring a country—*all* of it—to its knees within minutes. For this it should develop capacities to paralyse the 'acupuncture points' of the enemy at one fell swoop. The point to grasp, it was argued, is that the more modern a society becomes, the more interlinked and integrated its systems become. The aim should, therefore, be to paralyse systems controlling and managing air traffic, rail traffic, telecommunications, broadcasting networks, banking and financial transactions, national power grids, to 'blind and deafen' the adversary by killing or disrupting its satellites, its command and control systems. Information warfare is the 'assassin's mace' that would enable China to disorient and paralyse another country in this manner within minutes. Such an assault would hold several advantages, analysts pointed out. The damage that it could inflict—entire networks, and therefore entire sectors disrupted and paralysed across entire countries—would be vastly greater than any bombing raid could inflict. And it would do so at a fraction of the cost. Moreover, here was the closest thing to a true 'People's War'—ordinary citizens sitting at their desks in their homes and offices could take part in disabling systems and sectors in distant lands. Furthermore, the assault could easily be camouflaged: computers in distant, third countries could be suborned and the assault routed through them. By the late-1990s, reports were stating that China was already recruiting an 'army of hackers'.

No one could dub the new capabilities 'defensive'. Quite the contrary, every few months, new evidence surfaces that testifies to the capabilities that China has already acquired—for blinding and deafening adversaries, for getting into the networks of others, for spiriting away highly classified information, for distorting or erasing vital data. Several of the attacks trigger alarm—like the 'Titan Rain' which successfully targeted the US Department of Defense as well as a host of companies that were handling defence-related projects.

A wake-up call—that left us sleeping

In our own case, the report of the Munk Center was a sharp and direct wake-up call. Persons high up in the Tibet Government-in-Exile became suspicious. If an appointment was given to someone, say, in Austria that she could meet the Dalai Lama at such and such a time on such and such a date, she would soon start receiving threatening calls. The Tibetan officials sought the assistance of the group at the Munk Center, University of Toronto, which tracks information warfare developments.

From June 2008 to March 2009, computers used in the Dalai Lama's private office, in offices of the Tibet Government-in-Exile, in those of Tibetan NGOs were monitored, and their traffic tracked. It soon became evident that malware had been installed in them, and that documents were being exfiltrated from them—from the computer in the personal office of the Dalai Lama too. The texts that were suborned included highly confidential documents relating to negotiations of the Tibet Government-in-Exile with China, and the alternative negotiating positions it was weighing. The investigation established that

> the commands issued to the infected computers direct the infected computer to download files from additional command servers under the attacker(s)' control. In some cases, these servers act as control servers themselves; however, some appear to be used exclusively to host malicious files that infected computers are meant to download. The attacker(s) set commands on the control servers that instruct infected computers to download additional remote administration Trojans, such as *ghost RAT*, in order to take complete real-time control of the infected computers.

With the help of an array of techniques, including the setting up of a honeypot account, the exfiltration and malware were tracked to four control servers and six command servers.

It turned out that, as the study reported, 'Three of the four control servers are located in three different locations in China: Hainan, Guangdong and Sichuan. One of the control servers is located at a web-hosting company in the United States. Five of the six command servers are located in mainland China (Hainan, Guangdong, Sichuan and Jiangsu) and one in Hong Kong.' The IP addresses too were tracked down: they too were of Chinese entities. In each instance, the exfiltrated documents were being sent to multiple servers. In each instance, great ingenuity had been deployed to make the traffic seem to be normal http:// traffic.

The investigation uncovered 1,295 infected hosts, located in 103 countries. One-third of these were high-value targets. Among the computers from which documents were being exfiltrated, and which were being monitored, and which surfaced in just this single investigation, were those of India's embassies in Belgium, Serbia, Germany, Italy, Kuwait, the USA, and Zimbabwe, and the Indian high commissions in Cyprus and the UK.

The conclusion was chilling as can be:

> *GhostNet* represents a network of compromised computers resident in high-value political, economic, and media locations spread across numerous countries worldwide. At the time of writing, these organizations are almost certainly oblivious to the compromised situation in which they find themselves. The computers of diplomats, military attachés, private assistants, secretaries to prime ministers, journalists and others are under the concealed control of unknown assailant(s).
>
> In Dharamsala and elsewhere, we have witnessed machines being profiled and sensitive documents being removed. At our laboratory, we have analysed our own infected 'honeypot' computer and discovered that the capabilities of *GhostNet* are potent and wide ranging. Almost certainly, *documents are being removed without the targets' knowledge, keystrokes logged, web cameras are being silently triggered, and audio inputs surreptitiously activated.*

The investigators noted that alternative explanations are always possible—that the targets were just randomly picked computers; that some individuals were installing such malware and were monitoring the high-value targets for money or potential blackmail; that some third country, having suborned computers of Chinese agencies, was using them for espionage, etc. All considered, the investigators concluded:

> The most obvious explanation, and certainly the one in which the circumstantial evidence tilts the strongest, would be that this set of high-profile targets has been exploited by the Chinese state for military and strategic-intelligence purposes. Indeed, as described above, many of the high confidence, high-value targets that we identified are clearly linked to Chinese foreign and defence policy, particularly in South and South East Asia. Like radar sweeping around the southern border of China, there is an arc of infected nodes from India, Bhutan, Bangladesh and Vietnam, through Laos, Brunei, Philippines, Hong Kong, and Taiwan. Many of the high-profile targets reflect some of China's most vexing foreign and security policy issues, including Tibet and Taiwan. Moreover, the attacker(s)' IP addresses examined here trace back in at least several instances to Hainan Island, home of the Lingshui signals intelligence facility and the Third Technical Department of the People's Liberation Army.[12]

And how did we react? Newspapers carried an agency report about the findings on one day, and that was it. When I inquire what has happened to the work of firewalling our infrastructure that had been begun with the help of leading mathematicians and experts in this field at a time I had something to do with these matters, nine years ago, they tell me that things are more or less as they were. When I inquire

---

[12] For the foregoing, *Tracking Ghostnet: Investigating a cyber espionage network,* Information Warfare Monitor, Munk Center for International Studies, University of Toronto, March, 2009.

about the fences that have been set up around the cyber-systems that have been inducted into our defence forces, I am told they are 'rudimentary'.

Force projection

The new 'White Paper' on China's defence, *The Diversified Employment of China's Armed Forces*,[13] institutionalizes the doctrine—in the sense of giving primacy to high technologies including in particular 'informationization' of the forces, and setting out the objectives that modernization of the forces, their 'informationization', and their acquiring force-projection capabilities are designed to achieve. 'China's armed forces broaden their visions of national security strategy and military strategy, aim at winning local wars under the conditions of informationization' it declares.[14]

And force projection is writ large across the statement of policy. Setting out the tasks of Chinese forces, the 'White Paper' states, 'It is a strategic task of China's modernization

---

[13] *The Diversified Employment of China's Armed Forces*, Information Office of the State Council, The People's Republic of China, Beijing, April 2013.

[14] Ibid., para I.6. The theme is repeated in several contexts. In para I.8, we are informed, 'China's armed forces firmly base their military preparedness on winning local wars under the conditions of informationization, make overall and coordinated plans to promote military preparedness in all strategic directions, intensify the joint employment of different services and arms, and enhance warfighting capabilities based on information systems....' In II. Para 2, that 'Over the years, the PLA has been proactively and steadily pushing forward its reforms in line with the requirements of performing its missions and tasks, and building an informationized military...' The formulation is reiterated several times in connection with the specific wings: missile defence, police forces. And again in the 'Concluding Remarks': 'At the new stage in this new century, China's armed forces have effectively fulfilled their new historical missions, and enhanced their capabilities of accomplishing diversified military tasks, the most important of which is to win local wars under informationized conditions...'

drive as well as a strong guarantee for China's peaceful development *to build a strong national defense and powerful armed forces which are commensurate with China's international standing and meet the needs of its security and development interests...*'[15]

That is, Chinese forces are to be built (i) 'commensurate with China's international standing'; and to (ii) 'meet the needs of its security and development interests.''Development interests' are given a specific dimension two paragraphs later: '...the security risks to China's overseas interests are on the increase...'[16] It follows that, as 'China's international standing', as well as 'development interests' and the fact that China's overseas interests are under increasing risk, all require capabilities to protect, let us say, its oil assets in far-flung parts of the world, or Chinese technicians and workers working across continents, the PLA must have force projection capabilities. This becomes explicit in Part IV of the 'White Paper', 'Supporting National Economic and Social Development,' where, in the context of safeguarding China's 'overseas interests', we are told, 'With the gradual integration of China's economy into the world economic system, *overseas interests have become an integral component of China's national interests.* Security issues are increasingly prominent, involving overseas energy and resources, strategic sea lines of communication (SLOCs), and Chinese nationals and legal persons overseas...'—'legal persons' being Chinese companies engaged in overseas operations.

We may in passing note just two further points that arise from this statement, and bear on our security. The first is

[15] The phrases recur for emphasis: thus 'China's armed forces act to meet the new requirements of China's national development and security strategies ... China's armed forces provide a security guarantee and strategic support for national development, and make due contributions to the maintenance of world peace and regional stability.' C.f, *The Diversified Employment of China's Armed Forces*, op. cit., para I.3.

[16] Ibid., para I.5.

the omission that has been widely noted—that the 'White Paper' omits to mention China's oft-repeated pledge that it will not be the first to use nuclear weapons. To gauge the significance of this omission, notice how—just a while before the 'White Paper' was put out from Beijing—the US Secretary of Defense portrayed to the US Congress the Chinese doctrine on the use of nuclear weapons. In the mandatory Annual Report on China's military capabilities and developments, he told the US Congress,

> China has consistently asserted that it adheres to a 'no first use' (NFU) policy, stating it would use nuclear forces only in response to a nuclear strike against China. China's NFU pledge consists of two stated commitments: China will never use nuclear weapons first against any nuclear-weapon state, and China will never use or threaten to use nuclear weapons against any non-nuclear-weapon state or nuclear-weapon-free zone.

The report did note significant ambiguity even in that formulation:

> However, there is some ambiguity over the conditions under which China's NFU policy would apply, including whether strikes on what China considers its own territory, demonstration strikes, or high-altitude bursts would constitute a first use. Moreover, some PLA officers have written publicly of the need to spell out conditions under which China might need to use nuclear weapons first; for example, if an enemy's conventional attack threatened the survival of China's nuclear force or of the regime itself. However, there has been no indication that national leaders are willing to attach such nuances and caveats to China's NFU doctrine.[17]

[17] Office of the Secretary of Defense, *Annual Report to Congress: Military and Security Developments involving the People's Republic of China*, Washington, DC, 2013, p. 30.

The 'White Paper' leaves all to ambiguity: it omits the pledge. This is how it puts the matter:

> ... If China comes under a nuclear threat, the nuclear missile force will act upon the orders of the CMC, go into a higher level of readiness, and get ready for a nuclear counterattack to deter the enemy from using nuclear weapons against China. If China comes under a nuclear attack, the nuclear missile force of the PLASAF will use nuclear missiles to launch a resolute counterattack either independently or together with the nuclear forces of other services...[18]

One could argue that reference to the circumstance in which China is attacked with a nuclear missile force, means that it will unleash its nuclear arsenal only after it has been attacked, and that, therefore, the original pledge is implicit in the 'White Paper'. Given the care with which such statements are prepared, given in particular the importance the Chinese place on ambiguity, the omission of an explicit pledge is what has caught everyone's eye.

Another feature is worth noting in the way the statement concludes: 'If China comes under a nuclear attack, the nuclear missile force of the PLASAF will use nuclear missiles to launch a resolute counterattack *either independently or together with the nuclear forces of other services...*' That means that other components of the PLA—for instance, ground and naval forces—are also equipped with nuclear weapons.

Finally, there is the concern with developments in the Asia-Pacific region. This is what the 'White Paper' says about the region, and the countries that are active in it:

> ...The Asia-Pacific region has become an increasingly significant stage for world economic development and strategic interaction between major powers. The US is adjusting its Asia-Pacific security strategy, and the

[18] *The Diversified Employment of China's Armed Forces*, op. cit., III.12.

> regional landscape is undergoing profound changes... Some country has strengthened its Asia-Pacific military alliances, expanded its military presence in the region, and frequently makes the situation there tenser. On the issues concerning China's territorial sovereignty and maritime rights and interests, some neighboring countries are taking actions that complicate or exacerbate the situation, and Japan is making trouble over the issue of the Diaoyu Islands...[19]

The 'some country' is the US. Japan comes in for explicit mention. But the message could not be lost on other countries in the region—for instance, Vietnam, Philippines, Indonesia, Australia, each of which has entered into agreements of mutual assistance in the face of China's new profile and aggressive moves. And it should not be lost on us as we move to coordinate efforts with the very same countries in the region.

---

[19] Ibid., para I.2.

15

Putting our hopes in inevitability?

Until 2008, Deng's counsel held the field. Deng urged that as China was still poor and weak, it must avoid getting dragged into local wars, be they over spheres of influence or natural resources. 'Yield on small issues, with the long term in mind,' he is reported to have counselled. Do not strut around as the leaders, 'Don't stick you head out'. None of this, of course, prevented Deng himself from launching an assault on Vietnam to 'teach it a lesson'.

'Hide brightness, nourish obscurity,' Deng urged. Or, as the official translation of his four-character idiom went, 'Bide our time and build our capabilities.'[1] An influential Chinese general, at the time the vice commandant of the Academy of Military Sciences, made an addition: 'Build your capabilities, bide your time, quietly nurse your vengeance.' The addition itself was a telling one. But more, a new reality no less, was in store.

As Chinese growth took off, and especially after the financial crisis hit Western economies in 2008–09, officials in China concluded that China's time had come. Its diplomats

[1] For the preceding quotations, Michael Pillsbury, *China Debates the Future Security Environment,* National Defense University Press, Washington, D.C., 2000. Retrieved from http://www.fas.org/nuke/guide/china/doctrine/pills2/

became shrill.[2] Its claims became more and more expansive—for instance, over the Senkaku Islands in the north and over the Spratly Islands, the Paracels and the Natuna Islands in the south. The agreement with India on the principles that would govern border negotiations, as we have seen, suddenly came to be interpreted in ways that nullified the understandings that had been reached. The border talks froze. Incursions multiplied. Chinese soldiers came deeper and deeper into Indian territory. China moved aggressively to acquire not just economic assets abroad but also to build naval and military facilities. Alarm bells began ringing in several capitals.

In his important new book, *The Rise of China vs. The Logic of Strategy*,[3] Luttwak, of course, points out that this is not just a matter of maladroit conduct. It is of substance, of power: 'The post-2008 outbursts of provocative behavior certainly accelerated reactions to the rise of China. But those reactions had not been caused by the provocations, and could not be ended with conciliatory gestures, fence-mending state visits, or soothing language, because they reflect perceptions of power rather than assessments of Chinese conduct.'[4]

Edward Luttwak argues that

---

[2] I had a glimpse of this coming-out personally! I had been invited to deliver a memorial lecture at the London School of Economics premises in 2009. From there, I travelled to Brussels to deliver a lecture at one of the city's think-tanks. The subject was an innocuous one: on building and sustaining institutions. The lecture over, time for questions and answers. A short while into the exchanges, a Chinese diplomat started scolding and rebuking and reprimanding in a loud and minatory voice. His companion, another Chinese diplomat joined in. I was nonplussed. What have I said that has made them so angry? I was wondering. My host, who was seated next to me, turned to me and whispered, 'Don't worry. This has nothing to do with you. The same thing happened at two other meetings elsewhere in Brussels in just the last few days. This is the new China.'

[3] Edward N. Luttwak, *The Rise of China vs. The Logic of Strategy*, The Belknap Press of Harvard University Press, Cambridge, Mass., 2012.

[4] Ibid., p. 38.

- Explosive economic growth, rapid military rise and diplomatic influence just cannot go together.
- China is growing too fast, it is enhancing its military strength too rapidly and conspicuously for it not to alert and alarm its neighbours.
- Foregoing maximal military power would be the only prudent course for a country in China's position. As he puts his basic thesis:

  > The paradoxical logic of strategy is directly contrary to common sense: only in strategy can less be better than more. Specifically, a weaker army and navy are better than stronger ones if they exceed the culminating level of *systemically* acceptable strength, evoking more-than-proportionate adversarial reactions, both symmetric and asymmetric... As the strength of a rising Great Power continues to increase, friendly neighbours become watchful, allies edge towards neutrality, former neutrals become adversaries, and committed adversaries old and new are compelled to overcome their differences to combine against the Great Power rising too quickly. In a world of independent states, even the strongest rising power can be overcome by the gathering of adversaries summoned by the very increase of its very strength.[5]

  In a word, in his view China, paradoxically, may become weaker precisely because of its rising strength. Prudence would, therefore require that China 'renounce any but the slowest military growth'.[6]
- But that would never be allowed: neither the leadership nor, indeed, the people at large would countenance a course of that kind; furthermore, there are strong institutional interests—the weight of the PLA in decision-making, for instance—as well as personal interests—those of leaders

[5] Ibid., pp. 66–67.

[6] Ibid., p. 68.

in the political as well as military hierarchy whose weight as well as future are inextricably intertwined with the maximal strengthening of China's armed forces; and by now there are so many other organizations willing and able to pursue expansionism for their own aggrandizement: Luttwak lists, for instance, among the more bellicose, the Administration of Fishery and Fishing Harbor Supervision, the China Maritime Surveillance, the Maritime Safety Administration. Even more important are historical and cultural reasons that would preclude prudent restraint: the inability of Great States to be sensitive to the feelings that they are igniting in others—what Luttwak calls 'Great State Autism'; the inordinate, and in Luttwak's assessment, unwarranted pride that the Chinese have in their superior strategic thinking—in the last thousand years, it is only in 280 years that China has been ruled by Han dynasties; for the rest, the Chinese were conquered and ruled by those whom they looked down upon as barbarians— a 'stubborn faith in the superior strategic wisdom to be found in ancient texts, and the resulting belief that China will always be able to outmaneuver its adversaries with clever expedients, circumventing the accumulating resistance caused by its rise'. To compound it all, Luttwak writes, there is 'the structural insecurity of the leaders of the CCP, whose power has neither democratic legitimacy nor the ideological legitimacy that their predecessors could claim, regardless of the objective merits of that ideology'. The result is that Chinese leadership is given to 'the wild exaggeration of mostly very minor threats to the stability of the regime'; it is given to 'overreacting to very minor political threats, indeed to the mere auto-suggestion of nonexistent threats'. For these and other reasons—Luttwak marshals a broad array of facts and arguments to underpin his analysis—China will continue to strive to enhance its military strength to maximum limits at the fastest pace possible.

Reaction, therefore, is inevitable.

It has indeed set in.

It will not be without consequences: a large number of Lilliputians can tie up a Gulliver.

There is also a parallel from an unrelated field. For decades, the US propped up authoritarian regimes, and corrupt, thuggish rulers in Latin America. For decades, former colonial powers propped up equally venal rulers and regimes in Africa. As these regimes and rulers, to perpetuate themselves in power, oppressed their people, the US and other erstwhile colonial powers became the objects of people's hatred and wrath. In many ways, the same sequence was enacted in the Middle East. When China stands by Jose Eduardo dos Santos in Angola, Robert Mugabe in Zimbabwe, Joseph Kabila in the Democratic Republic of Congo, the oppressive rulers of the erstwhile Sudan—will it not eventually harvest the same anger?

The reaction

The reaction has set in, and Luttwak lists various measures that countries of the region are taking as a result. Every country in the region is strengthening its armed forces. Military exchanges and, in several cases, formal agreements have been put in place between several countries: among them are Japan, India, Vietnam, Singapore, Indonesia, Malaysia, Australia. These arrangements and agreements cover training, joint exercises, sharing of intelligence and assessments.

Public opinion has also changed. By 1992, Philippines had closed the naval base at Subic Bay and the Clark Air Force Base. But as China has begun to press its claims to the Spratly and Paracel Islands aggressively, Philippines has become more open to military cooperation, and to having ASEAN take a role in dealing with Chinese claims. Australia has announced that it shall allow US forces to be based in the Northern Territories. Since the aggressive Chinese manoeuvres around the Senkaku Islands, public opinion within Japan has witnessed a tectonic shift: the clamour for removing US forces has abated. In an unprecedented move, when asked in Parliament what his government would do if Chinese vessels entered Japanese territorial waters or landed on the Senkaku Islands, the new Japanese prime minister, Shinzo Abe, warned that he had ordered Japanese forces to respond with force. For the first time after it froze relations with India in the wake of Indian nuclear tests in 1998, Japan has agreed to consider sales of military equipment to India. Indonesia—which has always had a deep suspicion of the large population of ethnic Chinese in the archipelago—has been jolted by the nine-dash line coming as far as the Natuna Islands. Indian public opinion, too, as we have seen, has shifted: more and more now see China as the principal threat to the country; they see too that we have lost too much time, that we cannot today face it on our own, and must, therefore, enter into arrangements with other countries—the usual clamour against the US has muted. The US itself has announced that it will be reorienting its strategic deployments with Asia-Pacific as the pivot.

The reaction is not confined to the immediate periphery of China, nor just to military and territorial matters. Indonesians are seeing how disastrously and how rapidly their forests are being cut down to meet the insatiable demand of Chinese construction companies for timber. Vietnam has issued a decree that gives local officials the authority to deport foreigners who have been living in the country for over three months without a valid work permit. Applicants must also now show that they are qualified to hold positions for which locals are not available. The decree is said to have been issued and the regulations tightened to target Chinese migrant workers. Countries that depend on the Mekong have bestirred themselves to see how they should protect their interests as China pushes ahead in constructing dams in Tibet, with the clear and not distant objective of diverting Tibetan waters to north and east China. In faraway Brazil, even as the prosperity of parts of the country and sections of its population has got intertwined with China's rapid growth, a law has been passed imposing restrictions on foreigners buying land. Argentina has passed a similar law. In both instances, as Luttwak points out, the instigation came from the vast swathes of land that Chinese companies had taken over.

Even in Africa, the continent whose recent upsurge owes most to Chinese investments and projects, in particular the prosperity of whose elite owes an enormous amount to Chinese outlays, voices are beginning to be raised that economic relations with China are no different from the exploitative relations that the colonial powers enforced on the continent—namely, that China is taking away minerals and oil that the continent should be saving for its own industrialization; and, on the other, the cheap manufactures that it is dumping in return are already causing deindustrialization, even in a relatively advanced economy like South Africa. Michael Sata, the President of Zambia, ran for re-election in 2011, on an anti-China platform: he would throw them out for maltreating Zambian workers, he proclaimed; the Chinese are not *investors*, he declared, they are *infesters*. He won. The country has revoked the licences of the Chinese-owned Collum coalmine, charging the company with violating environment and safety standards, and with failure to pay mineral royalties. In Malawi, protests broke out in June 2012 in the northern town of Karonga against Chinese retail outlets. The government has invoked a law to confine foreign retailers to big cities. Namibia has banned foreign investment in medium-sized public transport companies and, of all things, in hair and beauty salons: Bloomberg quotes the minister in-charge as saying that, 'Much of this concern has been sparked by activities of Chinese business persons.' Gabon has begun renegotiations of a deal with the Chinese mining consortium, Comibel, for the Belinga iron ore deposits. Several countries have imposed restrictions on the landing of Chinese crews engaged in fishing, on sales of the catch, on financial remittances back to China. And so on—from the expulsion from South Sudan of the head of Chinese-Malaysian oil company for oil theft, to the banning of two Chinese firms from participating in a public tender in Algeria on the charge of their indulging in corruption.

Reporting that protest in Karonga and the decision of the Malawian Government to dust up an existing law confining foreign retail outlets to big cities, the Reuters dispatch talked of a 'grassroots backlash'—where governments are wary of acting against Chinese traders and investors, ordinary people are beginning to feel that they will have to take matters in their own hands and gear up for a fight. Violent incidents have begun to erupt:

> In many ways, the relationship between the two [China and Africa] has never been stronger. Bilateral trade has almost doubled over the past three years, to $166 billion in 2011 from $91 billion in 2009. In July, Chinese President Hu Jintao offered Africa $20 billion in cheap loans over the next three years. China, he said, would forever be a 'good friend, a good partner and a good brother' to Africa. But a growing number of Africa's billion people are less enthusiastic. Last November, four Chinese in rural South Africa were burnt alive in an arson attack on their home. In Zambia last month, miners in a dispute over pay crushed a Chinese supervisor to death with a coal truck. In Ghana, armed Chinese informal miners have clashed with gangs of local youths, triggering a government crackdown. In Angola a few weeks ago, 37 Chinese men were deported on suspicion of running a criminal gang that burnt its victims with gasoline before burying them alive, according to China's Xinhua state news agency. And from Senegal in the west to Kenya in the east, traders are up in arms about what they see as unfair competition from private Chinese

> merchants surfing into Africa on the back of a wave of big investments…[7]

The Economist reported in a similar vein,

> Africa now supplies 35% of China's oil. Two-way trade grew by 39% last year. China deserves credit for engaging a continent that desperately needs investment. Millions of Africans are using roads, schools and hospitals built by Chinese companies or financed with fees from resources they extracted. Not surprisingly, many African leaders have embraced the Chinese, especially when offered vast loans for infrastructure projects. By contrast, the leaders say, Western governments these days offer little more than lectures on good governance. But the honeymoon is coming to an end. Growing numbers of Africans are turning against the saviours from the East. They complain that Chinese companies destroy national parks in their hunt for resources and that they routinely disobey even rudimentary safety rules. Workers are killed in almost daily accidents. Some are shot by managers. Where China offers its companies preferential loans, African businesses struggle to compete. Roads and hospitals built by the Chinese are often faulty, not least because they bribe local officials and inspectors. Although corruption has long been a problem in Africa, people complain China is making it worse.

This backlash should worry the Chinese, the *Economist* wrote, in part because the rumbling in Africa is affecting its ability to get projects elsewhere:

> This antipathy should worry the Chinese government. Granted, it is unlikely to lose access to resources controlled by friendly dictators who have benefited personally from China's arrival. But its ambitions stretch far beyond

[7] 'Insight: In Africa's warm heart, a cold welcome for Chinese,' http://www.reuters.com/article/2012/09/18/us-africa-china-pushback-idUSBRE88H0CR20120918.

> securing resources. Chinese companies, private as well as publicly owned, are investing in farming, manufacturing and retailing. Many depend on co-operation with a wide array of increasingly unhappy locals. In Dar es Salaam, Tanzania's commercial capital, Chinese are banned from selling in markets. In South Africa their factories face closure at the hands of enraged trade unions. Moreover, China's investments spread far beyond Africa. Stains on China's reputation are harming its commercial plans elsewhere—and governments in other continents will be keener than African politicians have been to find reasons to put obstacles in China's way. A Chinese construction firm had an ear-bashing when bidding for a Polish motorway contract, in part because an Angolan hospital the company had built fell apart within months of opening its doors...[8]

Ghana, the *International Herald Tribune* reports, 'counts China as one of its most important economic partners.' It 'has oil and other coveted minerals, and the Chinese are busy there erecting government ministry buildings, a giant dam and even a stadium'. In such a country, the military police are chasing and rounding up Chinese workers and managers who have come for mining gold. 'The lucky ones have hidden out in cocoa farms and in Chinese-owned companies,' reports the *International Herald Tribune*, 'surviving on yams and water and moving about constantly and trembling at the prospect of being discovered by Ghana's security forces. The unlucky ones have been beaten, robbed and swept up by soldiers.' 'We have no food, no water, no sleep,' a terrified woman worker hiding in one such farm, says. 'Everyone is scrambling for a way to go back to China.' The military police swoop down,

---

[8] 'Rumble in the jungle,' http://www.economist.com/node/18586678. I am grateful to Gautam Mehta and Manishi Raychaudhuri, the head of research at BNP Paribas, for putting me on to some of the news trails for the foregoing.

wrest gold, cash and everything valuable. They drive away the cars. 'Then they poured out diesel we keep on the site to power the generators,' a miner explained, describing one such incident, 'and burned all of our excavators and camps.' 'A long furtive walk in the bush preceded a night-time dash to a Chinese-owned company in Obuasi that sheltered him from the authorities,' the *Herald Tribune* reporters write. 'We scurried to this company at night like rats crossing streets,' the young man tells them. 'Analysts in Ghana said the government has little choice but to act against the illegal miners,' the reporters note. The reason? 'Popular resentment', 'growing public agitation over the destructive, quite predatory, medium-scale mining operations engaged in mainly by the Chinese and some Indians…' 'The roundups have stoked fear among the Chinese migrants and anger at home,' the *Herald Tribune* reports, 'generating more than one million posts about the topic on one popular microblog…'[9]

So, there certainly is a reaction. There is apprehension—especially because China is looked upon as a predatory power, especially because others too believe what the Chinese believe: that the Chinese think long term, that the Chinese are better than all the others at thinking strategically and at putting those strategies into effect, that they are masters of cunning and deception.

To avail of the reaction

But for us to avail of the reaction, to avail of the apprehensions, we have to make an effort. The way we go about things, rather the way we don't go about things, it would seem that we want someone to not just put the morsel in our mouths, we expect him to move our jaws for us. Consider, what C. Raja Mohan, one of our acute observers on security-related developments,

[9] Adam Nossiter and Yiting Sun, "Chinese on the run in Ghana," *International Herald Tribune*, 12 June 2013.

had to say recently about the major forum that has emerged in South-east Asia, the Shangri-La Dialogue in Singapore. This is an annual event. Defence ministers and others responsible for security policy of all major countries in the region participate. 'China, which was initially opposed to the forum, now sends a very impressive delegation,' Raja Mohan wrote. The 2013 Dialogue was held in May. And India? Here are a few paragraphs from Raja Mohan's account—as you read them, ask, 'Will we be able, even in the slightest, to put the reaction to work when this is how we go about our responsibilities?'

'The MoD's [Ministry of Defence's] approach to the SLD [the Shangri-La Dialogue] has been unprofessional,' Raja Mohan wrote. 'Personal whims rather than a careful consideration of India's interests seem to define New Delhi's decisions.' Sometimes the Indian defence minister turns up, and sometimes he doesn't—in 2013, he didn't, even though he could have as he stopped in Singapore the very next day on the way back from his trip to Australia, and Thailand. Some years it is a junior minister; sometimes the National Security Advisor. This year it was the Chief of Naval Staff. And it is not till the very last minute that a decision gets taken as to who will represent India at the conference.

Nor is the choice without consequence: 'Representation at less than the cabinet level,' Raja Mohan wrote, 'is a protocol handicap when it comes to speaking slots and meetings on the margins of the conference. At this year's SLD, there was no Indian speaker in the prestigious plenary sessions.' To get an idea of the criminality of the negligence, it is best to read a few paragraphs in the words of Raja Mohan himself:

> Our foreign office can get the prime minister to sign up on high-sounding declarations on the Look-East policy and proclaim, 'strategic partnerships' with ASEAN nations. But when our Southeast Asian interlocutors turn to the MoD for follow-up, they run into a brick wall.
>
> In track-two interactions, ASEAN policymakers vent

> their frustration in dealing with the MoD—at the bilateral as well as the multilateral level. Many bilateral agreements with ASEAN countries on defence cooperation are languishing because of the MoD's inability to implement them.
>
> Worse still, the MoD is also very suspicious that all our armed forces are keen to develop deeper interactions with Asian militaries and the MEA [Ministry of External Affairs], which recognises defence diplomacy as a new quiver in its armoury.
>
> At a time when China and the United Sates have dramatically stepped up their defence diplomacy in Asia, the MoD seems out for lunch and siesta...
>
> No one expects the MoD's current leadership—both political and bureaucratic—to take bold new initiatives towards ASEAN. What surprises southeast Asia is the passive incoherence of the MoD's participation in the various defence forums of ASEAN—neither ready to lead nor willing to respond.
>
> Some tend to dress-up the MoD's feckless defence diplomacy as a deeply felt assertion of India's 'strategic autonomy'. Nice try. The real problem is the lack of political will in Delhi to take defence diplomacy in Asia seriously...[10]

Yes, there is a reaction to China's aggressiveness. Yes, countries all along its rim, as well as the United States want to engage with India to institute countervailing measures. Is this any way to put the opportunity to work?

And, of course, the fecklessness, the criminal neglect is not confined to responding to South-east Asian initiatives. It is germane. Of the innumerable instances that can be cited, one will do. Writing in 2009, General Ved Malik, former Chief of the Army, drew attention to the fact that a draft 'National Strategy paper prepared by the military staff has been gathering dust in the National Security Advisor's Office *since January 2007*'.[11]

---

[10] C. Raja Mohan, 'Missing Shangri-La', *The Indian Express*, 5 June 2013.

[11] *The Tribune*, 25 April 2009.

As I type this, we are in May 2013. Has the draft been approved since? Is it still lying on someone's desk? Upon inquiry, officers at Army Headquarters say, 'The armed forces have not been given the CCS/NSA approved "national security strategy" paper till date—which means the draft has either been shelved or is lying in limbo somewhere.' On asking further, Ajai Shukla, formerly of the Army and now a leading defence analyst, reports:

(a) It was a Draft National Security Strategy Paper, prepared by the Integrated Defence Staff and submitted to the Chairman Chiefs of Staff Committee, apparently on request from the National Security Advisor, M.K. Narayanan.
(b) The forces, having submitted the paper, heard nothing more about it. Upon inquiries being made by [a very senior and respected officer of the armed forces], [a person in the NSCS who is in a position to know], says that nobody knows anything about it.
(c) However, Shiv Shankar Menon, the current National Security Advisor, at a talk/briefing a couple of years ago did mention that there was this paper that needed to be circulated to all concerned and needed to be finalized. However, nothing more has been heard about it.

What could be the reason? Ajai Shukla tries to fathom one: 'While the strategy paper could have died of neglect, it could also be that the NSA's office was not impressed by it. Having been prepared by the IDS, it would have focused on the military aspects, perhaps to the exclusion of diplomatic issues. Instead of combining the diplomatic issues into the military ones, the NSA's office might just be sitting on it.'[12]

That the draft has not been finalized even though *six years* have passed is one aspect of the matter. The even more depressing fact is that the services have heard nothing of

---

[12] Personal communication.

the project of having a reasoned paper on national security, a paper for which they were asked to prepare a draft. Is this the way such an exercise should be conducted? Is this the way the forces should be treated?

'Defence diplomacy' in such circumstances?

'To give history a helping hand'

In a word,

- We have to be, and be seen to be serious about building our own Comprehensive National Strength;
- We have to be, and be seen to be ready to deploy it to protect our interests;
- We have to be as eager to join other countries as they have been to have us join them;
- We have to be ready to shoulder our responsibilities in an alliance;
- We have to do much more *for* and *in* other countries than we do at present. And we have to do different things. The Chinese set up halls of the people? We should set up children's hospitals in every African capital. They beat up workers, they troop in workers from China? We should impart skills to locals;
- For any of this to happen, we have first to pull up our boots at home.

When potential allies see the disarray in our governance; when they see us find reasons at every turn for *not* answering back; when they see the way even our force modernization and weapons procurement programmes get derailed; when they see inter-ministerial wrangling impede development of infrastructure in the very region that China is insisting is its own, Arunachal Pradesh; when they see that one Ghasi Ram can hurl an allegation, trigger a series of investigations and bring the construction of roads to Daulat Beig Oldie to a halt; when they see that a Lieutenant General of the Indian Army can be stopped by the wives of civilian employees of the Border Roads Organization from so much as entering his office—the wives demanding that control of the organization be handed over to civilians, their husbands: because this will speed up road construction or for the other obvious reason?; when they see the tardiness with which we responded to the urgings of South-east Asian leaders like the then Singapore Prime Minister Goh Chok Tong that we reach out to ASEAN, that we focus on growing faster—these leaders put the point gently, as if they were urging this in their own interest: 'Singapore needs two wings to fly,' they said; when they see the state of civil-military relations here—when others see all this, do they conclude that India is serious about building its strength? That it is willing to put that strength to work? That it will stand up for them when they are pushed by China? That it is even interested in collaborating? What would *we* conclude?

Hence, while there is a reaction to Chinese practices in Africa and elsewhere; while military exchanges among China's neighbours have begun; while agreements have been signed—these are a major step forward, no doubt, but they are just the first step—the fact is that no country will today come to our aid to shield our territory from China. No country will risk Chinese wrath in order to advance our interests vis-à-vis those of China. In 1962, only one country took an active and neutral position, and helped mediate a truce. That country was Sri Lanka. Were a similar situation to arise today, will even that one country do so again—what with our policy towards Sri Lanka having been made the football of political parties in Tamil Nadu?

A reaction has begun. It may be inevitable. But for us to avail of it, we have to do our bit. We have to 'give history a helping hand'.

For that, we have to be single-minded. We have to be clear about what is important and what is not.

Are we?

16

Shilpa Shetty trumps Arunachal, again

November 21, 2007: We were all at the weekly meeting of the BJP members of Parliament. Mr L.K. Advani was presiding. At the time, Arunachal Pradesh was represented in the Lok Sabha by two of our colleagues—Tapir Gao and Kiren Rijiju. They drew attention to the fact that Chinese incursions into Arunachal were not just continuing—these were becoming more frequent and the Chinese soldiers were coming deeper into our territory. They pointed to the statement of a senior official heading our forces deployed on the border: the official had felt compelled to disclose in a public statement that there had been 146 incursions in just 2007. The MPs—who knew the area well, who used to tour extensively across the state, to whom local inhabitants regularly and naturally brought information—said that the Chinese were now preventing locals from going up to regions where they had been taking their animals for grazing, that they were being supplied goods from Chinese shops…

They drew even sharper attention to an incident that had occurred just three weeks earlier. For as long as anyone could remember, there had been a statue of the Buddha—well inside Indian territory. Local inhabitants used to go up to it to pray and make their offerings. The local commander of the Chinese troops told Indian soldiers that the statue must be removed. Our soldiers pointed out that the statue was well within Indian territory, and so there was no question of removing it. The Chinese had come, and blown off the statue.

I raised my hand for permission to speak. It so happened that I was halfway through a book, *Why Geography Matters*, by the well-known geographer, Harm de Blij.[1] Setting the stage for his thesis, Blij had pointed out that one could get vital clues from maps, and why it was important to pay attention to them—especially when governments publish the maps. He recalled 'a telling experience' he had in 1990. A colleague of his, working then at the University of Baghdad, had sent him an official map that had been published by the Government of Iraq. The map had shown Kuwait as the nineteenth province of Iraq. At a meeting in Washington, Blij had drawn the attention of the then chairman of the Foreign Affairs Committee of the US House of Representatives to the map and its implications. The gentleman had told Blij not to worry, the US ambassador, he had said, was on top of things. A few days had not passed, and Iraq had marched its armies into Kuwait. The first Gulf War…

But it was the passage that followed which was of urgent interest to us, and I sought Mr. Advani's permission to read it. Blij had written:

> Cartographic aggression takes several forms. Some overt, as in the case of Iraq, others more subtle. In 1993 I received a book titled *Physical Geography of China*, written by Zhao Sonqiao, published in 1986 in Beijing. On the frontispiece is a map of China. But that map, to the trained eye, looks a bit strange. Why? Because in the south, it takes from India virtually all of the Indian state of Arunachal Pradesh, plus a piece of the state of Assam. Now this book is not a political geography of China, nor is the matter of appropriated Indian territory ever discussed in it. China's

---

[1] Harm de Blij, *Why Geography Matters, Three challenges facing America: Climate change, the rise of China and global terrorism*, Oxford University Press, New York, 2005.

> border is simply assumed to lie deep inside India, and the mountains and valleys thus claimed are discussed as though they are routinely a part of China. Make no mistake: such a map could not, in the 1980s at least, have been published without official approval. It should put not just India but the whole international community on notice of a latent trouble spot.[2]

At the time, BJP MPs used to be quite alert to issues concerning the country's borders and boundaries. Here were two colleagues from the state testifying to what the Chinese were doing in Arunachal, and here was a book that was warning about what was afoot—a book published far away, a book written by an author who had no interest in either running down China or upholding India's position on anything. The effect was palpable. Mr Advani said that the two MPs and I should address the BJP press conference that afternoon, and draw the attention of the media to the facts. Advaniji said that, in addition to explaining the background, I should read out the passage.

During sessions of Parliament, the press conference used to be held every afternoon. The large room was packed with journalists. After leaders of the party in the two Houses had dealt with events of the day, Tapir Gao and Kiren Rijiju narrated the facts. I set out the context—and read the foregoing passage.

I had hardly concluded and the usual clutch—pro-Congress, pro-Left—was up in arms. 'When was the book published?' one demanded. I couldn't get the relevance of the question: what has the date of publication got to do with the warning that the author had penned, even more so with the facts that the MPs have set out? I asked.

'No, no. As the book must have been available even during the NDA regime, what did your government do about the matter?' I hadn't looked up the date of publication. I did now.

---

[2] Ibid., pp. 44–45.

The edition I had in hand had been published in 2007! The copyright page recorded that the book was first published in 2005! The NDA Government had left office in 2004. The journalist subsided. In any case, I pointed out, trying to soften the deflation-by-date, the vital thing is not what the book says—the passage from the book just illustrates that, while others are concerned, we continue to sleep. The thing of vital consequence is what is happening on the ground, and this is what my colleagues here—who represent the state in Parliament—have just narrated.

'But what did the NDA do about the incursions?' another member of that clutch demanded. First, the head of the forces on the border has spoken about the incursions that have taken place this year, in 2007, I pointed out. But assume that incursions were taking place then, and that the NDA government did nothing. Does that in any way become a reason for not doing anything today? Please do have some mercy on our country, I said. Here is China claiming our territory; here it is, having begun that well-rehearsed series of steps which precede a grab. Are we going to divert ourselves from that reality by the usual '*tu-tu*, *mein-mein*, NDA *vs.* UPA?'

'No, Mr Shourie,'—it was the pro-Left journalist—'but you *have* to acknowledge that there is no agreed international border between India and China. So...' That is the Chinese position as articulated by your paper often, I said. Which side has prevented the delineation of the Line of Actual Control? Which side has ensured that the talks between the Special Representatives get nowhere?

By now enough diversion had been created. The press conference was soon over. My Arunachal colleagues were, of course, disheartened—'If this is how much the national press cares...' I was incensed. For years I had been seeing such clutches divert attention from life-and-death issues and been unable to do anything about it. Here was another infuriating instance.

Not only was the question at hand a matter of vital significance for our country. It was one on which we had the most recent historical experience to keep us alert. When Acharya Kripalani, Ram Manohar Lohia, K.M. Munshi and others had first drawn attention to Chinese maps that showed vast swathes of Indian territory to be part of China, Panditji had replied that he had taken up the matter with the Chinese and they had said that these were old, colonial, faulty maps, and, as they had just taken control of government, they had not had time to correct them. Later, these very maps were used to argue that the areas had always been part of China. Mao had then declared, 'Tibet is the palm of China, and the Himalayan kingdoms are the fingers of that palm.' Did the journalists not remember any of this?

An anchor from a news channel phoned. I saw your press conference, he said. We have been following this story for many months. Can you please come to our studio? No, I said, I really am very upset at what happened. But I give you my word, he said; we think this is an important issue, and we are going to follow it in the coming months also. I will send an OB-van to your house.

The van came. The late-night news. The earpiece in my ear. All set. Delay—quite understandable: some new eruption in Nandigram. Eventually, the anchor and I were talking.

'But are you sure about the facts or is the BJP indulging in its usual fear-politics?' the anchor asked. But why don't you ascertain them from the two MPs who represent the area? I responded. Better still, why don't you send your own correspondents and photographers to the area? I said. We will, we will, I assure you, he said. I was just making sure…

In any case, look at what the ambassador of China has himself said, I remarked. Remember, just days before Hu Jintao, the Chinese President, was to come to India, the ambassador declared, right here on Indian soil, that Arunachal is a part of China…

The anchor cut me short: 'But maybe he was saying it for rhetorical effect,' he said.

Rhetorical effect? I skipped a heartbeat. Is the Chinese ambassador also running after TRP ratings like the TV channels? Would an *ambassador* say such things just for effect? And that too the ambassador of *China*, of all countries? You mean *an ambassador*, you mean the ambassador of *China* of all countries would claim the territory of the country to which he is accredited, that he would lay claim to an entire state of that country for rhetorical effect? I asked. And remember, I pointed out, he repeated the claim in Chandigarh later. And look at the Government of China—it has not distanced itself from the claim advanced by its ambassador. On the contrary, its 'think-tanks' have held 'seminars' in the wake of the ambassador's statement. In these, 'scholars' and 'diplomats' and 'strategic thinkers' have declared to the man that Arunachal is 'Chinese territory under India's forcible occupation'; that it is 'China's Tawang region'; that it is part of 'the Administrative Zone of Southern Tibet' which must be brought under the control of the Tibet Autonomous Region. And you call this *rhetorical?* That is just lunatic.

The anchor was off to the next item: 'Be that as it may… Another controversy… Thank you, Mr Shourie. Always a pleasure talking to you. Moving now to a slightly less controversial story…'

'*Shilpa Shetty*,' he said, his voice rising, 'has not been in the news since the famous Richard Gere kiss, but we have her back today. Here she is, *Shilpa Shetty*…'

The sound on my earpiece cut. Shilpa Shetty had once again trumped poor Arunachal.

Both sets of exchanges—at the press conference as well as over the TV news channel—had been typical. In part, the problem is extreme, brazen partisanship—and this takes two forms. One is the premise of many, as of that leftist journalist: India can never really be in the right. You just have to see the play that Musharraf and his devious formulae got in many of our magazines. You just have to recall his brazen lies over Kargil: first, the claim that there were no Pakistani soldiers in the operation, so much so that he, the Chief of the Army at the time, refused to even take possession of the bodies of the soldiers; and then the claim in his autobiography that the Kargil operation was one of the most successful ventures of the Pakistan Army. You have to just recall such falsehoods, and see how they were glossed over by the Indian media. The presumption behind such fawning one day and such amnesia the next is that we are in the wrong in Kashmir, and so *we* are the ones who must bend, and go on bending till Pakistan expresses satisfaction. This premise is compounded in the case of many others by commitment: you can rely on several of our colleagues to see merit in China's stance on everything. The second variant is domestic predilection: in the Arunachal case cited above, that 'The BJP is evil incarnate; because the BJP has raised the issue, the issue itself must be trashed'. That is how the mortal danger from Bangladeshi infiltrators has been shouted out. That is how the dual-faced, anti-national politics of many in Kashmir is ignored. That is how appeasement of narrow sections for votes is routinely seen as 'social justice'. That is how what was happening in regard to Arunachal was being shouted out.

And then there is what has become the nature of the media: the obsession with the sound bite on the one side and with the next 'breaking news' on the other. Issues like Kashmir, the nuclear deal, the way China is translating its economic strength into military might—these require more than a sound bite. The media has no time for that.

Similarly, to deal with China, to counter Pakistan's proxy war, the country must sustain a policy for twenty-thirty years. And for that, you have to keep readers and viewers focused on that issue for decades at a time. But the media is fixated only on what it can project as 'breaking news' in this shift—what was 'breaking news' in the last shift is 'old hat' by this one.

Even more than partisanship, and the current obsession of the media with the next 'breaking news', the problem is superciliousness—this has become the reigning ideology today. This was brought home to me directly one day. We happened to meet while flying to Mumbai—the owner of one of the country's foremost newspapers and I. I accosted him about what his paper was printing on Kashmir—every allegation, every smear that any and every secessionist thug was spitting out at our country and our forces was being carried on the front pages of his paper as fact. Aren't you reading the nonsense—and it is dangerous nonsense—that your paper is printing on Kashmir? I asked. And I gave examples from the preceding few days. The entrepreneur listened, the tolerant smile never leaving his face. And then exclaimed: '*Arun bhai, yehi to farq hai aap mein aur hum mein. Aap abhi bhi hamara paper padhte ho*!'—That is precisely the difference between you and us, Arun *bhai*. You still read our paper!

That he no longer bothers to read his paper was just a pose. His real message was, 'Kashmir, did you say? I am above such trifles...'

Are these not ways to tempt an aggressor?

When journalists are to busy themselves with 'lifestyle journalism'; when local candidates can ensure that papers carry the 'paid news' they send; when companies can get the coverage they want by entering into 'private treaties'; when sundry politicians with a mass base of six journalists can manipulate papers and channels—will foreign governments not sense and use the opportunity?

Make no mistake: China watches all this. It watches the feeble, confused, contradictory ways in which our governments, and even more our society, reacts each time it advances a claim. And it pursues its policy:

- Claim
- Repeat the claim
- Go on repeating the claim

- Grab
- Hold
- Let time pass.

And they will reconcile themselves to the new situation. Has the policy not succeeded in regard to Tibet? No Indian prime minister will dare mention the word 'Tibet' or 'Taiwan'—lest doing so offends China. But China will go on claiming what it wants—for reasons that we must understand!

But why think of Tibet and Taiwan? Has the six-step policy not succeeded in regard to Aksai Chin? As we noted when we began, in spite of the unanimous resolution that the Parliament passed at the time under Panditji, is there an Indian leader who will today demand that China hand back Aksai Chin? And recall that the area that they have seized in Aksai Chin is 37,244 square kilometres. The Kashmir Valley is how large? 15, 948 square kilometres—that is, the area that the Chinese have already usurped is *two and a half times the area of Kashmir.*

We should understand the Chinese. We should understand their aims, their ways. We should understand what they think of themselves. We should understand what they think of us.

17

Understanding them, understanding what they think themselves and us to be

'I also recall seeing the record of conversation between R.K. Nehru[1] and Chinese Premier Chou En-lai in 1962, some months before the border war erupted in October that year,' Shyam Saran, the distinguished diplomat,[2] narrated recently. 'R.K. Nehru drew attention to reports that China was leaning towards the Pakistani position that Jammu and Kashmir was disputed territory. He recalled to Chou an earlier conversation, where when asked whether China accepted Indian sovereignty over J&K, he had said, rhetorically—Has China ever said that it does not accept Indian sovereignty over J&K, or words to that effect. At this latest encounter, Chou turned the same formulation on its head, to ask, Has China ever said that India has sovereignty over J&K?'[3]

As we have seen, earlier in the book, Pandit Nehru had himself had a taste of—or, allowed himself to be taken in by—such half-sentences. As he was to recall later, when Chou en-Lai had come to India, Panditji had taken up the question of Chinese maps: these showed large swathes of India to be

[1] Former Secretary General, Ministry of External Affairs.

[2] Former Foreign Secretary and Special Envoy of the Prime Minister; currently chairman, National Security Advisory Board.

[3] Shyam Saran, 'China in the Twenty-first Century: What India needs to know about China's world view', Second K. Subrahmanyam Lecture, Global India Foundation, New Delhi, August 2012.

parts of China, he had told Chou, and that creates problems. Chou En-lai remarked that these were 'old, Kuomintang maps' and that they—the new Government of China—had not had time to verify them. Panditji took that to be an endorsement of the Indian position in regard to these maps. The maps continued to show large parts of India to be part of China. When he and other Indian officials raised the matter with Chinese authorities again some years later, they were told, in effect, O, yes, these are old maps. We hadn't had time to verify them at the time. We *have* verified them since, and they correctly set out China's territory!

In 2005, the same sequence was repeated, as we have seen. An agreement on 'Political Parameters and Guiding Principles' was signed. This set out the principles that would govern negotiations about and settlement of the boundary between the two countries. To recall an example: one of these principles was that the boundary shall follow natural contours, and that settled populations would not be disturbed. The Indian government took this to mean that China had come to accept India's position on Arunachal and, in particular, on Tawang being a part of India. Settled populations will not be disturbed—exactly, said the Chinese soon. That only means that all of Tawang and Arunachal shall be in China: those residing there will not be disturbed!

The same sort of thing has been happening all across the South China Sea. On the basis of their 'nine-dash map', the Chinese have pressed claims to the Spratly and Paracel Islands. (It used to be the 'eleven-dash map'—one that would entitle them to take in not just these, but also large chunks of Vietnamese possessions. By just striking out two 'dashes', the Chinese magnanimously let Vietnam off!) In any event, the Indonesians, though gravely suspicious of the Chinese, must have thought that, at least as far as the dashes were concerned, they were safe enough—being in the large outside the nine-dashes. But suddenly, the Natuna Islands seemed to be a no-man's land! Edward Luttwak recalls what happened. The Natuna Islands are a thousand miles from the nearest Chinese coast on Hainan Island, he points out. But the Chinese kept saying that there is no dispute about these islands with Indonesia. That set the Indonesians thinking! And then in 1995, the spokesperson of the Chinese foreign ministry stated, 'There is no dispute between China and Indonesia on possession of the Natuna Islands,' only to add, 'We're willing to hold talks with the Indonesian side to settle demarcation of this area'![4] The expression 'There is no dispute' suddenly acquired a new meaning! Of course, there is no dispute—the place is ours. But, being friends, we are prepared to negotiate about it with you!

Several countries will be able to add instances. The point that Shyam Saran made was generic, and goes beyond pasting blame on them. It is not just that in these particular instances the Chinese hoodwinked others. But that they would be surprised, if not incensed if you concluded that they had done something wrong. 'Much of the misunderstanding and lack of communication that has characterized India-China relations may be sourced to the failure on India's part to be conversant with Chinese thought processes,' Saran observed. 'It is easy to accuse the Chinese of betrayal, as Nehru did after the 1962 war, but a clear awareness that deception is, after all, an integral element of Chinese strategic culture, may have spared us much angst in the past. Such awareness should certainly be part of our confronting the China challenge in the future.' Recalling the 'Ruse of the empty city', Saran remarked: 'There is no moral or ethical dimension attached to deception and the Chinese would find it odd being accused of "betrayal", in particular, if the strategy of deception had worked. What is required from our strategists and diplomats is to understand this important instrument in the Chinese strategic tool-box and learn to deal with it effectively.'

---

[4] Edward Luttwak, *The Rise of China vs. The Logic of Strategy*, The Belknap Press of Harvard University Press, 2012, pp. 189–90.

A second feature is just as important, in that it has consequences that traverse many dimensions. We are often told that the Chinese think very long term—in terms of decades, of centuries, in 'civilizational-time', we are instructed. That has immediate implications for the type of weapons systems, of the types of warfare that a country in their sights must be prepared to contend with: to safeguard ourselves against such systems we must begin as far in advance of the deployment of such systems of warfare as would be required to build up counter-capacities. And we must not just begin years and decades in advance, we must sustain the effort over those decades. The same thing goes for maps, and verbally advanced claims. The Chinese will posit a claim. The unwary may think that it was just something they said. They will go on repeating that claim. The unwary will think, 'O, that is something they just keep saying.' But over the decades, it would have seeped into history, so to say. It would have become 'the long-held claim'—a sort of constructed memory. The mere repetition of the claim would have given it a basis, and led to the inference that it is something that the Chinese shall not let go.

Sanjeev Sanyal points to two additional implications of thinking on a civilizational time-scale that we would do well to bear in mind:

> First, since it is thinking in civilizational terms, the Chinese regime is willing to strategize in very long cycles. Second, the Chinese will put an unusually large premium on creating levers of power even when it may be irrational or immoral to actually exercise this power (i.e., there will be constant effort to create strategic leverage even when there is no obvious need for it). Thus, it would keep alive a North Korea even as it trades actively with South Korea. Indian strategizers would do well to keep these in mind when dealing with Beijing.[5]

---

[5] Sanjeev Sanyal, 'China's Rise and Its Implications for India', Working Paper, Indian Council for International Affairs, 2010.

China's ancient strategic texts set great store by stratagems, deception, conspiracies. These ancient texts are a living presence in the Chinese mind. This has three consequences. Luttwak stresses that as several of the maxims and stratagems are obviously of lesser efficacy when circumstances are so different today than they were when the texts were composed, on many occasions Chinese thinking can be quite off the mark. Second, being heirs to this hoary tradition, the Chinese are apt to think that they are specially gifted at carrying conspiracies through, at deceiving others, and getting the better of them. As he shows, this confidence can be quite misplaced. In any event, successful or not, the fact that the Chinese place such high value by conspiracies, deception, at suborning personnel in other regimes, etc., gives them in the eyes of others the reputation for these very skills and stratagems, and that certainly works to their disadvantage. There is a third consequence also. As they themselves put so much faith in conspiracies, in strategic and tactical deception, in bribing and the rest, they believe that others set the same sort of store in deception, in conspiracies and the like.

As a result, they are much given to conspiracy theories, to detecting hidden motives into events and statements and proposals—this way of looking at others has immediate consequences: it colours the way they are apt to construe what is from our point of view the most straightforward step that we may have taken, or the straightforward proposal that we may advance.

In their reckoning, everyone is forever conspiring, and China is the common, sometimes the sole target. Japan is forever being portrayed as a country that, through its 'China Threat Theory', through its skill at 'strategic misdirection', is instigating the United States into suspecting and confronting China. Japan is thought to be misdirecting the United States so as to keep the latter tied to itself in military matters, to continue to defray the expenditure for defending Japan, and, in general, to invest an inordinate proportion of its resources in military expenditure—the latter would leave the field clear for Japan to overtake the United States economically, and eventually to replace it as the world hegemon.

A single example of how '1+1' makes eleven in such constructions will suffice. Behind the façade of humanitarian concerns, the NATO bombardment of Kosovo in 1999 had deeper geostrategic objectives, we are told. Analysis after analysis of this campaign—a campaign that led to major rethinking among the Chinese on future warfare, which led them to conclude also that the decline of the US would take longer than they had earlier thought to be the case—elaborated on this deep design in almost identical terms. Here is a typical passage from Pillsbury's accounts of these analyses:

> Kosovo is located in the middle of the Balkan Peninsula and the peninsula is at the meeting point of Europe, Asia, and Africa. It is an important corridor joining the north, south, east, and west and leading to Asia and Africa... The United States knows full well the importance of the Balkan region and has regarded it as a 'new priority for consideration'... In this region, it can strengthen its security system in the Mediterranean and the North Atlantic to the west; can consolidate the 'southern wing of NATO' to the south through converging it with its Middle East strategy; can infiltrate and expand in the Black Sea and the Caspian Sea regions to the west, that is, the outer Caucasus and Central Asia regions, weakening and squeezing out Russian forces and influence, and taking a step further, can press on to China's northwestern boundary to coordinate from afar with its Asia-Pacific strategy; and finally, can exercise restraints on its European allies to the north, especially the NATO move southward. In this way, the United States will be able to properly fulfill its ambition of making Europe more important and practicing hegemony in the world.[6]

[6] Michael Pillsbury, *China Debates the Future Security Environment*, National Defense University Press, Washington, DC, 2000. Retrieved from http://www.fas.org/nuke/guide/china/doctrine/pills2/

As almost every point in the world is on the way to somewhere else, much the same could be said of operations centred on almost any spot in the world!

As everyone is always conspiring, as everyone is always propelled by carefully concealed motives, what we do is manifestly going to be seen far from what it seems to us. That is even more so in our case, for, as we shall see in a moment, the Chinese think of Indians as congenitally devious and deceitful. Nor does this proclivity merely colour the construction one places on what the other is saying or doing. It becomes a justification for deceiving him in turn. The circle is thus completed!

A vital determinant, little known in India

The next feature that we have to bear in mind requires a word as preface. The fact is that even among Indian literati, in fact especially among Indian literati, discourse about India and China is asymmetrical—that is in part due to the fact that most of us know little about China; but the principal reason is that such discourse, as there is, has been dominated for ever so long by the left, for whom China has been Medina if not Mecca itself. As the point might stir sensitivities, in the following paragraphs I will take examples only from the much-acclaimed work of a Sinophile—a former British Marxist who quite looks forward to the day when the West would have declined, and China would be remoulding the world to its distinctive order—Jacques Martin. To cite just one symptomatic expression, while it is well known that traditional China was just a third of the area that is today claimed to be China, and even though he himself acknowledges that 'China's provinces are far more diverse than Europe's nation-states, even when Eastern Europe and the Balkans are included'; even though he himself acknowledges that dialects within China are as incomprehensible to persons from other regions as one

European language is to Europeans from other countries, Martin's entire thesis is that China is a civilizational state: that its civilization is distinctive, that that civilization pervades and underlies all of China. On the other hand, his view of India is that, 'India too can be considered a candidate [of being regarded as a civilization state] but, unlike China, India, as we know it today, was a relatively recent creation of the British Raj, its previous history being far more diverse than that of China.'[7] In a word, a suitable observer from whom to cull a few examples.

Inequality? In China, the richest 1 per cent of households own 41 per cent of the country's privately held wealth.[8]

Rulers forever? Jacques quotes the historian Wang Gungwu: '...in the last thousand years, the Chinese can claim to have ruled their own country for 280 of those years.'[9]

Imperial conquest of peoples and lands? No, not in the reckoning of the Chinese; they have looked upon their expansion not as 'conquest' but as 'unification'.[10]

Article 370? Here we are tied hand and foot by Article 370. And China? One of the most consistently and ruthlessly used instruments of Chinese imperial expansion and subjugation—of much of what is today 'China', certainly of Xinjiang, Tibet, Inner Mongolia—has been to populate the conquered lands with Han Chinese. As a result, in the 'Mongolian Autonomous Region', 'there are four times as many Han as Mongols, thereby rendering the latter relatively impotent'.[11] In 1950, Han were around 6 per cent of the population of Xinjiang, China's main producer of oil and gas; they now account for 'at least 40 per cent, perhaps more

---

[7] Martin Jacques, *When China Rules the World*, Penguin, London, 2012, pp. 245, 257–58.

[8] Ibid., p. 195.

[9] Ibid., p. 300.

[10] Ibid., p. 299.

[11] Ibid., p. 316.

than half.'[12] A few pages later, Jacques gives figures closer to the official version: '...The Han now account for around 8.3 million of Xinjiang's population of 22 million, almost as many as the Uighur, with the Han concentrated in the urban centers, notably the capital, Urumqi, where they comprise most of the population of 2.3 million, and in the oil- and gas-producing regions in the north.' He adds, 'As in Tibet, the socio-economic structure of the workforce reflects a very marked ethnic divide, with the Han dominating commercial activities, the bureaucracy, oil and gas, and the Uighurs living in the smaller towns and the rural areas...'[13] As for Tibet, the Dalai Lama—expelled; the six-year old boy who in 1995 was named as the Panchen Lama by the Dalai Lama—'apprehended' by the Chinese and not seen since. 'In addition, China has encouraged large-scale Han migration in Tibet in an effort to alter the ethnic balance of the population and thereby weaken the position of the Tibetans, who for the most part live in the rural areas and in segregated urban ghettos, unlike the Han, who comprise over half the population of Lhasa and are concentrated in the urban areas. Given the rapid rise of Han migration encouraged by the new direct link between Beijing and Lhasa, it is possible that the proportion of Han in TAR [the 'Tibet Autonomous Region'] could rise rapidly in the future. In what appears to have been a typical case of divide and rule, China chose to dismember the Tibetan population by putting heavily Tibetan areas under non-Tibetan jurisdiction in the neighbouring provinces of Sichuan, Qinghai and Gansu...'[14]

'Century of humiliation': Much of what China does today is explained away as the result of a determination not to let the 'century of humiliation' be repeated—the century from 1842 when the Treaty of Nanjing was imposed on China to

[12] Ibid., p. 316.

[13] Ibid., pp. 321–22.

[14] Ibid., pp. 318–19.

1949 when, with Mao's victory, 'China stood up'. That the Chinese should work to ensure that no power will ever again be able to impose unequal relations on them is something everyone would endorse. On the other hand, if anyone in India so much as mentions a thousand years of foreign rule, he is dubbed—especially in India—as a 'communal jingoist' and worse! And this was foreign rule in the worst sense, under which the overwhelming majority of Indians just did not have rights available to Muslims in the first instance and to whites in the second—an inequity so monstrous that the unequal relations that were imposed on China by those treaties in the nineteenth century, wholly repugnant though they were, pale into the second order of smalls. Moreover, in regard to the unequal treaties which were imposed on China—and they *were* imposed, they *were* unequal—Luttwak makes a telling observation: 'It was not the inequality that rankled, but rather the reversal of the usual pattern of inequality, in which it was the emperor who subjected foreigners, and not the other way around…'[15]

Atrocities: The Chinese forever keep reminding others as well as themselves of the atrocities that the Japanese committed on them—so much so that they seek to determine what the Japanese shall state in textbooks for their children. But if anyone in India so much as mentions the immeasurable massacres that the Muslim invaders perpetrated or the atrocities that the British committed, he is one who is 'obsessed with the past'.

So, there is this asymmetry within India in the discourse about China and about India—and it certainly has consequences for our ability to see what adversaries are up to. But there is another point about Chinese attitudes that bears even more directly on how they perceive India and Indians and how they will deal with us.

It will surprise most in India to learn how deeply embedded

---

[15] Edward N. Luttwak, *The Rise of China vs. The Logic of Strategy*, op. cit., p. 35.

racialism is in the Chinese culture and psyche. Several standard works testify to this—two easily accessible ones are the well-known studies by Frank Dikotter and the one edited by Steven Harrell.[16] But for reasons stated above, a few observations of Martin Jacques will be enough—no one can accuse him of a bias against the Chinese; and he incorporates and carries further with his first-hand observations the work of Dikotter and others.

Race is deeply embedded in Chinese thinking, culture, in their very psyche, Martin Jacques points out, and race shall be one of the four or five main features of the new world order that China will establish, he forecasts. Skin colour has always carried great significance among the Chinese, he recalls. A white complexion was always highly prized, and was likened to as 'white jade'. The Buddha himself, Jacques quotes Dikotter observing, was converted from a 'swart half-naked Indian to a more decently clad divinity with a properly light complexion'—rather as Jesus was whitened in the Western tradition, Jacques adds. The Han Chinese referred to themselves as 'white'. Skin colour made visible the class distinctions, Martin Jacques explains. It is only in the nineteenth century, when the Caucasian whites began imposing those unequal treaties on the Chinese, that, to distinguish themselves from the whites on the one hand and from the dark-skinned people on the other, the Chinese began to refer to themselves as 'yellow'.

Our ancestors have been condemned times without number for looking upon foreigners as *mlechha*—unclean. The Chinese routinely referred to them as 'barbarians', and not just the Mongols and others who conquered them, but all who had not absorbed and internalized the superior

---

[16] Frank Dikotter, *The Discourse of Race in Modern China,* Hurst and Co, London, 1992, and *The Construction of Race in China and Japan,* Hong Kong University, 1997; and *Cultural Encounters on China's Ethnic Frontiers,* Steven Harrell [ed.], University of Washington Press, 1995.

Chinese culture. Among these, as Jacques recalls, one set was called *shengfan*, the 'raw barbarians'; the other, those who had been conditioned into Chinese mores, as *shufan*, the 'cooked barbarians'. Foreigners were routinely described as 'devils', with Caucasians being designated as 'white devils'. Like several others have done, in particular African students who studied in China, Martin Jacques describes the repulsive treatment to which Africans have been subjected at the hands of the Chinese.

And these intense racial prejudices are shared in common by the elite and common folk, by academics and men of letters.

'...The pervasiveness of racism applies not only to China,' Martin Jacques notes, 'but also to Taiwan, Singapore, Hong Kong and even overseas Chinese communities. Thus it is not only a function of isolation or insularity, of China's limited contact with the outside world...' Overseas Chinese tend to keep to themselves as a community, he notes. They commonly look down upon the majority race of the place in which they have settled or are residing, often referring to the host population as 'foreigners'.

What about Marxism-Leninism-Maoism? Did it not erase race-consciousness? 'Under Mao, the language of race was replaced by that of class,' Jacques points out. 'However, the underlying attitudes of the Han have remained little changed. There is an ingrained prejudice among great swathes of the Han Chinese, including the highly educated, towards the ethnic minorities. According to Steven Harrell, a writer on China's ethnic minorities, "there is an innate, almost visceral sense of superiority"...'

And the surprise of surprises! The appellation 'Han Chinese' itself, Martin Jacques points out, came into existence only in the later nineteenth century. It was coined by a nationalist writer: 'The term "Han Chinese" was an invention, nothing more than a cultural construct: there was no such race; the Han Chinese were, in reality, an amalgam of many races. The purpose of the term was overtly racial, a means of inclusion and exclusion...'[17]

Martin Jacques lists the features that will characterize the new world order that China shall set up once it attains dominance, among them being the fact that other states shall be steered into a relationship of being tributary states of China. Given the culture and history of China, one of the major features of that new order, Martin Jacques's analysis ineluctably suggests, shall be racial hierarchy—with the carriers of its ancient culture, the Han, at the top. As we are not just lying on China's periphery, as we are the browns lying right on China's periphery, their attitudes towards us cannot but be conditioned, among other things, by this racial presumption.

In no doubt about India, Indians

Race apart, China has a clear idea about India—that it is a potential nuisance. It views us as one of the 'claws of the crab'—the crab being the US whose aim is to contain China; a crab with South Korea, Japan, Taiwan, Vietnam, Australia and India as its claws. The recent moves for closer relationship between the US and India, advantageous though they are for us, have had the incidental effect of reinforcing this perception.

For decades, Chinese strategic writers have persistently held that four countries pose a threat, often the tone is that they pose an imminent threat to China. These four are the US, Japan, Russia and India. Chinese analysts have insisted that the objective of the four is the 'dismemberment' of China.[18]

---

[17] On the foregoing, Martin Jacques, *When China Rules the World,* op. cit., pp. 297, 308–41.

[18] A convenient summary of the standard Chinese view is Michael Pillsbury, *China Looks at the Future Security Environment,* op. cit. This informative study is based on the writings of 200 Chinese scholars, strategic thinkers, defence personnel.

In their writings, Japan and India are often clubbed. As Pillsbury noted, several strands seem to mingle to produce a deep prejudice about both countries. There was the Marxist premise that, as these were capitalist countries, they would by definition be predatory. There was the heritage of China's ancient statecraft—that one should be vigilant about nearby rivals, especially of those with whom one has territorial disputes, and seek partnerships with distant states. And then there are history and culture. Pillsbury recorded the views of General Li Jijun, then vice president of the Academy of Military Sciences, who wrote that Japan's strategic culture is fundamentally ruthless, bloodthirsty, and a 'self-made freak'.

India has consistently been seen and portrayed 'a half-scale' version of Japan with that 'self-made freak' strategic culture. Both are portrayed as being on the way to being taken over by religious-militaristic-nationalist regimes. India is consistently portrayed as ambitious—as recklessly ambitious, reckless in that its fantasies are always causing it to punch beyond its weight. The clash between these 'Great Power ambitions' of India and reality—the declining influence of India in international affairs—will further enflame militarism, and religion-based nationalism, the analysts maintain. Pillsbury cited a Report written by Chou En-lai which attributed to India the ambition to be the regional hegemon, and traced this grandiose dream to Indian leaders having interbred with their British colonial masters, to their having a 'blood relationship' with their British masters. The report explained that the Indian middle class 'took over from British imperialism this concept of India being the center of Asia', and that its rulers want to have 'a great Indian empire' that dominates Asia. These Chinese analysts are forever quoting two sentences of—of all persons!—Pandit Nehru and reading into them meanings that Panditji could never have imagined could be wrung out of them: from his *Autobiography*, the sentence, 'Though not directly a Pacific state, Indian will inevitably exercise an important influence there'; and, another sentence to the effect that, given India's size, history, culture, either it must play a major role in the world or none at all. These stray sentences are taken by the Chinese—and that specifically included Mao and Chou personally—to establish that the 'goal pursued by this ambitious Nehru is the establishment of a great Empire unprecedented in India's history'. Reading their own history—with its system of tributary States—which even a Sinophile observer like Martin Jacques writes shall be one of the characteristics of the New World Order under China—they explain that a small national State 'can only be a vassal in Nehru's great empire'.

The contempt that Mao and Chou had for India, for Indians, leaps through their exchanges with Kissinger and Nixon.

Moreover, having been an instrument of the British for so long, the Chinese say, India is always only too willing to become an instrument of others. It became the instrument of the Soviet Union. It is becoming the instrument of the US. To inveigle these larger powers into becoming its accomplices, India, like Japan, repeatedly plays the 'China Threat Card', the analysts assert.

The common objective of all these countries is to contain China, and eventually to dismember it. India also has a proximate objective: to help create an independent Tibet—so that it has a buffer between itself and China. This 'political plot' of India accords with the objective of the US, Japan, etc., as the latter also aim to dismember China—in the first instance by getting Tibet and Xinjiang to become independent.

Accordingly, China has pursued a consistent strategy of containing India in return, of keeping it confined to, and busy in South Asia.

With this aim, it has given aid to Pakistan for all sorts of purposes—including the development of atomic weapons and acquisition of missile technology. And it does so on hoary counsel. Recall the counsel of *The Wiles of War*, 'Murder with a borrowed knife'—that is, instead of doing anything overtly aggressive yourself, find the entity that is naturally predisposed to do your enemy in; and arm, encourage, instigate it. Tibet has been militarized—to put the Tibetans down, no doubt; but is it only to put them down? And, even if it were only to put the Tibetans down, the *capacity* that China acquires for doing so has consequences for us. China has redoubled its efforts in Sri Lanka, Maldives, Seychelles and Mauritius. In large part because of the short-sighted policies of the West and of India itself, Myanmar had become a dependency of China. China put that phase to good use. It acquired access to ports of Myanmar. It took on lease the Coco Islands just 30 miles from the Andamans. It is building and thus acquiring access to deep-sea ports round us: Chittagong in Bangladesh and Gwadar in Pakistan—the latter alone is being built at a cost of US$ 3 billion. It is also upgrading the naval base in Omara for Pakistan. Along with constructing the port at Gwadar, it is building highways that will link Gwadar to locations within Pakistan but also to Urumqi in Xinjiang. It is building the port at Hambantota in Sri Lanka.

As we have noted above, it has advanced novel interpretations of the terms of the 2005 agreement regarding the political parameters within which and the principles on which negotiations on the border shall proceed. It has repeatedly refrained from exchanging maps of the Line of Actual Control, thereby leaving the line ambiguous, and then, asserting that the line is unspecified, gone on advancing into India. It has been conducting more and more aggressive patrolling of the border. It has taken to being more and more explicitly aggressive and unambiguous in regard to its claims to Arunachal Pradesh: it denied a visa to an IAS officer who was part of a contingent scheduled to visit China—on the ground that being from Arunachal and therefore a citizen of a part of the Administrative Zone of Tibet, he needed no visa! It has shifted its stance on Jammu and Kashmir, raising doubts about the state being a part of India, and rubbing this in in various ways: it began insisting that it would give only stapled visas to residents of Kashmir; in 2010, it refused to give a visa to the general heading the Northern Command of the Indian Army on the ground that Jammu and Kashmir fell under the Command. It has taken up and is executing a series of projects in the part of Kashmir which is under Pakistani occupation

Few of the measures it has been taking will perhaps be as consequential as the schemes it has begun implementing for diverting Tibetan waters to north and east China. The dams it has begun building across the Brahmaputra are just one limb of these schemes.

Furthermore, in every international arena, there is a pattern to its actions vis-à-vis India. It expended much effort to keep ASEAN from establishing closer links with India—it campaigned to have ASEAN+3 (ASEAN, Japan, South Korea and China) and not ASEAN+4 which would have included India. It summarily rejected the G-4 framework for the expansion of the Security Council. It did not agree to let India enter the Shanghai Cooperation Organization—through which it is institutionalizing its influence in Central Asia. In the end, it agreed to grant us 'observer status'—but only along with Pakistan and Iran; and only when we agreed to it getting the same status in SAARC and BIMSTEC: for the latter, it was vigorously supported not just by Pakistan and Bangladesh but also by our 'traditional friends', Sri Lanka and Nepal.

The incident at the Asian Development Bank was typical. The Government of India sought technical assistance from the Asian Development Bank for preparing a project. The ADB agreed to provide it. China objected: part of the eventual project would be in Arunachal, which is China's territory, it maintained; the ADB cannot undertake the project. The Indian response, I was told in Manila, was so 'ambivalent and muted' that China prevailed. Not only was the project never taken up, not only was the proposal 'left to die', the ADB was compelled to adopt a new policy: if a territory is in dispute—and in the case of China this comes to mean, 'any territory over which China *just raises a dispute*'—the ADB will not take up any project in the area without talking to both sides to the 'dispute'.

Three points before we move on to summarize the lessons that all this holds for us.

First and foremost, for none of this is China to blame. It is pursuing its interests as it perceives them. In many instances—from the way we let Myanmar be pushed into the lap of China; to the incursions that China has made and the territory that it has been able to go on acquiring in India; to the chasm that has developed in our economies and technologies, we are the ones who are responsible.

Second, China sees that, while it has been advancing its interests in this aggressive manner for decades, we have not stood up to halt it.

Third, while each of the issues on which it has pressed ahead vis-à-vis India is important in itself—no country whose leaders proclaim the sort goodwill that successive Chinese leaders routinely do when they visit India could be taking such steps inadvertently—the issues were just the occasion for taking those hostile steps.

For the real issue, in the Chinese mind, is something else entirely. 'The structural problem is leadership,' Shen Dingli, the deputy head of the South Asia Research Institute in Shanghai, explained. 'The question is who leads in Asia.'[19]

And beyond.

---

[19] Peter Ford on the escalating 'war of words' between India and China, in the *Christian Science Monitor*, http://www.csmonitor.com/2009/1020/p06s04-woap.html. Cited in Mohan Malik, 'India balances China', *Asian Politics and Policy*, 2012, Volume 4, No. 3, pp. 345–76, at p. 351.

18

Bal hoa bandhan chhutey...

- We must be Arjunas—with one singular aim, to forge a strong India. That objective must take precedence, it must override all others. A society in which people are obsessively pursuing money the way most are in India today—including, as has become obvious in the last few years, so many of the leaders; a society in which everyone is pursuing his particular issue—environment, civil liberties, rights of tribals, the tiger, whatever—just will not be able to meet the challenges that confront the country. Each of these concerns is important but it must give way to building the strength and security of the country.
- Do not take the burdens of the world on your shoulders, as Panditji felt duty-bound to do. Attend first and foremost to what concerns your country directly.
- The head of the government, in particular, must not plunge into saving the world: bear in mind the enormous, literally enormous amount of time that Panditji had to devote to Korea, Indo-China, Congo. A general in the trenches—especially in other people's trenches—will have no time for thinking out the strategy that is best for his own armies.
- If you are not able to do anything at one turn, build up your capacity so that you are not helpless at the next one: that we could not do anything when the Chinese

first invaded Tibet is no excuse for not having prepared ourselves in the years that followed.

- Do not be carried away by welcomes and the 'emotional upheavals' that you see on fleeting visits. Be as wary of the earnestness of a Chou En-lai acting the eager student. He is not waiting for your instruction. He is playing on your vanity to fool you.
- It is ruinous for a country when its leaders insist on being unilaterally friendly and trusting of those who control a potential adversary; when its commentators feel that the way they can establish themselves to be objective is to be supercilious, to bend backwards and be unilaterally 'fair'.
- Be alert to what our neighbours are doing, to the strengths they have acquired; and just as much to what our rulers are doing, to what they are agreeing to do when they talk to leaders of other countries. Memorize the delusions of 1949–1962. Memorize the warnings that were ignored. To do so, diligently plough through the record of the time. Most of this is now in the public domain.
- Know the Chinese. Know what they think of themselves. Know what they think of us. Know the objective they have set for themselves. Know what they have concluded they have to do to and around India for attaining that objective.
- Do not expect a China to be grateful because you have championed its cause—at Bandung, much less at the Climate Change Conference in Copenhagen.
- Never take its silence to be consent.
- Nor its ambiguous word: memorize what Chou En-lai said to Panditji about the maps being old, Kumintong maps; memorize what Panditji assumed this to mean, and what followed. Memorize what Chou En-lai told R.K. Nehru about recognizing India's sovereignty over Jammu and Kashmir, and what R.K. Nehru took that to mean. Remember what it now says 'not disturbing settled

populations' means, and what in 2005 we had taken that expression to mean.

- Nor indeed its consent—do not take that to be the final word.
- Not even if that consent is in writing: no compunction restrained China from repudiating the 17-point agreement with Tibet fifty years ago, just as no compunction has restrained it now from standing on their head the principles and political parameters that were agreed in 2005 for settling the border question. The only thing which will matter is our strength on the ground vis-à-vis the strength an adversary will hurl at the theatre of operations. It follows that, while we must strive to settle the border dispute with China, we have to bear in mind that no settlement will survive if the country does not have the strength to beat back anyone who violates it.
- We must recognize a danger as far in advance as it would take us to institute the measures that are required to meet it: it did little good to see in mid-1962 the danger that Chinese forces posed.
- What is lost can seldom be recovered. As we have seen, the Resolution that Panditji moved in Parliament and which the Parliament adopted unanimously said in conclusion: *With hope and faith, this House affirms the firm resolve of the Indian people to drive out the aggressor from the sacred soil of India, however long and hard the struggle may be.* Who will today insist that the Chinese be driven out from Aksai Chin?
- Rushing troops around at the last minute, buying weapons at the last minute, learning how to counter new types of warfare at the last minute—all this *has* to be done when the avalanche descends, but by then it is of little use. Nor does the emotion and enthusiasm with which people respond when the aggressor actually launches operations. The emotion and enthusiasm are indispensable—the more so the longer are the hostilities. But they are no

substitute for having prepared oneself in the years that precede the onslaught. As Clausewitz would say, 'The best strategy is always to be very strong'—both terms are equally important: '*always*' as well as '*very strong*'.

> *Bal hoa bandhan chhutey sab kuchh hote upaaye…*
> *Strength accrues, shackles snap, every move becomes a stratagem…*

'The weak are never at peace,' K.P.S. Gill, who saved Punjab for our country, writes. 'There is … one general principle that must guide our explorations, perspectives, plans and projections,' he writes.

> *The primary and most effective strategy to avoid war is to prepare for it.* It is one of the ironies of the human condition that, if you love peace, you must be ready and willing to fight for it. The weak, the vulnerable, the unprepared and the irresolute will always tempt the world and call misfortune and ruin upon themselves. This is tragic, but it is the inexorable lesson of history. It is strength that secures respect and dignity; conciliation, appeasement, and a desperation to avoid confrontation at all costs—these will only bring contempt and aggression in their dower.[1]

- And that strength must be what the Chinese characterize as Comprehensive National Strength. The Soviet Union was the second most powerful country militarily; it collapsed without a shot being fired—as its economy was stagnant and its society uncreative. Till the other day, Japan was the second-largest economy in the world, but it counted for little as it had foregone commensurate military strength and thereby handed over its defence and foreign policies to the United States.

---

[1] K.P.S. Gill, 'The Fundamental Idea,' in *Freedom from Fear: Occasional Writings on Terrorism and Governance,* South Asia Terrorism Portal, *http://www.satp.org.satporgtp/kpsgill/terrorism/00Mar13Outlook.htm*

- True, as Panditji repeatedly emphasized, basic, all-round strength requires comprehensive development programmes, and bringing them to fruition will extend into the 'long run'. But the long run is no substitute for the short run, as it too often seemed to be in Panditji's thinking. Indeed, it is made up of a series of short runs. Both sorts of steps are imperative—those that will safeguard us here and now, as well as those that are required to build our strength eventually.
- It is certainly not enough to be stronger than we were yesterday. We have to be stronger than are those who are out to harm us.
- We must be stronger than our rivals will be years from now: that is, we have to begin acquiring the capacity to counter a capability that our rival is building—for instance, in 'magic weapons', in space, in information warfare—taking into account the gestation period, the number of years it will take us to acquire that countervailing capacity.
- We must benchmark ourselves against the strongest rival who is likely to seek to hobble and harm us—in our case, and in our neighbourhood, that is China.
- As a country that does not plan to strike first, we have to equip ourselves for the entire range of possible assaults. All too often, in India, our discussions veer off into '*either/or*'—*either* lethal, light and wired forces *or* special forces *or* corps-level forces. But the angle of vision should be, '*and also*'. No single formula, no single type of force, no magic switch will suffice. And today, perhaps for the first time since Independence, resources are not the constraint: we just have to recall the colossal amounts that governments today throw away at 'welfare schemes' to see that we certainly have the resources for a great a leap in defence and foreign policy operations, including foreign aid—just the leakages from these 'welfare schemes' will suffice.

- But, in addition to deploying resources, we need to think anew. Today, as each strike orchestrated by Pakistan reminds us, as each incursion by China reminds us, we are a country without options. The time when large armies could be sent across international borders is gone—unless the difference between the adversaries be as large as that between the US and Grenada, or Iraq and Afghanistan, and even then, as the last two instances show, the outcome the larger power can manage may well be no better than camouflaged disaster. 'Doing a Kashmir' to the aggressor when that is what he is doing to us; throwing vast sectors of the aggressor into disarray without firing a shot or crossing a border—those are the sorts of capacities that we must acquire.
- But capacities for such options cannot be built in a week just because the terrorists have struck, or a posse has crossed into our territory. They can be built only over twenty-thirty years, they can be acquired only through unremitting effort over twenty to thirty years. It can never get built if, as has been happening, each government that comes, stops, if it doesn't reverse initiatives that its predecessor had commenced.
- Acquiring a capacity includes acquiring the reputation that we *will* use the capacity we have acquired. Others should see us as a porcupine, not a peacock. The response must be swift. It must be seen to be in retaliation for what has been inflicted on us. It must personally hit those who organized and instigated the assault against us. And/or it must inflict an unacceptable level of damage on their country. That is why, for instance, it is no more than an announcement of helplessness to keep proclaiming, 'We will crush terrorists if they come *into* India,' or, to be more current, 'We will send the intruders back, we will get them to pull up their tents'. Why will the controllers of those terrorists, for instance, stop sending terrorists across when they know that all

that India will attempt to do is to kill the terrorists who are *inside* India?

- All instruments must be put to work for the same, designated purpose. We have only to recall the role that manipulating the international environment played in ensuring victory for the North Vietnamese to see how foreign and defence policies must move in tandem. And not just in a crisis. Even this elementary lesson is very important for us as our ministries and departments work in silos.
- *We* must acquire the requisite capacities. Yet, over the last thirty years, we have allowed ourselves to fall so far behind China that, as of today, we cannot stand up to it on our own. Several lemmas follow from this:
    - We must strive to knit a network of alliances. Working with others is often exasperating but, as Churchill is reported to have said, the one thing worse than fighting a war with allies is fighting a war without allies! Reflect for a moment: Which are the countries that will do China's bidding on Security Council reform? Which will risk anything in our interest?
    - We must seek alliances knowing full well that each country, if it joins up, will do so for its own reasons, that most often these will be complex, they will entail a balancing of many conflicting assessments within that country.
    - We must work for an array of several intersecting alliances; different countries will join us on different issues: e.g., some are today apprehensive of Islamic terrorism, others are apprehensive of China's rise; some would be interested in exchanging intelligence information and assessments of possible futures, some in maritime cooperation, some in coordinating responses to China's projects for diverting Tibetan waters to north and east China. We must have programmes and personnel for cooperating with each of them on issues that are of concern to them.

- The situation has changed substantially in the last five years. A reaction has set in among several countries to the rise and the aggressiveness of China. Several are now uncertain, indeed they are apprehensive about what China may do in the future. But to avail of this reaction, to put these apprehensions to work, we have to do much, much more *with*, *for* and *in* those countries than we do at present. Proclaiming a 'Look East' policy; signing agreements for 'strategic partnership' with these countries is of little consequence unless we follow these up with concrete measures—unless *we* follow these agreements up with concrete measures.
- We should forge alliances not just with countries, we should also forge them with nationalities and sub-nationalities within countries—with the Baluch, the Pashtun, with the peoples who are being suppressed in Gilgit-Baltistan, in POK; with the Tibetans, of course, but also with other minorities in China—the Uighurs, the Mongols.
- Indeed, we should seek to build alliances and working relationships not just with nationalities and sub-nationalities within countries but also with groups of academics and others. So many groups within China and abroad—at the Universities of Cambridge, of Toronto, and in several hubs of software development—are working to get around Chinese censorship, to get facts out about events in China, to get information to the Chinese. Others are working to find out what China is doing in regard to information warfare. Still others are working to nail theft by Chinese and Chinese firms of intellectual property and high technology. Are we even in touch with them?

• Hence, alliances are a must. But at the same time, we must not be, and must not be seen to be dependent on any other country. Nor must our actions be subject to the approval of any other country—a country that our adversaries can dissuade. That is, while we must work out alliances, our adversary must know that we will act on our own if necessary. Look at the way China has been able to dissuade France, Germany, the US time and again just by cancelling a visit, just by holding out the possibility that a contract may not come through. If we are seen to be susceptible to persuasion by one of these countries, would that country not be pressed to make us see merit in the Chinese position?

What is the inference that an adversary will draw when, while referring to the Pakistan-trained and -based terrorist attack in Mumbai, he hears the then US Secretary of State, Hillary Clinton, tell the House Appropriations Subcommittee, 'We worked very hard, as did the prior administration, *to prevent India from reacting*. But we know that the insurgents and *al Qaeda* and their syndicate partners are pretty smart. They are not going to cease their attacks, inside India, because they are looking for exactly the kind of reaction that we all hope to prevent. So we do have a lot of work to do, with the Indian government, *to make sure that they continue to exercise the kind of restraint they showed after Mumbai*, which was remarkable, especially given the fact that it was the political season.'

And when he hears her testify that that work continues? For Mrs Clinton told the House Committee that, when the US President met Manmohan Singh on the sidelines of the G-20 meeting, they discussed '*the issue of how India can do more to tamp down any reaction, on any front, like Mumbai could have provoked*.'[2]

Would he not conclude that there is a lever in Washington that can be used to 'tamp down' India?

---

[2] Hillary Rodham Clinton, Secretary of State, Remarks before House Appropriations Subcommittee on State, Foreign Operations, and Related Programs, Washington, DC, 23 April 2009.

- Nor should we expect, to say nothing of relying on even the closest allies to do our work for us. Every country will proceed by what is in its national interest; by what is in its national interest *as perceived by a handful*; by what is in its national interest as perceived by a handful *at that moment:*
  - Scholars acquainted with the history of the Communist Party of Vietnam recount the difficulties that Vietnam faced during its long struggle: in spite of the strongest opposition in the highest reaches of the Communist Party, Ho Chi Minh and his closest associates were forced to compromise at Geneva in 1954: the USSR wanted to ease relations with the West, China was loath to get into another war with the US so soon after Korea. It faced difficulties of another sort when these two allies, on whom it was relying for assistance, fell out among themselves for reasons that had nothing to do with what it was doing to liberate South Vietnam.
  - For long Saddam Hussein was good as a counterweight to Iran, then he became evil; one day, the exchanges and signals were such that he could make himself believe that, were he to press his claim to Kuwait, the US would be indifferent as it was not interested in *inter se* issues among Arab States; the next, his lunge into Kuwait became the reason for an all-out invasion. One day the Taliban are fearless freedom fighters against the Soviet Union; the next, they are vermin who have to be squashed. Just as suddenly, they are not all bad—there are the 'good Taliban' who have to be engaged, and the 'bad Taliban' who have to be exterminated.
  - Today, many look with hope to the American announcement of reshaping their policy with Asia-Pacific as its pivot, and infer that, at last, the US is taking the threat from China seriously. But even as

it announces the pivoting, the US—perhaps as part of that very refocusing—seeks to engage China in a sort of G-2 framework.

- Do not pose the question as 'all or nothing'. The choice that the other fellow sees is not 'war or peace', but 'limited war', 'proxy war'; not 'amity or violence,' but 'the violence of peace'.
- Often, a country is confronted with a determined challenge. Sometimes it just *has* to face war. The choice is not up to the country alone. The country cannot avoid hostilities when the adversary is bent on 'teaching it a lesson', when the adversary has concluded that the country must be made an example of, when it has concluded that others need to be shown who is boss. A people who have been continually fed discouraging notions—about the horrors of war, about how a war here will trigger a World War, and thus bring about the end of civilization as we know it: each of these being expressions that Panditji used incessantly—are being psychologically incapacitated.
- Nor is it enough to occasionally acknowledge the threat, and write the occasional note on file that necessary preparations be made: Panditji himself wrote quite a few notes to this effect. Sundry ministers have spoken in the same vein more recently—recall that in the months preceding 26/11, the prime minister, Manmohan Singh, the home minister, the National Security Advisor had each warned that terrorists were liable to use the sea route to come into India. They delivered their warnings at international conferences on security also! And, as if they were mere consultants, declaimed that 'necessary steps must be taken'. Someone has to ensure that those steps have actually been taken on the ground.
- Never, but never underplay what the adversary has done. This was the fatal flaw. Panditji had insisted China would not act aggressively. It did. Panditji kept minimizing what

the Chinese were doing, he started exculpating them, he in fact started finding reasons for what they were doing—in part because he had insisted it would not act that way, and in part because he still did not want to take the steps that the actions of China demanded. To our peril, as we have seen in regard to incursions across the Line of Actual Control, in regard to the series of steps that China has been taking to directly thwart our interests, the same pattern—of denial, of minimizing—continues to this day. Instead of concealing the truth, take the people into confidence at each stage. Tell them the *whole* truth. That is the only way they will be conditioned for the sacrifices that will eventually have to be made.

- When leaders are pygmies of the kind that crowd our public life today, there is no help. Glance again through the statements of the present government with which this essay commenced, the statements that put wishful constructions on what the Chinese are saying. Do they suggest that the country and its rulers have learnt anything at all from the blunders that cost us so dearly in 1962? Statements apart, recall what the government has actually been doing. Do you think that the cravenness that it displayed while handling the Olympic Torch in 2008 is seen in Beijing as careful handling for which it should be grateful or as fright of which it can take advantage? Look again at the cover of this book. Do you think that the Chinese see that bow by the prime minister of India as courtesy that they should reciprocate or as cravenness that is their due from a weakling?
- But, equally, when the leader is indeed as exalted and as knowledgeable a person as Panditji, he must exert all the more to ensure that he does not shut out contrary assessment and counsel.
- Build up capacity all along our Himalayan borders. Ensure that no PIL, no frivolous allegation, no 'environmental clearance' shall impede this work.

- Remember that our security is inextricably intertwined with Tibet—with the survival of the Tibetan people and of their religion and culture. Do not repeat the blunder of Panditji when he decided that India should not take up in any international forum, the Chinese invasion of Tibet, certainly not at the UN: the others got a chance to reason, 'As the country most affected by the invasion, India, is not interested in taking up the matter, why should we?'
- Because of the disarray in our governance, the gap between China and India has already grown into a dangerous chasm. Unless we mend our ways, we will be fomenting an irresistible temptation to an aggressor. Be certain that China sees the disarray in our political life; the paralysis of our institutions; the discord between the armed forces and civilian authorities; the evaporation in governance from vast swathes of the country; the sway of local mafias making India into a sort of decentralized Russia; the preoccupation of the media with trivialities. It would be worse than foolish to think that China does not see all this, that it does not see the opportunity in it.
- Yes, China has problems. But these are not going to solve our problems. At best, they will give us a little more time than we might otherwise have to get our affairs together. Even if one assumes that China will inevitably be pulled down by its problems, there is danger. How will the rulers of China react when confronted with such a situation? Will a foray abroad, a lunge at someone on their periphery not be a way to deflect the anger of their people? Hence, leave China's problems to China. Focus instead on the strengths that China has acquired, and on what these imply for us. Instead of consoling ourselves with accounts of problems that China has, we should discern the factors that have enabled it to register the successes it has attained, and match them.

- Nor is the task confined to governments. The disarray that we see in governance is truly representative of disarray and distractedness in our society. It is not just our governments that have to focus. We have to. In particular, those who dominate discourse in our county today have to keep their eyes on national security, on national strength.
- Even those of us who are nowhere near the defence establishment, who are nowhere near governments, can do a great deal. Recall an example that we came across earlier—the report of the Munk Center on how the Chinese had penetrated computer networks, including those of our embassies and ministries:
    - How many of us have computers?
    - How many of us surf the Internet?
    - How many of us saw the news-report about how an inquiry originating in the Dalai Lama's office had uncovered a vast operation centred in China through which computers in close to 130 countries were penetrated—everything in them was made transparent; information from them, even the keys that the users struck, were being relayed in real time to servers back in China; everything in them was opened to being controlled by manipulators far away? How many of us saw the news item about this study?
    - How many of us then went on to download and study the report? After all, the Munk Center and the authors had put the full text on the Internet the very day that the papers reported their findings.
    - We should track down information that bears on our security, and disseminate it like the chain-letters of old, except that we can now use the infinitely more potent Internet. We should learn from groups and individuals in China. They outwit the authorities there: thousands and thousands of bloggers dodge

Chinese authorities and their censorship to acquire and spread information. When we have computers; when we surf the Internet; when there is no one to block information here in India; when, in spite of these advantages, we do not use the freedom and facilities we have and acquire the information that is so vital to our security and broadcast it, do we not neglect to do what is in our power to help create the environment that is needed to shore up the security of our country?

- To help weld a national resolve, to provide alternatives to the people, to the leadership, we require much, much greater intellectual work:
  - Work that looks decades ahead: to likely transformations in the nature of warfare; to the likely evolution of countries—those on whom we rely today, those that oppose us today; to the likely availability of non-renewable resources, to the vulnerabilities in their continued and uninterrupted supply.
  - Work that dissects the here and now: work that weighs options that the country should have when the next attack on Parliament or the next Mumbai occurs, or the next incursion, and spells out what needs to be done to acquire those options.
  - As it is necessary to recalibrate the balance between the 'generalist' civilians and the armed forces, personnel of the latter must undertake detailed analyses of the political decisions that affected our wars, that affect our preparedness today: the decision to halt our men as they advanced in Kashmir, having driven out the invaders; the decision to refer the matter to the UN, when even Pakistan had not demanded that be done; the fatal assessment of China in the 1950s and early 1960s; the fine set of decisions that led to the creation of Bangladesh in 1971; on the other side, the Shimla

Agreement; the decision to lift an obscure preacher, Bhindranwale, to counter the Akalis; the decision to boost ULFA, and then the Bodo National Front to counter the Assam students; the decision to allow training grounds to the LTTE, and then to send the IPKF to squash the LTTE; the bus to Lahore on the one side, and Operation Parakram on the other; the compromises surrounding Rubiya Syed, Hazratbal, Charar-e-Sharif, Kandahar; the stop-go stances towards Naxalites, towards ULFA.

- In addition, a very detailed roster must be prepared of the costs that have been inflicted on the country, and on security personnel by specific decisions at the administrative level, and the failure to take decisions when these were required.
- Equally, we should study our successes: the way secessionist movements have been defanged in Tamil Nadu, in Andhra; the way insurrections have been quelled in Punjab, in Tripura; the way Naxalites have been crushed in Andhra by the Greyhounds in spite of the politicians.

The studies must be detailed, they must be absolutely candid. And they must not just be internal papers prepared at the Defence Services Staff College or the National Defence College to be studied by course participants and then locked away. They must be widely publicized: so that people learn the cost of alternatives, so that our leaders learn to cease and desist, so that all learn to heed professional advice, in particular the advice of the armed forces.

So that such work may be done, several universities must be enabled to have war-studies departments; the business community should be enabled to set up truly autonomous, truly first-rate think-tanks; and journalists should specialize in security matters. The most important thing in this regard is to desist from making bodies like the National Security

Advisory Board yet another parking lot—for accommodating persons who cannot be given places elsewhere.

All this should happen. But I would put much greater store by ex-servicemen: they must use their vast experience to write and speak—few carry the credibility today that they do; most certainly, the politicians and civil servants do not; and none can lay claim to the first-hand experience that they have had on these matters. And they must not just speak, they must speak out, loud and clear.

- Today the political leadership—and I don't mean just the present government—does not lack just expertise, it lacks even elementary competence to assess the situation, to weigh options; it has the shortest of short horizons, when, as we have seen, to counter Pakistan's proxy war, to meet the challenge from China we need to pursue policies for decades at a stretch. In addition, as we see every day, the political establishment is hopelessly fragmented: it is not able to do the obvious things that are required for national security—in the hope that doing so will get it into the good books of Muslims, it throws away vital instruments—POTA, for instance; it drags its feet in cooperating with potential allies—Israel, for instance; it goes on and on with debates and accusations about a federal centre to coordinate efforts against terrorism. The bureaucrats are little different: they are little politicians themselves, more and more of them are tagged on to some godfather in politics; their horizons are all too often as short as those of the politician they serve—their next posting, their CR, maintaining the hegemony of the bureaucracy in, say, the defence ministry. And they are parochial to boot: witness what they engineered with the Sixth Pay Commission—even as the crisis in staffing the armed forces stares the country in its face. The damage that was done by some Joint Secretary barring the Punjab police from using the requisite weapons to counter terrorists, weapons it had in its almirahs; the harm that was done by rejecting pleas for snowmobiles in Siachin... these have been documented time and again. Yet the tradition remains to defer to bureaucrats and itinerant ministers; to, as we saw in regard to that paper on national security, wait upon them to decide between alternatives.

The tradition of deferring to those occupying chairs in ministries has its roots in a time when leaders like Sardar Patel and Panditji ruled. That time is long gone. Moreover, the tradition of deference has transmuted into a tradition of subservience. And this has been kept going by conjuring ghosts—'Unless we keep them in check, they may engineer a coup.' For reasons that have been sketched above, this attitude of subservience needs to be re-examined. No one is saying that higher decisions must be just handed over to the armed forces. But surely, they must be made participants in arriving at those decisions—and they must feel that they are partners.

Several lemmas follow:

- The first, of course, is that the leadership of the defence forces must provide, it must *insistently* provide strategic advice to civilian leadership.
- It must do so to the point of resignation, if necessary. Senior officers of the defence forces are too easily discouraged by the discomfiture of General Thimmayya forty-five years ago, by the ministerial reaction to the statement by General Rodrigues that the armed forces could not but be affected by the deterioration in governance. I have never been able to comprehend how persons who are willing to risk their lives for the security of the country are not prepared to risk losing an assignment at Army Headquarters, a promotion, a decoration. After all, what else can the politician or civil servant conspire and accomplish? And the fact is that, while he may be able to accomplish that little bit in regard to an officer or two, he just cannot do so on any scale or for any length of time.

Legitimacy is no longer either with the political class or the bureaucracy.[3]

- And that advice must be tendered as the unified stand of all three Forces. The top officers must not let the

[3] There is a key lesson from the American experience in Vietnam. Notice how those who were directing the US Armed Forces at the time viewed their diffidence in retrospect:

> It was clear during the Vietnam War and even more so since its conclusion that the Joint Chiefs of Staff and other senior military leaders disagreed with their civilian superiors on fundamental issues of war policy...
>
> Yet not a single member of the Joint Chiefs of Staff or senior field commander ever resigned in protest. 'Not once during the war did the JCS advise the commander-in-chief or the secretary of defense that the strategy being pursued most probably would fail and that the United States would be unable to achieve its objectives,' noted retired army general Bruce Palmer Jr. That at least the Joint Chiefs of Staff should have resigned has been the post-war judgment of many influential officers. 'Somewhere in 1967 or early 1968,' argued Phillip B. Davidson, Westmoreland's chief intelligence officer, 'one or more of the Chiefs should have stood up and told the president publicly that what he was doing in Vietnam would not work, and then resigned.' Harry Summers Jr. believed it 'was the duty and responsibility of his military advisors to warn (the president) of the likely consequences of his actions, to recommend alternatives, and, as Napoleon put it, to tender their resignations rather than be an instrument of their army's downfall'. Army Chief of Staff Harold K. Johnson later regretted his failure to resign: 'I should have gone to see the president. I should have taken off my stars. I should have resigned. It was the worst, the most immoral decision I've ever made.' Chief of Naval Operations David McDonald also lamented (in retirement), 'Maybe we military men were all weak. Maybe we should have stood up and pounded the table. I was part of it and I'm sort of ashamed of myself too. At times I wonder, "why did I go along with this kind of stuff?"', Jeffery Record, 'How America's own military performance in Vietnam aided and abetted the 'North's' victory,' in *Why the North Won the Vietnam War*, Marc Jason Gilbert (ed.), Palgrave, New York, 2002, pp. 116–36, at p. 132.

slightest inter-service rivalry, or consideration get to the politician or civil servant: for the politician as much as the bureaucrat will use the slightest cleavage to do nothing, to let the existing arrangements continue, at best to do the least, most convenient thing. Neither is competent to adjudicate disagreements between the forces. Each will use the disagreements only to fortify his position as arbiter. That is another key lesson of the Vietnam War, and two brief passages from the collection of studies that we just encountered nail it:

> The inter-service rivalries that the Kennedy and Johnson administrations inherited were so acute as to preclude all but minimal cooperation on behalf of a common objective. The Joint Chiefs of Staff were a committee of equals with a relatively weak chairman, and the individual service chiefs had no mandate other than to advance their own parochial agendas. Accordingly, they tended to serve up conflicting advice, lowest-common-denominator advice, or no advice at all. The JCS were unable to provide useful and timely unified military advice and to formulate military strategy. In the crucial decision-making period of mid-1964 to mid-1965, they could never seem to offer more than what amounted to single-service solutions stapled together...
>
> Such a cacophony of views made it impossible for the JCS to meet their legal obligation of providing the president the best military advice. It also permitted those disdainful of military opinion in the first place to ignore whatever advice was proffered. As a populist, Lyndon Johnson had an innate mistrust of the military. 'It's hard to be a hero without a war,' he once told the historian Doris Kearns. 'That's why I'm so suspicious of the military.' McNamara also had little use for military opinion, which he regarded as hidebound and simpleminded...[4]

[4] Ibid., p. 120.

Do the words not apply, do they not apply literally to our case: 'The Joint Chiefs of Staff were a committee of equals with a relatively weak chairman, and the individual service chiefs had no mandate other than to advance their own parochial agendas. Accordingly, they tended to serve up conflicting advice, lowest-common-denominator advice, or no advice at all... they could never seem to offer more than what amounted to single-service solutions stapled together...'

- Of course, it is often argued that for the services to tender unified advice, government must first institute the equivalent of the American Joint Chiefs of Staff with one head, etc. That, of course, should happen, but, as the American example itself shows, constituting such a body with one formal head will not make up for moral timidity. More than that, the record of the last few decades of governance in India leads us to not put as much store by formal structures as on intense, incessant, perpetual informal discourse—among Chiefs of course, but also all along the line between officers of the three Services.

Finally, more than any particular thing, it is the general environment that determines how prepared we will be. It determines how long we will stay the course. In determining the outcome of a contest, the fighting spirit of the soldier is as important as weaponry. It is equally a commonplace that today, when war is 'unrestricted', when technology has obscured the difference between front and rear, between soldier and civilian, what determines the outcome is not just the spirit of the soldier or even that of the fighting forces as a whole; the morale and perceptions and the readiness of the general population to bear sacrifices are just as important, all the more so the longer the engagement lasts: the US was defeated as much by the sapping of morale *within* the US during the Vietnam War as by setbacks on the battlefield. 'But you never defeated us in a battle,' an American strategist is said to have told his Vietnamese counterpart years later at a conference. 'That is true,' said the latter, 'but irrelevant.'

The key is the confidence with which a society goes after those who assault it: today, as we have noted above, we cannot investigate cells of terrorists, we cannot pursue suspects—the hands of security forces are tied; we cannot stem Bangladeshi infiltrators; we are not able to hang Afzal Guru for years on end—even after the Supreme Court has confirmed the death sentence for attacking Parliament. The nature of discourse is such that the state apparatus is perpetually on the defensive.

A key determinant is the extent to which people are prepared to shoulder sacrifices. But how will they put up with sacrifices when they have been told day in and day out that every question has two sides? When they have been taught that nationalism is 'chauvinism'? There has been so much talk about Kandahar, about the government having humiliated the country by giving in to the demands of the hijackers and releasing the terrorists. I can testify from personal knowledge, and as one who throughout opposed any deal with the terrorists, to the enormous pressure that the media's coverage put on the senior leaders in those days. The channels and newspapers had just one focus, the relatives of the passengers on that plane: the country was bombarded with images of relatives of the hostages shouting and wailing and beating their chests, 'The government is doing nothing to get our sons and daughters released ... Bring our relatives back, we don't care what happens, we don't care what you do...' That is not to say that mistakes were not made by government. On the contrary, the fatal mistake was made when the plane was allowed to leave the Amritsar airport. But that mistake having occurred, the senior leaders were weakened by this pounding on the TV screens.

This is where the greatest confusion prevails. The consequence is a debility much more severe than the fact that we are not keeping up with the latest weapons, etc. It isn't just that there is no consensus on what our strategic objective vis-à-vis, say, China is. There is no informed discussion about it. What is it that MPs, that the media regard as vital to our national interest today? Aksai Chin? Siachin? Arunachal? Waters off the coast of Somalia? Will they see the country as being imperilled by any of these? Will they see that something vital to their own, personal existence is imperilled? Worse, given the adversarial nature of discourse and of politics today; given the ephemeral preoccupations of the media; given the way superciliousness has been made into the reigning ideology of large sections of the media; given the laziness by which—once its reporter has got one person to say he is 'for' a proposition and another to insist he is 'against' it—the typical channel proceeds as if its job is done; given all this, on every issue, national resolve is dangerously dissipated. The result is as obvious as it will be fatal. We often hear it said, we Indians ourselves say, 'Americans can't stand the sight of body-bags.' In our case, the problem has become the opposite one: we don't *see* the body-bags. I have yet to come across a newspaper reader who can recall the *number* of CRPF personnel who were blown up by the latest mine or even *where* they were blown up. And this at a time when, as we noted above, war has become 'unrestricted', when it has become 'total', when it has erased distinctions between 'front' and 'rear', between soldier and civilian.

With this as the prevailing situation, people will be for a course of action as long as the going is good. The moment there is a reverse, they will take recourse to doubt: about our locus standi—as in regard to Kashmir every other day; as in regard to the India-China border. Ever so often, the most momentary difficulty becomes the occasion to urge that we give in. Recall what happened during the agitation that was whipped up in Kashmir when the state government decided to lease land so that toilets and shelter could be constructed for pilgrims going to the Amarnath shrine. So-called 'national' papers and magazines carried columns, 'Time for us to give up Kashmir, to cut it loose...' The agitation was soon over. Elections were soon held. Another elected government assumed office. Had we listened to the advice of the columnists, Kashmir would have been ceded. It would have been ceded *yet again*! Ever so often, it seems that were a part of the country—Tawang—to be hacked off one day, all that would happen is that it would fill the slot of that day's 'breaking news', and that week's 'War of Words': who is responsible for the loss—Panditji? Indira Gandhi? UPA? NDA?

The lessons are manifest.

We must educate the people. Look at the cry that goes up after each terrorist attack: 'Bomb terrorist camps in Pakistan.' But there are no fixed camps; second, bombing solidifies people behind regimes: from the bombing of Germany during the Second World War to the bombing of Hanoi and other targets in North Vietnam, that is what happened: will the same not happen if all we did was to lob a few bombs inside Pakistan? Should we not educate the people, even more so the politicians about such options?

We must exhume the connections of, the selective humanism of liberals, civil rightists, the self-acclaimed peace advocates. As the Taliban went about killing innocents, as they went about prohibiting young girls from going to school, a diplomat asked, 'Why don't we see them lighting candles at Wagha pleading with the Taliban to moderate their Islam?'

In a word,

- We must make nationalism respectable again
- We must make pursuing the national interest legitimate

Of course, overriding all this is the condition of governance, of the type of leaders we select—from top to bottom. Just as no amount of firepower can make up for a corrupt, illegitimate, ill-trained, ill-equipped, ill-motivated local police force, no amount of excellence in analysis or reportage can make up for a venal, ill-prepared, short-sighted leadership that is chasing money, that is obsessed with the next election, that is prepared to throw away essential instruments and thereby sacrifice national security if doing so holds the promise of bringing a few votes, that hasn't competence enough to comprehend the advice that is put up, that hasn't the resolve to act on it. Yes, there is massive corruption among Chinese leaders. Yes, there is enormous nepotism among them. But observers who have interacted with leaders in both India and China affirm that at the tasks that it is handling, the Chinese leadership is far more competent at every level than the Indian one. *That* is the central difference between China and India. That is the root-gap that we have to bridge—and we have to do so 'with the urgency of a man whose hair are on fire'.

Index